Public Sector Organizations

Series Editors

B. Guy Peters
Maurice Falk Professor of Government
Pittsburgh University
USA

Geert Bouckaert
Public Governance Institute
KU Leuven
Belgium

Organizations are the building blocks of governments. The role of organizations, formal and informal, is most readily apparent in public bureaucracy, but all the institutions of the public sector are comprised of organizations, or have some organizational characteristics that affect their performance. Therefore, if scholars want to understand how governments work, a very good place to start is at the level of organizations involved in delivering services. Likewise, if practitioners want to understand how to be effective in the public sector, they would be well-advised to consider examining the role of organizations and how to make organizations more effective. This series publishes research-based books concerned with organizations in the public sector and covers such issues as: the autonomy of public sector organizations; networks and network analysis; bureaucratic politics; organizational change and leadership; and methodology for studying organizations.

More information about this series at
http://www.springer.com/series/14525

Sorin Dan

The Coordination of European Public Hospital Systems

Interests, Cultures and Resistance

Sorin Dan, PhD
Lecturer in Management
Emanuel University of Oradea
87 Nufărului St., 410597
Oradea, Romania

Public Sector Organizations
ISBN 978-3-319-43427-8   ISBN 978-3-319-43428-5   (eBook)
DOI 10.1007/978-3-319-43428-5

Library of Congress Control Number: 2016957715

© The Editor(s) (if applicable) and The Author(s) 2017
This work is subject to copyright. All rights are solely and exclusively licensed by the Publisher, whether the whole or part of the material is concerned, specifically the rights of translation, reprinting, reuse of illustrations, recitation, broadcasting, reproduction on microfilms or in any other physical way, and transmission or information storage and retrieval, electronic adaptation, computer software, or by similar or dissimilar methodology now known or hereafter developed.
The use of general descriptive names, registered names, trademarks, service marks, etc. in this publication does not imply, even in the absence of a specific statement, that such names are exempt from the relevant protective laws and regulations and therefore free for general use.
The publisher, the authors and the editors are safe to assume that the advice and information in this book are believed to be true and accurate at the date of publication. Neither the publisher nor the authors or the editors give a warranty, express or implied, with respect to the material contained herein or for any errors or omissions that may have been made.

Cover image © Neuhold

Printed on acid-free paper

This Palgrave Macmillan imprint is published by Springer Nature
The registered company is Springer International Publishing AG
The registered company address is: Gewerbestrasse 11, 6330 Cham, Switzerland

ACKNOWLEDGMENTS

Throughout the course of working on this book, I greatly benefited from the support of a number of people and institutions. First of all, I would like to thank Prof. Emeritus Christopher Pollitt who supervised my PhD dissertation on which this book is based. Prof. Pollitt encouraged me to think academically—theoretically informed and socially relevant. In his wisdom, he found the perfect balance between professional guidance and personal, friendly support. Secondly, I would like to thank Prof. Trui Steen, who co-supervised my dissertation, for her intelligent and helpful feedback which contributed to my thinking about some of the ideas that I was struggling with. She made an important contribution to both the form and content of the dissertation. The Public Governance Institute at KU Leuven where I worked on this book was a supportive environment which provided many opportunities to grow as a young researcher in public administration, management and governance. I would like to thank Prof. Geert Bouckaert for constant encouragement in his own unique and intelligent way, Prof. Annie Hondeghem, Prof. Marleen Brans and the many colleagues at the Institute (the Instituters) who contributed in various ways during the four years I spent in Leuven (2011–2015). Anneke Heylen, Maaike Vandenhaute, Inge Vermeulen and Anita Van Gils were very helpful throughout this time in providing much-needed administrative assistance and guidance. Other colleagues made a significant contribution. I would like to especially thank Prof. Steven Van de Walle who initiated and developed the Coordinating for Cohesion in the Public Sector of the Future (COCOPS) project along with Prof. Gerhard Hammerschmid. Without the COCOPS project, this book would have probably not existed. I would also like to thank Prof. Per Lægreid for being a source of support along the way. He organized a seminar on coordination in the public sector in Bergen that I attended and co-chairs the European Group for Public Administration (EGPA) Permanent Study Group on Public Sector Organizations where I presented the theoretical part of this book. I am also grateful to the colleagues, and their institutions, who hosted me during my four stages of field research in Estonia, Norway and Romania, respectively. They comprise Prof. Tiina Randma-Liiv, Prof. Lars Erik Kjekshus and Prof. Marius Profiroiu. Riin Savi's help during my two stays in Estonia was highly useful. An important component of this book is its empirical research. Thus I would like to thank the many interviewees with whom I spoke in each country. They gave of their time, input and experience and improved my understanding of hospital reform and coordination. Last but not least, I would like to thank my family, close relatives and friends for bearing with me and doing their best to understand what this book is all about. Writing a book on hospitals (and sometimes, in hospitals) while not being a (medical) doctor, I must admit, can be confusing at times, but they were careful to deal with me with tact. Special thanks go to my friends with whom I was constantly in touch while in Belgium and to my friends from Prime Time of the International Baptist Church of Brussels (IBC). If I were to summarize in a few words, what I learned while working on this book is that management is important, coordination helps, culture matters, and different interests, goals, norms and values are instrumental to the intriguing and important world of organizational reform of public hospitals.

I would like to thank Jemima Warren of Palgrave Macmillan and Vinodh Kumar V of SPi Global for their help and support.

CONTENTS

1 Introduction   1

2 Public Management Reform and Coordination   9

3 Theoretical Framework   49

4 Research Design   59

5 Coordination of Public Hospitals in Estonia   75

6 Coordination of Public Hospitals in Romania   131

7 Coordination of Public Hospitals in Norway   179

8 Discussion and Conclusions   219

Appendix   243

Index   255

LIST OF FIGURES

Fig. 3.1   Theoretical framework of coordination of public hospitals   50
Fig. 3.2   Principal-agent relations in public hospital systems   56
Fig. 4.1   Type of public hospital systems   60
Fig. 5.1   Change in the number of hospitals in Estonia, 1981–2013   79
Fig. 5.2   Number of acute hospital beds per 100,000 inhabitants
            in Estonia, 1992–2013   80
Fig. 6.1   Number of acute hospital beds per 100,000 inhabitants
            in Romania, 1992–2013   141
Fig. 6.2   Gross Domestic Product per capita in Romania in USD,
            1995–2014   158
Fig. 6.3   Public sector expenditure on health as percent of Gross
            Domestic Product in Romania, 1995–2013   159
Fig. 7.1   Number of acute hospital beds per 100,000 inhabitants
            in Norway, 1992–2013   183
Fig. 7.2   The structure of the public hospital system in Norway, *2014* 184

LIST OF TABLES

Table 2.1	Definitions of coordination	35
Table 2.2	Dimensions of coordination	37
Table 3.1	Characterization of hospital system culture	54
Table 4.1	Interviews by country and organizational setting	64
Table 5.1	Healthcare policy initiatives in Estonia, 1991–2013	77
Table 5.2	Type of hospitals in the HNDP, Estonia	86
Table 6.1	Healthcare policy initiatives in Romania, 1992–2014	134
Table 6.2	Number of hospitals in Romania, 1990–2014	136
Table 7.1	Healthcare policy initiatives in Norway, 1984–2014	181

CHAPTER 1

Introduction

This book asks whether the increased autonomy and decentralization associated with the New Public Management (NPM) have impacted on the coordination of organizations within the public sector. Below, we set out the background to this issue and explain why it is important. Ideas and practices once typical of the private sector have become increasingly common in public sectors around the world. Often times, they have been promoted under the umbrella of fashionable terms such as "change," "modernization" or NPM. Although not entirely new, these ideas gained momentum, starting in the early 1980s, in some Western democracies and then increasingly became promoted as a solution—and sometimes *the* solution—to public administration problems across the world. Great variation exists, however, in their spread and implementation across countries and sectors. Two of these proposals for change are the disaggregation of bureaucratic forms of organization and decentralization. The expectation has been that these reforms would improve operational flexibility, responsiveness to the needs of service users and ultimately quality and performance. Following these reform proposals, administrators are supposed to make use of greater discretion in the application of managerial principles and techniques. Managers and the entities they lead are expected to exercise initiative, to be proactive and to act rather than just react to imperatives from politicians, as it was traditionally common in public administration. This granted flexibility, however, is exercised in a

© The Author(s) 2017
S. Dan, *The Coordination of European Public Hospital Systems*,
DOI 10.1007/978-3-319-43428-5_1

framework of accountability, often with contracts stipulating performance targets. Missing the targets may lead to "name and shame" and other sanctions, while hitting the targets may bring about more and bigger contracts and budgets—or further increases in managerial freedoms ("earned autonomy" as it was termed in the UK). Therefore, the autonomy of public managers, even if increased, is still always limited and varies across time and public sectors, and can be more realistically termed semi-autonomy.

A second major reform that has been widely experimented with in the public sector is decentralization. Decisions, it is argued, ought to be made as close to the citizen as possible. In this way, it is assumed that information and understanding of local needs improve, which can further translate into better decision making. There is also an ambition to reduce the overload and delay associated with highly centralized decisions. However, the trend toward decentralization is neither new nor uniform across public sectors. Some governments have taken steps to recentralize certain functions after earlier efforts to decentralize, while others have been initially reluctant to decentralize, but recently have taken more confident steps in this direction.

These developments—commonly bracketed under the umbrella of the NPM—have stimulated enormous interest from both academics and practitioners. NPM has left—and is still leaving—a major mark on the history of administrative thought and practice. Some have praised NPM, while critics have questioned its logic and emphasized that NPM has reinforced or led to a loss of coordination as a result of decentralization and disaggregation of formerly more integrated public organizations. Instead of a greater dose of NPM, the critics recommend a different kind of treatment: a treatment that is more holistic and aims at joining the system up again in a more coordinated and integrated fashion. NPM ideas have led to increased specialization in the public sector. In such a model, different types of expertise are divided across different entities horizontally and/or vertically across different levels of government from central to regional and/or local government. It is argued that specialization may have improved flexibility, professionalism, performance and a customer orientation—common to the private sector—but it may have also led to fragmentation and coordination problems in the public sector as a whole. These concerns have increasingly stimulated debate and have sometimes led to policy reversals. To address these issues, post-NPM initiatives have been proposed in various countries. They are known in the public administration and management literature under different names, such as joined-up government or whole of government, but in essence, they all share one major aspiration, that is improved coordination. This involves thinking about the public sector or at least specific policy sectors as a whole—as systems—rather than as disparate units and organizations.

The healthcare sector has not been immune to the changes in governance and management that have swept across the world in the past decades. Considering the complex, resource-intensive and politically sensitive nature of specialized healthcare, it is not surprising that hospitals have been key targets of reform. They have traditionally constituted a major part of European secondary and tertiary care. Therefore, it was to be expected that NPM would have an impact on the organization of hospitals. Under growing financial stress, public hospitals have been drawn into the management and performance movement and have been expected to deliver greater performance. Much of the reform in public hospitals—as in other public services—was and is stimulated by fiscal deficits and budget cuts in social spending, combined with a desire to restrain mounting expenditures caused by an aging European population. A major component of organizational reform has been the need to do more with less and to find ways to reduce spending and diversify funding to sources other than the public purse. Concurrently, in many hospital systems, in both developed and developing countries, organizational reforms have resulted in greater decentralization. Autonomy is in many cases pursued as part of a larger reform program which can include decentralization, recentralization or both—decentralization of some functions and tasks and recentralization of others. The specific setting of this book comprises public hospital systems in selected European countries:

1. a Nordic country—Norway
2. a Baltic, EU member state since 2003, formerly part of the Soviet Union—Estonia
3. a nation in Central and Eastern Europe (CEE), a former communist state and an EU member state since 2007—Romania.

The aim of this book is to investigate the principal assumption undergirding post-NPM—the alleged problems of coordination. Have increased autonomy and decentralization affected coordination and if so, how and why? Coordination can be studied at different levels (national, regional, local and organizational), but the explicit focus in this work is on national coordination (or central coordination—we use these terms interchangeably throughout the book). By national or central coordination, we understand the coordination by national public healthcare institutions—mainly ministries of health or social affairs—of the system of publicly owned hospitals.

RESEARCH QUESTIONS

The book addresses the following research questions. For ease of presentation, the research questions have been divided into three parts. These correspond to the following sequential steps that are followed in answering questions:Step 1

RQ1:   Has hospital autonomy changed national coordination of the system of publicly owned hospitals in Estonia, Norway and Romania?
RQ2:   Has decentralization changed national coordination of the system of publicly owned hospitals in Estonia and Romania?
RQ3:   Has recentralization changed national coordination of the system of publicly owned hospitals in Norway?

Step 2
RQ4:   What theory best explains similarities and differences in coordination problems between the selected cases?

The present work first seeks to fill gaps in the academic literature. A reading of the literature connecting reform with coordination has revealed at least one broad theme (Bouckaert, Peters, & Verhoest, 2010, pp. 7–12; Christensen & Lægreid, 2007; Van de Walle & Hammerschmid, 2011, pp. 8–12). The disaggregation of bureaucratic monoliths into public organizations with some degree of organizational autonomy is said to have reinforced coordination problems. However, the nature and extent of these problems have been insufficiently studied (Bouckaert et al., 2010, pp. 32–33). For instance, coordination problems may affect the performance of the system of hospitals as a whole. This is one of the possible effects that can occur in a context of greater organizational autonomy with increased freedom of action for individual hospitals and decentralized service provision. Furthermore, if hospitals pursue their own goals (such as improving market share or expanding their range of services), the efficiency and financial sustainability of the system as a whole may be affected. These goals may be different from those of the central coordinating bodies, which can reinforce conflict and pose coordination problems. It is possible that it is more cost-effective, for instance, for some services to be provided only in specific hospitals. The literature has only marginally—and often only rhetorically—addressed such questions.

A first look at hospital reforms in the three countries indicates that more research has been conducted on evaluating the reforms in some countries than others, with Norway on top, followed by Estonia and Romania. Only in recent years has Romania started to experiment with decentralizing its public hospital network. Since the major hospital reform of 2002, Norway has shifted toward greater centralization, accompanied by greater autonomy given to hospitals as a result of the creation of health enterprises. Estonia in the first decade after its independence promoted decentralization and the creation of autonomous hospitals, organized either as foundations or limited companies operating under private law. Romania, by contrast, has maintained strong central control. In recent years, however, the government has shown an increasing interest in experimenting on a large scale with the decentralization of government hospitals. These efforts were translated in 2010 into a major reform which transferred ownership of most local and county hospitals to local public authorities. Those of national and regional importance were (and still are) owned by the Ministry of Health. In all selected countries, reforms aiming at increasing autonomy of public hospitals have been part of a larger agenda of decentralization (specifically in Estonia and Romania) and recentralization (most evidently in the case of Norway). There are evident differences between the three countries but equally some similarities in terms of the reforms pursued and alleged coordination problems faced. Health policy makers in all three cases have promoted broadly similar ideas at different points in time and in different political, administrative, financial and healthcare contexts. Analyzing reform and coordination problems in contrasting contexts can shed light on the advantages and disadvantages of reform across different countries. Norway has a developed and well-funded welfare and healthcare system, and is very different when compared with Estonia and Romania, which are still relatively underfunded. Financial status and a developed healthcare system constitute key enabling factors for certain outcomes, but it does not necessarily mean that they "solve all problems." Though these conditions may facilitate coordination, they do not necessarily rule out problems of coordination. Having more money does not necessarily mean having greater coordination. Health policy makers in each of the three countries have grappled with finding an optimal balance between local, organizational autonomy and central coordination. This makes these countries relevant candidates for comparative research into the coordination of public hospital systems. This area of research is also relevant because knowledge of problems associated with NPM can provide academics and practitioners with a more solid foothold in proposing and evaluating post-NPM initiatives—which have become increasingly popular. The increasing spread of these initiatives raises important questions about the underlying gaps and problems that they seek to fill.

There is a growing body of literature, as we shall see in Chap. 2, on governance and coordination in the public sector generally and healthcare specifically. Similarly, the autonomy and decentralization of public organizations have received much attention in the public administration and management literature. This book builds on these two bodies of knowledge, and aims to contribute to the existing literature. The book:

- Directly compares two eastern and one western European system and shows that such comparison, although it does not follow a most similar research design, is both feasible and productive. This research finds that problems of coordination can occur in different systems, and therefore to study public sector coordination comparatively, one can choose to select cases that display differences between them and look for factors that can explain a similar outcome
- Covers one country where only very limited research on hospital reforms has previously been published (Romania)
- Sets out new primary evidence in the form of original interviews and documentary evidence which has not previously been cited in academic research
- Employs two theoretical approaches in a comparative and complementary way, and argues that conflicting interests and goals and hospital system culture help explain coordination in European public hospital systems
- Proposes an analytical framework for analyzing coordination in public hospital systems and finds the framework to be useful in that it encourages researchers and practitioners to think specifically about the implications of coordination.

STRUCTURE OF THE BOOK

The book comprises eight chapters. Chapter 2 reviews the literature and shows how the subject matter of this book is embedded in the broad academic discourse. This consists of the public administration and management literature—particularly NPM, governance and coordination—on the one hand, and healthcare and hospital management and governance, on the other hand. It provides a theoretical review of the concept of coordination, and shows how different theories have dealt with coordination in a public sector context. The chapter also reviews existing analytical and empirical approaches to coordination. In Chap. 3, we propose an analytical framework geared to the central coordination of publicly owned hospitals. The framework builds on two theories—principal-agent theory and sociological institutionalism—and seeks to explain why coordination problems occur across the three cases. Chapter 4 includes the research design: the case selection and methods. The book uses an explanatory comparative case study approach to understand how reform affects coordination in hospital systems in the three country cases: Estonia, Norway and Romania. This evidence is supplemented with relevant documentary data and statistical information. Chapters 5–7 constitute the core of the book, and they describe, evaluate and explain the relationship between organizational reform in public hospitals and coordination problems. Each of these three country chapters ends by discussing the compatibility between empirical findings and the theoretical propositions derived from the two theories. In each country chapter, we seek to explain the relationship between organizational reform in public hospitals and central coordination by means of the theoretical framework introduced in Chap. 3. Chapter 8 concludes by comparing the empirical and theoretical findings across the three cases and discusses the implications of the results for theory and practice.

BIBLIOGRAPHY

Bouckaert, G., Peters, B. G., & Verhoest, K. (2010). *The coordination of public sector organizations. Shifting patterns of public management.* Basingstoke: Palgrave Macmillan.

Christensen, T., & Lægreid, P. (2007). The whole-of-government approach to public sector reform. *Public Administration Review, 67*(6), 1059–1066.

Van de Walle, S., & Hammerschmid, G. (2011). *Coordinating for cohesion in the public sector of the future; COCOPS project background paper.* COCOPS Working Paper No. 1.

CHAPTER 2

Public Management Reform and Coordination

The NPM is not as new as it used to be. In some parts of the world it is getting older and older, while in others it appears to have the features of an elixir: young and vigorous. Some parts of the world even may not have yet been introduced to it. Some academics have declared the demise of NPM (e.g. Dunleavy, Margetts, Bastow, & Tinkler, 2006a), whereas others think it has reached middle age (Hood & Peters, 2004). Practitioners, however, may well use NPM ideas to reform their organizations, but say little in practice about the existence of a distinct NPM model (Bekker, 2013). Coined 20 years ago, NPM has now received considerable attention in both academia and government. Starting with certain pioneering OECD countries, governments across the globe have tried to implement NPM ideas to reap the benefits of the promises they make: creating a better government which operates more efficiently and effectively and delivers high-quality public services either directly or indirectly through semi-autonomous agencies. For more than 20 years, scholars of public administration and management have tried to conceptualize NPM, to delineate its scope and reach, to understand its origins and to assess its various effects, implications and adaptations (Brans, 1997; Ferlie, Pettigrew, Ashburner, & Fitzgerald, 1996; Hood, 1991, 1995; McLaughlin, Osborne, & Ferlie, 2002; Pollitt, 1995; Pollitt & Bouckaert, 2011; Pollitt & Dan, 2011). This has created what some scholars call a "substantial branch industry in defining how NPM should be conceptualized and how it has changed" (Dunleavy et al., 2006a, p. 469).

© The Author(s) 2017   9
S. Dan, *The Coordination of European Public Hospital Systems*,
DOI 10.1007/978-3-319-43428-5_2

Stemming from the reform agenda of certain OECD countries starting in late 1970s, NPM was a convenient label to group under the same umbrella a number of similar doctrines of administrative change that dominated the reform agenda of those countries (Hood, 1991). In addition to being construed as a set of similar ideas, NPM is understood as a specific, though not universally labeled and recognized, set of tools, mechanisms and practices. Pollitt and Bouckaert (2011, p. 10) distinguish a set of five such practices:

- Greater emphasis on "performance," especially through the measurement of outputs
- A preference for lean, flat, small, specialized (disaggregated) organizational forms over large, multi-functional forms
- A widespread substitution of contracts for hierarchical relations as the principal coordinating device
- A widespread injection of market-type mechanisms (MTMs) including competitive tendering, public sector league tables, performance-related pay and various user-choice mechanisms
- An emphasis on treating service users as "customers" and on the application of generic quality improvement techniques such as Total Quality Management (TQM)

This does not mean that NPM has only been framed in this way. Various labels and interpretations have been added (and are being added) since it first became part of the academic discourse (Dunleavy et al., 2006a, p. 469). Commentators have rightfully noted that NPM is not a stable, coherent theory, but rather a doctrine and a set of practices that are associated with an entrepreneurial government that is more disaggregated than a traditional bureaucratic structure, employs business-like techniques and makes greater use of performance management and control tools. In the words of Dunleavy et al. (2006a, p. 470), the three "chief integrating themes in NPM have focused on disaggregation, competition and incentivization." Autonomy is the close cousin of disaggregation. Scholars have argued that there was not one single coherent theory that fed into the NPM (Pollitt & Bouckaert, 2011). Nevertheless, economic theories, typically neo-classical and rational choice, are often considered to form the core of the theoretical basis of NPM. These include public choice theory (Downs, 1967; Niskanen, 1968, 1971; see also Boyne, Farrell, Law, Powell, & Walker, 2003 for an application to public services in the UK), principal-agent theory (Jensen & Meckling, 1976; see also Buchanan, 1988; Verhoest, 2005) and property rights theory (Preker & Harding, 2003). Business-type managerialism was a second strand of ideas that influenced the NPM. Unlike neo-institutional economics, generic management theory takes a more optimistic view of motivation and the ability of leaders to inspire and guide staff, and to reset organizational cultures. These two streams have created tension within NPM (Balle Hansen, Steen, & de Jong, 2013, p. 31; Hood, 1991, p. 6). NPM promoters have argued that NPM ideas would lead to significant improvements in how the public sector operates and responds to public needs. As major review of the NPM literature across Europe argued: "In most of the pro-NPM literature it was assumed that the application of 'business methods' would result in a public sector that was cheaper, more efficient, and more responsive to its 'customers'" (Pollitt & Dan, 2011, p. 8). This report found that NPM can be associated in some situations with positive changes, but that the picture is far from uniform. In many cases, NPM did not reach its expectations, and furthermore in some cases, it has led to deteriorations. Hood (2011) and Pollitt (2013) are puzzled by how little we know about the extent to which the expectations of NPM have been realized: "Indeed, what will surprise many readers is how little we seem to know after decades of research about whether and how far NPM 'worked' in what is commonly said to have been its main original concern, namely to cut costs and improve efficiency" (Hood, 2011, p. 738; Hood & Dixon, 2012). How exactly the components of NPM were each expected to lead to these benefits—the mechanism—was only partially spelled out by NPM enthusiasts. It was believed that what worked in business would also work in government. For example, contracts are supposed to encourage closer definition of services—to stop mission creep—and a defined budget or price would stop budgetary creep. MTMs were designed to foster competition and were expected to steer bureaucrats to become customer-minded rather than self-centered. It was assumed that this shift would eliminate monopoly and encourage efficiency, quality, innovation and effectiveness in service provision. The measurement of performance, particularly outputs, was seen as a response to bureaucratic self-seeking behavior that needed control if it was to be responsive to user needs. By measurement and performance information, control in the right direction became—at least in theory—possible. The interest in NPM reforms has led to many changes in how governments work in countries where it was intensely implemented, but has not transformed all the older structures, processes and services of the traditional Weberian bureaucracy. To be sure, there is a continuum depending on how intensively NPM was allowed to make its mark, but even in now strongly NPM countries, it has not transformed everything (Dunleavy et al., 2006a). NPM coexisted and coexists with features of the Weberian bureaucracy and, more recently, with post-NPM approaches, grouped under various labels such as digital-era governance (Dunleavy, Margetts, Bastow, & Tinkler, 2006b), neo-Weberian state (NWS) and new public governance (NPG) (Osborne, 2006, 2010; Pollitt & Bouckaert, 2011), public value (Moore, 1995), whole of government (Christensen & Lægreid, 2007) or joined-up government (Hood, 2005). This new "third wave" of reforms has been advanced to address the challenges, contradictions and (perceived or real) unintended consequences of NPM such as policy fragmentation, lack of coordination or issues of policy and social cohesion (Dunleavy et al., 2006a; Van de Walle & Hammerschmid, 2011). While in the countries where NPM has gone furthest, there is a need for a more systematic impact assessment focused on the outputs and especially the outcomes of NPM reforms (Pollitt & Dan, 2013), in Central and Eastern Europe, this would be too lofty a goal. Although NPM-type reforms have started to be adopted in some countries in the region since the 1990s, few of them have been successfully implemented (Bouckaert, Nemec, Nakrošis, Hajnal, & Tõnnisson, 2008, Nemec, 2008). Implementation problems are not exclusive to administrative systems in CEE (see e.g. Askim, Christensen, Fimreite, & Lægreid, 2010; Micheli & Neely, 2010; Roberts, 1997 for examples from Western states). However, one can see a clear pattern of issues of implementation of innovation in public management in a number of states in CEE (Dunn, Staroňová, & Pushkarev, 2006). As is the case elsewhere in Europe, there has been little evaluation of NPM-type reforms that were successfully implemented.

Autonomy Reform

A consequence of autonomy reform is expected to be a change in the degree and scope of formal, de jure autonomy of public sector organizations. A change in autonomy is seldom viewed as a goal in itself. Rather it is usually considered one of the means by which performance can be improved (Chawla, Govindaraj, Berman, & Needleman, 1996; Govindaraj & Chawla, 1996). A standard definition used in the political science and public administration literature views autonomy in terms of discretion, choice or legal right to exercise decision-making responsibilities within a certain accountability and control framework (Bryner, 1987; Shumavon & Hibbeln, 1986). Autonomy, as this definition implies, is not an absolute concept. Regardless of the type of public sector organization, autonomy is never absolute in a democratic society. Even in the case of privatization, autonomy, though significantly higher than in the other forms of organizational reform, is not absolute since privatized entities operate within a certain regulatory framework established and monitored by governmental regulatory agencies. Therefore, the literature suggests that a more realistic term to describe the degree of autonomy would be semi or partial autonomy (Chawla et al., 1996; Verhoest, Van Thiel, Bouckaert, & Lægreid, 2012). Autonomy is construed in the public administration literature as a multi-dimensional concept (Verhoest, Peters, Bouckaert, & Verschuere, 2004). It encompasses various functional forms such as managerial autonomy, legal autonomy, policy autonomy and financial autonomy. Great variation exists, however, in how much autonomy is granted along these various dimensions which in themselves are not readily distinct. The literature also recognizes that *de facto* autonomy may be different from formal, *de jure* autonomy (Bossert, 1998; Verhoest et al., 2012). Similarly, although formally autonomous public organizations may be given the same degree of discretion, in reality, they may use it differently—some may overuse it while others may not use all of its dimensions or use them differently (Verhoest et al., 2012). A semi-autonomous organization may enjoy a certain degree of autonomy relative to central government, local government and other stakeholders. Moreover, semi-autonomy is not a static right—it can alter in either sense over time. These contribute to a complex web of semi-discretionary dynamic powers. Disaggregation of large public bureaucracies into single-purpose semi-autonomous agencies, it was believed, would improve flexibility of operation. Organizational size was chastised by public choice theorists, and it was strongly believed that small is better: Smaller organizations are more outward-focused, more "managerial," are easier to control and more likely to adapt to changing needs in their environment.

The creation of agencies has been at the center of NPM, but empirically evaluating the success of autonomy in the public sector is no easy task. While much has been written and commented about agencies in the past two decades, clear evidence of effects is still scarce and fraught with a host of methodological problems. A number of patterns have emerged as a result of international comparative research into agencies in European public sectors (Dan, 2014; Verhoest et al., 2012). First, there is mixed evidence concerning the outputs and outcomes of agencification. Second, there is evidence in different countries and sectors on improved processes following an increase in autonomy (Dan, 2014). In concrete terms, this is manifested in modernization of management infrastructure and greater orientation toward the needs and demands of service users. Third, a number of unintended consequences of autonomy have become apparent. The most frequent are concerns about organizational stability, fragmentation and diminished central, system-level coordination and governance. Transparency and accountability are two other dimensions related to the effects of agencies, but evidence is more mixed in these cases. Some studies have identified diminished transparency and accountability while others found evidence that these improved in a context of agencification. These contribute to a nuanced picture of the effects of the creation and on-going operation of public sector agencies. A special issue in the *Transylvanian Review of Administrative Sciences* (2011) discusses the specifics of agencies in this region (see also Nakrošis and Martinaitis, 2011 and volume V number 2 Winter 2012/2013 "The Politics of Agency Governance" in the NISPAcee Journal of Public Administration and Policy). The following findings have been reached (Dan & Pollitt, 2015, p. 1309): (1) there is limited empirical evidence of the impacts of agency reform in Central and Eastern Europe; (2) the contributions in the issue are mostly descriptive outlining the agency landscape and developments in agencies in each country (see preface to the special issue); (3) the approach to the creation of agencies has most often been piecemeal rather than systematic; (4) less funding and capacity to develop and implement agency reform were available compared to Western countries (Van Thiel, 2011); (5) coordination mechanisms are still under development, which makes further agencification problematic leading to fragmentation in those countries which pursued a more aggressive agency agenda (Randma-Liiv, Nakrošis, & Hajnal, 2011); (6) in high-corruption environments granting greater autonomy to agencies and service delivery organizations may lead to rent-seeking and waste; and (7) some country cases have found a number of positive effects, such as improved results.

Decentralization Reform

Political science, public administration and health policy scholars have developed a number of definitions and types of decentralization. Rondinelli & Cheema (1983) and Mills, Vaughan, Smith, and Tabibzadeh (1990) distinguish between four forms of decentralization, that is de-concentration, delegation, devolution and privatization. De-concentration is defined as shifting powers from central government to local governments *within the same* administrative structure. Delegation, by contrast, is conceptualized as granting powers to semi-autonomous agencies operating at arm's length from the government which still exercises strategic control, but relatively less control on operational and management matters. Devolution is defined as a transfer of ownership from the central government to *separate* administrative structures at the regional, county or local level. Although autonomy reform as such is not formally recognized as a form of decentralization, it is clear that delegation is the organizational reform that would most closely reflect what is nowadays understood by autonomy reform. Pollitt, Birchall and Putman (1998, pp. 7–9) analyze four main types of decentralization: political versus administrative, competitive versus non-competitive, internal decentralization as contrasted to devolution and finally vertical and horizontal decentralization. They distinguish between these types in the following way:

- Political decentralization involves decentralized authority to elected representatives, whereas in the case of administrative decentralization, authority is decentralized to managers and appointed, rather than elected, bodies
- In competitive decentralization, there is competitive tendering, while non-competitive decentralization does not involve competition
- Internal decentralization occurs within the same organization, whereas devolution includes decentralized authority to a separate, legally established, organization
- In horizontal decentralization, authority is shared within an organization, while vertical decentralization follows a more top-down logic.

Other dimensions and taxonomies of decentralization exist in the public administration and management literature. Along similar lines with the previous classification, in the *Oxford Handbook of Public Management*, Pollitt (2005, pp. 374–376) differentiates political decentralization from administrative decentralization, territorial from non-territorial, competitive from non-competitive decentralization, internal from external and lastly vertical from horizontal decentralization. He notes that what these different types have in common is the notion of "authority being spread out from a smaller to a larger number of actors." Pollitt, Birchall, and Putman (1998) analyze decentralization reform of the UK Conservative governments in late 1980s and the first half of the 1990s and look at the impact of the reform in three sectors: hospitals, schools and housing. Their general conclusion is that the three sectors experienced during that time an intensification of activity, efficiency improvements and a shift toward a cost-conscious and consumer-oriented culture. The benefits seem to outweigh certain drawbacks such as concerns about equity, fragmentation and representative local democracy. The latter in particular was found suffering in a context of heightened administrative, management-centered decentralization favored by the Conservatives. However, they did not find conclusive evidence that decentralization convincingly led to these benefits and drawbacks—it was one of the many possible contributing factors (Pollitt et al., 1998, p. 179). Nemec (2007) discusses general lessons from decentralization reforms in the context of Central and Eastern Europe. He argues that decentralization may have both negative and positive impacts depending on country-specific conditions. In a weak democratic system with little respect for the rule of law, high levels of corruption and low implementation capacity, decentralization is likely to give rise to clientelism and rent-seeking behavior. Under such circumstances, it is likely that the positive expectations of decentralization will not be achieved. However, this does not mean that decentralization is inherently unproductive and that it is impossible for decentralization reform to work well (Nemec, 2007).

NPM AND HEALTHCARE REFORM

NPM ideas and related concepts and practices such as entrepreneurialism or managerialism are not new to the healthcare sector. These ideas had been influencing public healthcare organizations such as hospitals, general practices and insurance funds before NPM became part of the academic debate in the 1980s. Entrepreneurial behavior in healthcare, as it is sometimes called, has been observed in various healthcare areas, including at least the following: the hospital sector, the pharmaceutical industry, social care, third-party payers, primary healthcare and oral healthcare services (Saltman, Busse, & Mossialos, 2002). Looking at general trends in Europe in the 1990s, this same study observed that entrepreneurial behavior was growing in hospitals, pharmaceutical markets, social care and third-party payers. Similarly, it observed that entrepreneurialism was strong but not changing in primary healthcare and oral healthcare services. Due to complexity, size and a strong management component, management reforms have found fertile ground in hospitals and have raised questions about how to best regulate the entrepreneurial behavior of hospitals while at the same time enabling, steering and coordinating it so as to flourish for the public good. NPM ideas became increasingly salient in reforming public hospital management starting in the 1980s and continuing on in the following decades. Years later, a sizable body of literature has accumulated. In reviewing this literature, we focus on the studies that specifically evaluate or discuss decentralization and autonomy of publicly owned hospitals.

A first strand of literature on NPM in hospitals looks at micro-level management and performance. Some identify this body of research as the "management matters thesis" (Boyne, 2003; Moynihan & Pandey, 2005). What underlies this research in healthcare is a "clear recognition that only so much can be achieved by appealing to individual practitioners, and that more effort needs to be expended on understanding how the organization and management of care affects outcomes" (West, 2001, p. 41). The unit of analysis in this body of research is the healthcare organization and its subdivisions. While not ignoring larger governance concerns, this literature seeks to understand particularly what role management has on the performance of public organizations. Some authors view hospital management as "operational governance" (Saltman, Durán, & Dubois, 2011). This is used to distinguish the micro level from the meso and macro levels of governance. The meso level encompasses governance processes at the level of the boards of healthcare organizations, whereas the macro level includes processes at the level of the entire healthcare system. Academics have stressed that the organization and management of public hospitals have an impact on hospital performance, but evidence of how and how much management matters is still patchy. After a review of the literature, one author pointed out that "although few would now question that management does not matter in delivering quality healthcare, knowledge about the nature of the relationship is incomplete" (West, 2001, p. 40). West (2001) concluded that overall "there is some evidence that management matters as well as the combined efforts of individual clinicians and teams" (p. 40). This study was particularly interested in identifying variables associated with hospital performance and quality of care including "structural features of the organization," that is decentralized versus centralized decision-making processes, "organizational processes" such as human resource management practices, internal communication and participatory management. Importantly, the author stressed that a key point in the literature was the need for participatory decision-making, involvement and autonomy (West, 2001, pp. 46–47). A major caveat of this literature, however, is that the bulk of research has been in Anglo-Saxon countries—although organizational reform is not restricted to these countries (Bloom, Homkes, Sadun, & Van Reenen, 2010; Smith, Mossialos, Papanicolas, & Leatherman, 2009; West, 2001). A number of lines for future research were identified (West, 2001; see also Flood, 1994). They included: (1) a need for theoretically informed research; (2) longitudinal rather than cross-sectional designs need to be used in order to address causal links and sequential temporality more systematically; (3) there is no single theory that can yet explain the complexity of the relationship between the organization and management of hospitals and performance; (4) future research should account for the role of culture in managerial decision-making; and (5) overwhelmingly research has focused so far on Anglo-Saxon countries, particularly the USA.

Both economic and general management theories were deemed to undergird the adoption of NPM reforms in public hospitals (Bloom et al., 2010; Preker & Harding, 2003; West, 2001). The key expectation of these theories is that autonomous organizations are uniquely positioned to deliver performance—if only they were equipped with the proper incentives. Being granted the needed discretion to operate and make decisions, management, it is argued, does matter (Bloom et al., 2010). It is assumed that service delivery organizations need to enjoy a certain degree of discretion so that decisions can be made locally on the basis of the specific circumstances of each organization and on patient preferences. Therefore, allocative efficiency is presumed to improve following disaggregation (Collins, Njeru, Meme, & Newbrander, 1999; Govindaraj & Chawla, 1996). Technical efficiency of operations is likewise assumed to improve. A flexible delivery organization is expected to be in a better position to innovate constantly and to find cost-effective and creative solutions to improve quality, to address financial problems and adapt to changing patterns of demand. As a result, public accountability and patient satisfaction are supposed to improve (Collins et al., 1999; Govindaraj & Chawla, 1996). Autonomy enables organizations to design, in economic parlance, the optimal production function by using the optimal level and set of skills of personnel, availability of medication and equipment. Likewise, if management is empowered with the adequate decision-making capacity, it can motivate personnel by designing tailored incentives, which in turn are expected to lead to performance improvements. An expanded choice of services available to patients is an additional expected benefit. The expectation is that performance of service delivery organizations will improve without a significant decrease in equity or access to services. No other consequences were originally envisaged by NPM proponents. Issues of fragmentation, coordination and their implications for systemic performance and policy coherence were not part of the original model. Much weight is placed on the performance of operations at unit level measured by the production of outputs (Schick, 1996). Under the inspiration of NPM ideas, healthcare reformers have opted for a combination of reforms aimed at greater decentralization, autonomy, corporatization and privatization (Atun, 2007; Busse, van der Grinten, & Svensson, 2002; Preker & Harding, 2003). Some authors viewed these reforms as sequential steps toward (ultimately) privatization, potentially one building upon the other, depending on the context, problems and characteristics of each hospital system (Preker & Harding, 2003). However, reforms of public hospitals have not been pursued in isolation. Their various elements have been adopted in combination with other healthcare policies and in other cases as a comprehensive reform program. Some reforms envisaged the transfer of ownership of public hospitals from the central government to local municipalities (decentralization) combined with greater autonomy granted to hospitals (Saltman et al., 2011). It is worth noting here that the direction of reform in European hospital systems has not always been toward greater decentralization *and* greater management autonomy. Greater decentralization and management autonomy have been followed in some countries by efforts to recentralize certain functions (Habicht, Habicht, & Jesse, 2011; Hagen & Kaarbøe, 2006; Vrangbæk, 2007). Recentralization, however, does not necessarily imply diminished hospital autonomy. Reforms in public hospitals in Norway in 2002, for instance, transferred ownership from county governments to the central government (recentralization), but operational autonomy of hospitals increased as a result of the creation of health enterprises. In some studies of decentralization in healthcare, the granting of autonomy to providers is seen as a form of decentralization (Bossert, 1998; Bossert & Beauvais, 2002). It is in this context that NPM-type reform in public hospitals finds its place and needs to be investigated. It is but one of a panoply of changes in public hospitals. Autonomy reform is expected to make hospital managers manage. Corporatization is thought in terms of the creation of health enterprises subject to private law or at least given the structural or organizational form of a corporation while still under public law. Corporatization is often associated with an intense use of corporate, managerial techniques such as performance management and measurement systems or quality improvement schemes. Autonomy reform, however, is also expected to enable service delivery organizations to make greater use of managerial tools to manage performance. Therefore in this respect, differences between autonomy reform and corporatization are not always clear cut. Finally, privatization is defined as the transfer or sale of ownership to private providers. Collins et al. (1999) specifically underlined that hospital autonomy is a multifaceted concept. Hospital autonomy, they argued, forms a dynamic continuum. The authors emphasized that "autonomous hospitals may still be owned by the government but have the ability to act under their own authority to achieve their primary missions. Although established by the government, autonomous hospitals share some of the characteristics of private organizations that should allow them to operate more efficiently" (p. 130). A systematic contribution to the literature on framing autonomy in the public sector is found in Bossert (1998). This framework is then applied to a series of case studies of decentralization of public hospitals in developing countries (Bossert & Beauvais, 2002). Based on principal-agent theory, the study built a framework called "decision space map" which consists of the range of choice available to local decision makers along specific functional dimensions. This complex framework is flexible enough to be used for assessing not only decentralization (the "decision space" of local policy makers) but also the decision space in semi-autonomous public hospitals.

Empirical research on decentralization and management autonomy of public hospitals stresses the limited evidence of the implications and impacts of these reforms (Bossert, 1998; Bossert & Beauvais, 2002; Chawla et al., 1996; Collins et al., 1999; Govindaraj & Chawla, 1996). Despite much policy experimentation, academic research has not kept up with the speed of reform on the ground. Pollitt, Birchall and Putman (1998) investigated the creation of hospital trusts in the UK's National Health Service (NHS). The type of decentralization in this case was administrative—it involved granting authority to appointed managers rather than to elected local officials, which is common to political decentralization in various other European countries. The UK reforms involved devolution through the creation of new autonomous entities. The study reached the following findings. First, it found the following benefits that accompanied the reform: greater managerial flexibility, less red tape, greater cost consciousness, improvements in hospital identity and closer connection to local general practitioners. These benefits concern internal processes, which may have had in the short, medium or long term a positive effect on hospital outputs and outcomes. They found less conclusive evidence of improvements in efficiency and, especially, in clinical outcomes as a result of trust status. Other important factors were at work, and the specific effect of the trust status could not be isolated from the rest. Second, the research identified the following drawbacks: increased fragmentation and "self-seeking behavior" within the NHS, concerns about the coherence of the system as a whole and concerns about equity. As the authors put it, however, none of these problems were significant and shared across the board. The general conclusion was that the trust status did not bring about the benefits to the extent that they were expected, but at the same time, none of the interviewees thought that a return to the previous state was desirable (Pollitt et al., 1998, p. 75). Govindaraj and Chawla (1996, p. 8) in a study of public hospital autonomy in developing countries made qualified statements about the effects of autonomy: "While a priori one can only conjecture as to whether, on balance, the positives of providing increased autonomy outweigh the negatives, the popular consensus seems to be that greater hospital autonomy can lead to significant gains in efficiency, effectiveness, public accountability and the quality of care, without a significant compromise of equity." These gains are hypothetical, and convincing evidence is scarce. One such study is Bloom et al. (2010). This research showed that the autonomy of hospitals in a number of Western countries (Canada, France, Germany, Sweden, Italy, UK and the USA) and "good management practices" are associated with greater quality of patient care, productivity and clinical outcomes (Bloom et al., 2010). More specifically, the study found:

- significant variation in management practices and effectiveness of hospitals between countries and in particular within the same country;
- great potential for improving hospital performance through good management practices;
- larger hospitals are managed more effectively than smaller hospitals;
- for-profit and non-profit hospitals perform better compared to public hospitals across all countries included in the study;
- good management practices are associated with significantly lower mortality rates and greater financial performance;

- competition helps improve managerial standards;
- Greater managerial autonomy leads to improved management performance.

In their analysis of autonomy and corporatization in public hospitals across a number of developed and developing countries, Preker and Harding (2003) reached a number of pertinent preliminary conclusions. First, they identified key internal variables that need to be properly coordinated if reform is to be successful, namely decision rights, extent of market exposure, residual claimant status, accountability arrangements and explicit policies and reimbursement of social functions. The authors argued that insufficient managerial control and autonomy prevented needed reform. Managerial autonomy ought to be comprehensive and coordinated across various parts of the hospital system in order for reform to be successful. Moreover, the study identified key external environmental factors that could facilitate or prevent successful reform. They include the influence of political factors, interest groups and powerful stakeholders as well as a number of other characteristics of a country, political system or specific hospitals, such as the level of informality, corruption or respect for the rule of law. On the basis of country case studies, the authors arrive at the ingredients for a "requisite theory," an approach that has become increasingly popular in public management research more generally (see also Pollitt & Dan, 2011 who similarly identified a number of contextual factors affecting the impacts of NPM reforms in Europe). Alonso, Clifton and Diaz-Fuentes (2013) have recently compared the efficiency of traditionally managed hospitals with that of hospitals operating under a new management model and find no significant difference. The study analyzed efficiency scores specifically for hospitals in capital city Madrid which has adopted new management formulas in part of its hospital network. Compared to traditional models, all the various new models are subject to private law, and staff management follows the labor legislation, whereas in "old" models, staff management followed a statutory regime. Another difference is the service delivery model which in the models can be public, private or mixed compared to public only in the original "administrative management" model (p. 8). To obtain efficiency scores, the study constructs input–output ratios. The inputs used include the number of beds, the number of full-time employed physicians and the number of full-time nursing staff. For outputs, the authors use the number of discharges and the number of outpatient visits. The study found no clear pattern in the relationship between new management models and technical efficiency. Among the best performers, they find both hospitals operating under a traditional management model and hospitals which have adopted a new model. The same is true for the hospitals with the lowest technical efficiency scores. The paper concluded that what mattered was not the management model, but the quality of the management itself—regardless of the model. It is important to note, however, that adopting a new management model does not "harm" either—some of the most efficient hospitals included in the study had adopted a new management formula. In conclusion, the existing evidence of the effects of NPM-type management models in European hospital systems is mixed. Some studies have found no significant difference between, on the one hand, traditional models and, on the other hand, new managerial type of models. Other studies, however, have found certain improvements.

Theorizing Coordination

Thinking about coordination can be traced back as far as there have been written documents about government. As social and economic life became increasingly complex and differentiated, interest in coordination has continuously grown. Studies looking at coordination emphasize a number of problems in the scholarship and treatment of the topic. These problems range from definitional and conceptual ambiguity and insufficient theorization to problems with operationalizing the concept in empirical research (Alexander, 1995; Bouckaert, Peters, & Verhoest, 2010). One or more of these limitations are frequently mentioned both in the past and in the current literature on coordination. There have been few detailed pieces of work dealing explicitly with coordination. However, since the practice, if not the concept of coordination, has a long history, ideas about coordination are not new. Different schools of thought embracing different theoretical traditions have been dealing with the topic in one way or another. What can be noticed is that interest in the idea and practice of coordination has grown and is blooming in the current era of integration and "joining-up." The theoretical approach to studying coordination cannot be separated from that of other areas of research in political science and public administration (Bouckaert et al., 2010, p. 34). Theories in political science and public administration are relevant for understanding what drives and hampers coordination in the public sector. Almost 20 years ago, in one of the most detailed treatments of the topic, one scholar argued that what was missing in the study of inter-organizational coordination was not some grand theory, but a focus on the "mechanics of coordination" (Alexander, 1995, p. 47). Instead, attention has tended to focus either on the relatively abstract and general or on the very concrete and particular. In his view, the abstract and general represented theories explaining why coordination occurs while the concrete and particular stood for various tools of enacting coordination. What was missing, he argued, were the structures of coordination—the intermediate level—or what is often referred to currently as the mechanisms of coordination—following the now classical three-point typology of hierarchy, market and networks. Nevertheless, various scholars have stressed that "the general and abstract," if present in current scholarship, have somehow been left behind and decoupled from the more daily mechanics of coordination, which reigns supreme in much of the work on the subject (Jennings & Krane, 1994). This view was also shared by Alexander (1995) who claimed that the starting point in tackling the study of coordination is the theory (or theories) behind various conceptualizations of the term. These various theories can explain the different understandings and explanations of the concept (p. 7). Omitting them may leave the reader wondering what the basis is for the overall narrative, what particular theoretical lens structures the narrative and what assumptions are embedded in that narrative. The words of Frederickson and Smith (2003, p. 3) speak specifically to this point:

"There is no more clever theorist than the scholar who claims to have no theory. Simply to arrange the facts, describe the research findings, and claim no theory may appear to be safe. But theory of some kind will have guided the selection of which facts to present, how to order those facts, and how to interpret them. All theories have weaknesses, and denying theory while doing theory has the big advantage of not having to defend those weaknesses. Denying theory while doing theory helps to avoid the stereotypes of, say, decision theorists or rational choice theorists […] These are all compelling reasons to avoid theoretical boxes and categories, but these reasons do not diminish the centrality of theory in all of public administration."

The subject of coordination is a "nebulous" one, spanning various academic disciplines, policy areas, organizational forms and theoretical traditions (Hood, 2005, p. 20). There is no one single coherent theory of coordination (Malone & Crowston, 1994). The theories that are most commonly used to tackle the topic are governance, organizational and institutional theory and rational choice. We treat organizational theory and institutional theory in the same section. The reason for this choice is the close relation between the two, with institutional theory building on organizational theory. This part emphasizes how new ideas in organizational theory—the roles of cultures, norms and informality—have challenged the work of classic organizational theorists. This change in focus from formal structures to the informal has contributed to a growing interest in institutional approaches to administrative science generally and coordination specifically. The choice of these perspectives is based on their centrality in the fields of political science and public administration, and by extension to the more specific area of coordination. They also constitute a combination of "old" and "new" and a mix between structure and behavior. Many of the theoretical summaries and handbooks in our field include these four theories (Bevir, 2011; Frederickson & Smith, 2003). Our theoretical review begins with governance, continues with organizational and institutional theory, with a focus on culture, and ends with rational choice, a major component of which is principal-agent theory.

Governance and Coordination

There is much discussion on the merits and clarity of the concept of governance currently, and coordination is a recurrent theme in this literature. As one author puts it, the major advantage of the concept of governance is that "it provides for a rather abstract frame in order to cover a broad array of institutional arrangements by which the coordination, regulation and control of social systems and subsystems is enabled and facilitated" (Schneider, 2004, p. 25). It is difficult to pin down exactly what governance means and of what it consists. Unlike the "pure" versions of rational choice theory, which claims to be highly deductive and predictive, it is more difficult to draw precise expectations about coordination on the basis of governance theory. A relevant salient focus linking governance with coordination is the interest in modes (or mechanisms) of governance. Command and control, steering and rowing or self-steering by societal actors are some examples of modes of governing frequently discussed in the governance literature. These same modes of governance refer to mechanisms of coordination. In a discussion of the topic, the three "classic" mechanisms—hierarchy, market and networks—are all thought of both as coordination mechanisms (Bouckaert et al., 2010; Hollingsworth, Schmitter, & Streeck, 1994) and as governance mechanisms (Bevir, 2011;

Pierre & Peters, 2000, see also Kaufmann, Majone, & Ostrom, 1986 for an early work). The level of generality, as shown below, can explain this apparent interchangeable use of the terms. In an approach that views governance as a modern variant of the theory of the state, coordination is a function of state governance (Schneider, 2004). The state with its institutions has the goal to coordinate, control and integrate various parts of complex societies. Governance can be construed as a theory of the various forms of social coordination (Bevir, 2009, p. 164; Schneider, 2004, p. 25). The hierarchical mode of governance is contrasted to a socio-cybernetic view where no single sovereign authority governs alone, but governs with other actors or governs other actors collaboratively in networks. The role of the governing body is to manage these networks and coordinate the overall process. Coordination takes precedence over control and is more closely linked to the concept of governance. However, as Pierre and Peters (2000) emphasize, the state perspective on governance does not become obsolete in the face of a network-dominated social and political life. Their approach to governance is centered on the state—not on networks or societal actors. In defense of this approach, the authors argue that "the role of the state is not decreasing as we head into the third millennium but rather that its role is transforming, from a role based in constitutional powers towards a role based in coordination and fusion of public and private resources" (p. 25). The state maintains its governing role, though it is different from what previous mainstream state theory posited. Two of the main functions of governance are steering and coordinating. Steering derives from cybernetics—the science of control. Pierre and Peters (2000, p. 23) stress two related problems related to steering as a governance function. The first one concerns the capacity of governments to steer society in a multiple-actor environment. The second one refers to what objectives governments can still steer toward in such a setting and who sets these objectives. Discussing governance as practice as well as the constraints on governing, Chhotray and Stoker (2009) show that governance is a political activity characterized by coordination and decision-making in a context of multiple interests and views. Governance and coordination are thus closely intertwined. Coordination is described as one of the tasks of governance among others, including (de)composition and coordination, collibration and steering, and integration and regulation (Eliassen & Kooiman, 1993, p. 66). Decomposition and coordination are seen as mutual governance tasks. For instance, the creation of agencies—a form of decomposition—calls for coordination of the system as a whole. Steering and collibration differ in their level of formality. Steering is seen as a more common form of governing than collibration, but more sensitive to implementation problems (Dunsire, 1993). Steering involves the definition of norms and indication on how the norms can be reached (Eliassen & Kooiman, 1993, p. 67). According to Dunsire (1993), collibration is seen as exerting influence on power relations in order to move in a preferred direction.

The need for coordination in a setting with multiple interconnected actors leads to changes in governance structures and processes as well as to the need for cultural change. Are public managers, educated and socialized in a command and control setting, prepared to take a step back and sit at the table with other actors over which they previously had hierarchical control? Effective policy in such a context involves effective coordination. The quality of coordination becomes a key factor determining policy effectiveness. If coordination becomes an important determinant of effective policy, then policy makers may choose (and have chosen) to first tackle coordination problems before expecting effective policy to occur. For instance, a need for greater coordination was the main official reason underlying the coordination reform in Norway. An official report of the Norwegian Ministry of Health and Care Services stated: "There is a great deal that is going very well, but many people still do not receive the help they need, when they need it. Insufficient coordination is the main reason that our ill elderly as well as people with chronic diseases, substance abuse problems and mental health disorders too easily lose out in Norway's current healthcare system" (Ministry of Health and Care Services, 2009, p. 1). Academic and policy work analyzing Norway's coordination reform has equally identified the need for coordination as a key component of reform (Ringard, Sagan, Sperre Saunes, & Lindahl, 2013). Coordination may not be the end goal, but it is an intermediate goal on which policy outcomes may depend. Although coordination is a recurrent theme in governance theory, there are few specific insights or key concepts, in our view, which can be directly relevant to our research. Another drawback is that governance does not put forth theoretical expectations on coordination which can then be explored or assessed empirically. We need to draw on other theories to inform our study, which we do in the following two sections.

Organizations, Institutions and Coordination

It can be argued that coordination has always been an element of organizations though not necessarily the most important one. The need for creating structures and processes to coordinate intra and inter-organizational activities has always existed, but methods of coordinating have changed.

Organizational practice and theoretical developments have shaped the more "mundane" tasks of ensuring that the various parts of an organization are in some way connected. Alexander (1995, p. 48) distinguished two branches that looked at inter-organizational coordination: organization theory, on the one hand, and political science, policy science, planning and public administration and implementation, on the other hand. He noted that the former is more systematic and is a subset of the broader literature in inter-organizational relations and behavior. This body of literature is mainly concerned with describing and explaining inter-organizational behavior and processes of how coordination occurs. The latter is less systematically developed and views coordination as a (usually) desirable goal, not just as a subject of inquiry. An implication of this distinction for our purposes is that coordination has received relatively more theoretical elaboration in the organizational theory perspective (Mulford, 1984) than in the more practitioner and goal-oriented perspective common to policy and administration research (Jennings & Krane, 1994). In an early essay, Gulick (1937, p. 3) noted that "the theory of organization has to do with the structure of co-ordination imposed upon the work-division units of an enterprise." He memorably made a case for the need for coordination: "When many men work together to build a house, this part of the work, the coordinating, must not be lost sight of" (p. 5). Classical organizational theory was concerned with the study of formal organizations particularly with how "coordinated interaction is authoritatively achieved within formal organizations." In the Weberian tradition, organizations are seen as places of "imperative control" or "imperative coordination." The aim of formal organizations was to foster rule-based compliance for regulating behavior. Classical management theory and science in the tradition of Frederick Taylor emphasized productivity gains in production processes through an optimal design of work which needed to be rigorously controlled and coordinated (Taylor, 1911). Henry Fayol's (1916) *Administration Industrielle et Générale* identified coordination as a separate function of management. Coordination was understood as the design and operation of organizational processes to bring separate elements together. The central goal undergirding this literature was rationalization and optimization of industrial production. The means to achieve this goal was through vertical control so that self-interested workers would pursue not their own interest but the general interest of the organization. It was assumed that goal conflict was part of the equation. Coordination was necessary due to a high degree of division of labor and specialization which were—and still are—seen as grounds for coordination problems today (Christensen & Lægreid, 2007, p. 97). In a context of economic enterprises aiming at efficiency and profit maximization, coordination was seen as a process, not as a goal in itself. Subsequent schools of organizational theory began to question the central tenets of the classical school. What followed has been a process of "institutionalization" within organizational theory to the extent that it has become increasingly difficult to distinguish organizational theory from institutional theory. Clearly there is much overlap: some elements in institutional theory and new institutionalism—for instance the place of informal routines and the role of culture—are also part of the organizational culture school within organizational theory. What is clear, however, is that various criticisms were put forward that challenged the classical school (e.g. Tsoukas, 2003, pp. 608–609). They include, first, the lack of social embeddedness of organizations. Organizational structures, it is argued, are to some extent a product of societal metaphors, symbols and myths. Second, the mainstream approach to organizational theory focused on static structures and failed to explain how organizations and organizational structures change within their embedded environment. Third, individuals are "beings" possessing feelings and emotions that create bonds and epistemic communities of practice where socialization occurs. This socialization takes place within the professions characterized by their own culture and influence. This moves the focus from individual explanations of social processes to group explanations. A particularly salient line of research has been the role of the medical profession—as an archetype of the power that professionals can wield. These epistemic communities and processes of socialization can foster coordination in low-conflict environments, but they may hinder it in high-conflict settings (Peters, 1998a). Conflict is thus a key ingredient to the effectiveness of coordination.

Culture and Coordination

The role of informal norms and cultures has gradually received increasing attention leading to the organizational culture and sense making school of thought and furthermore to institutionalism in the mid-1980s in its historical and particularly its sociological strand (Hall & Taylor, 1996; Peters, 1999; Powell & DiMaggio, 1991). Cultural perspectives have influenced the study of coordination. Alexander (1995) devoted one chapter to analyzing how coordination can be supported or obstructed by informal factors. These include kinship and community, ideology and values, education, profession and "clans." Informal links can act as a glue fostering coordination, but they may equally pose barriers to effective coordination in case of conflicting or unrelated goals and interests, incompatible values or professional boundaries. Institutions of various forms—both formal and informal—can coordinate individual action and organize effort and create what March and Simon (1993, p. 2) call "systems of coordinated action among individuals and groups whose preferences, information, interests or knowledge differ." Culture can be a unifying theme that provides "meaning, direction and mobilization" to organizational life (Kilmann, Saxton, Serpa, & Associates, 1985). Sociological institutionalism provides the most detailed treatment of culture of all versions of the new institutionalism (Hall & Taylor, 1996). As Peters (1999, p. 107) notes "the view that institutions must shape behavior is the dominant perspective within the sociological study of institutions, with emphasis on the manner in which individuals within organizations become habituated to accepting the norms and values of their organization." A broader conception of institutions in sociological institutionalism distinguishes it from institutional approaches in political science. In the sociological view, institutions include "symbol systems, cognitive scripts, and moral templates" that provide "frames of meaning" shaping behavior (Hall & Taylor, 1996, p. 947). This leads to a blurry relationship between institutional explanations and cultural explanations and a reconceptualization of what constitutes culture to include routines, symbols and scripts in addition to attitudes and values. These are expected to influence the preferences and identity of actors. A logic of appropriateness guides actors to behave in a way that fits the culture of their organization or system (Hall & Taylor, 1996). Healthcare institutions and systems are characterized by certain cultural factors that presumably set them apart from one country to another. Some researchers have welcomed the developing interest in healthcare system cultures:

> As well as being sets of institutional arrangements, health systems are clusters of assumptions, values, traditions, norms and practices. Institutions—organizations, rules, routines, procedures and assumptions—themselves are cultural products; in turn they shape cultures. Health systems are cultural systems. (Freeman, 1999, p. 91)

A cultural approach in sociological institutionalism does not put forth clear expectations about the influence of culture on coordination. The same is true for the new institutionalism more generally (Peters, 1998a, p. 298).

Culture is, unfortunately, notoriously difficult to conceptualize and operationalize in research (Freeman, 1999; Schedler & Proeller, 2007). However, we find this approach helpful for our purposes. In a context of international comparative research of this kind, which explores culturally different hospital systems, it is expected that culture may play an important factor. Culture can have an impact on coordination as it does on other institutional processes. This impact, however, needs to be distilled considering the specific research setting.

Principal-Agent Theory and Coordination

The assumptions of rational choice theory form a distinct lens of viewing social life and are worth discussing in relation to coordination. Rational choice theory as an umbrella term that groups various theories around the assumption of rational individual behavior is commonly related to neo-classical economics, agency theory (or principal-agent theory), public choice theory, property rights theory and transaction cost theory. More than any other theoretical perspective on coordination, rational choice theory has focused on how coordination can be achieved—the mechanisms of coordination—and has embraced the market as the main, and sometimes the only, coordination mechanism. Mainstream microeconomic theory assumes that coordination of market-based economic action is realized through the "invisible hand" of the market. The interaction of sources of supply and demand is expected to yield an optimal allocation of resources. Organizational economics, however, has challenged the assumption that price theory provides the only possible method of coordination (Coase, 1937). It claimed that hierarchy also needed to be considered. Under certain conditions, hierarchy may be a better way to ensure coordination than a market (Williamson, 1975). Neither market nor hierarchy is a slogan that has become increasingly common in the past decade (Bouckaert et al., 2010; Fountain, 2001). Networks, fuelled by the development of the internet and modern information and communication technologies, are seen as a third coordination mechanism (Gretschmann, 1986; Peters, 1998a). Unlike Williamson (1975), who saw hierarchies and markets as the only pure organizational forms, scholars argued that networks can give rise to efficiencies and benefits not possible within the other two forms. Networks, they argue, possess their own logic and a distinct comparative advantage (Powell, 1990; Powell, Koput, & Smith-Doerr, 1996). This discussion implies that coordination can be fostered through a combination of the three mechanisms depending on country and sector-specific conditions (Bouckaert et al., 2010). The narrow rationality assumption of rational choice theory has been vividly challenged since the bounded rationality school. Two broader lines of criticism have been advanced. The first one concerns the reality of rationality, and a second one focuses on the collectively problematic effects of individual behavior even when the rationality assumption does hold (Hay, 2004). On the one hand, the claims of mainstream rational choice theory are highly deductive and predictive, and are based on a naturalist approach to social phenomena. Some scholars have challenged this narrow view and argued that economic action is embedded in broader social structures that affect individual behavior (Granovetter, 1985; Perrow, 1986). One of the concerns of public policy and administration professionals is the effect of rational individual thinking and action on collective public goals. In this respect, public choice theory occupies a central place, looking for instance at the collectively irrational effects of budget-maximizing bureaucracies (Hay, 2004, p. 42). Public choice has been associated with NPM which, as we have seen, has exerted much influence on the public sector. A key pillar of NPM—and a main target of attack from NPM enthusiasts—was the monolithic, integrated bureaucracy which was deemed inefficient, ever growing and slow to respond to local needs and a changing environment. Downs (1967, p. 160) emphatically argued: "The increasing size of the bureau leads to a gradual ossification of operations...the bureau becomes a gigantic machine that slowly and inflexibly grinds along in the direction in which it was initially aimed. It still produces outputs, perhaps in truly impressive quantity and quality. But the speed and flexibility of its operation steadily diminish." To respond to these perceived flaws, proponents of NPM recommended the creation of semi-autonomous agencies operating at arm's length from government and enjoying some degree of management autonomy (James, 2003; Pollitt, Talbot, Caulfield, & Smullen, 2004; Preker & Harding, 2003; Verhoest et al., 2012), and/or corporatization or privatization.

Principal-agent theory, as a variant of rational choice, has been particularly concerned with issues of ensuring coordination. One concern in this theory is the choice of coordination mechanism that needs to be put in place to solve the agency problem—imperfect information and conflicting interests and goals between the principal and the agent. A main focus of the theory is the design and adjustment of instruments that can foster coordination and reduce information asymmetry and conflict. These may include outcome-based contracts to reduce agent opportunism, and information systems and performance indicators to hold the agents accountable (Eisenhardt, 1989). This is a main aspect that distinguishes coordination from a principal-agent theory perspective (commonly based on hierarchy and some form of control) from voluntary market-based coordination common to price theory. Agency theory combines price theory mechanisms (market incentives) with hierarchical mechanisms (Shafritz & Ott, 2001, p. 246). Some researchers have drawn on principal-agent theory to investigate coordination in both the private and public sectors. Calvert (1995), for example, discusses how institutions can address coordination problems by specifying rules and standards, rewards and punishments and through organizing effort. This research shows that a coordination problem is characterized by more than one individual sharing a common goal, the achievement of which is obstructed by different opinions about what goals are best. Asymmetry of information and disagreement over what decisions to make may further complicate the relation. This approach builds on neo-institutional economics and the rational choice strand within neo-institutional theory. In this view, the narrow rationality assumption has been qualified under the influence of structure over agency. The focus in rational choice, however, has changed from assuming universal self-interested rational behavior to understanding the circumstances under which actors behave rationally (Hay, 2004, pp. 43–44). If coordination is affected by individual, non-cooperative behavior, then this question can help explain coordination processes generally and coordination problems specifically. As one prominent representative of neo-institutional economics, principal-agent theory does not necessarily assume absolute rationality. In an influential overview of agency theory, Eisenhardt (1989, p. 59) points out that one of the "human assumptions" of the theory is bounded rationality along with self-interest and risk aversion. The author claims that "agency theory offers unique insight into information systems, outcome uncertainty, incentives and risk." The author goes on to say that "agency theory is an empirically valid perspective especially when coupled with complementary perspectives." The study concludes that "the principal recommendation is to incorporate an agency perspective in studies of the many problems having a cooperative structure" (p. 57). Other researchers have drawn upon principal-agent theory and have found its insights helpful in analyzing public hospital decentralization internationally, especially when it involves central–local relationships (Bossert, 1998; Bossert & Beauvais, 2002). They have used principal-agent in a healthcare context characterized by non-dyadic, complex relations and concluded that the theory can accommodate multiple principals and agents (Bossert, 1998). We favor these recommendations and, as we shall see in more detail in the next chapter, incorporate principal-agent theory as a complementary perspective to a cultural approach grounded in sociological institutionalism to shed light on central coordination in European public hospital systems.

COORDINATION: CONCEPTUAL AND ANALYTICAL APPROACHES

Researchers have defined coordination in various ways, but few authors openly connect their understanding of the term to a specific theory. It is not at all clear that organizational theorists, for instance, define coordination differently from how rational choice or governance theorists do. Themes and foci of coordination differ across theories, as we have seen, but this does not necessarily hold for conceptualizations of the term. For this reason, we believe it is more natural to review various definitions and ways to operationalize the concept separately. We see reasons for doing so given the eclecticism of the concept. One such definition was proposed by Malone and Crowston (1990, p. 358) who allowed a simple dictionary definition of coordination—"the act of working together harmoniously"— to inform their work. They developed this definition further and argued that coordination is "the act of managing interdependencies between activities performed to achieve a goal" (p. 361). Along similar lines, Hall, Clark, Giordano, and Rockel (1976, p. 459) wrote that coordination is "the extent to which organizations attempt to ensure that their activities take into account those of other organizations." Lindblom (1965, p. 23) defined coordination as "mutual adjustment between actors or a more deliberate interaction which produces positive outcomes to the participants and avoids negative consequences." Peters (1998a, p. 296) referred to coordination as "an end state in which the policies and programs of government are characterized by minimal redundancy, incoherence and lacunae." Other authors have provided their views of coordination. Table 2.1 summarizes these definitions emphasizing what coordination is and what it is meant to achieve (see also Beuselinck, 2008).

We see that coordination is defined at different levels. Some scholars take a broader stance and discuss coordination between organizations (interorganizational coordination) while others focus on coordination within one specific organization. What is also clear is that coordination is meant

Table 2.1   Definitions of coordination

What coordination consists of	*What coordination is meant to achieve*	*Source*
Instruments and mechanisms of coordination	– To enhance the voluntary or required alignment of tasks and efforts of organizations – To create greater coherence, and to reduce redundancy, lacunae and contradictions within and between policies, implementation or management	Bouckaert et al., 2010, p. 16
The practice of aligning structures and activities	– To improve or facilitate the likelihood of achieving horizontal objectives – To reduce overlap and duplication and at a minimum to ensure that horizontal objectives are not impeded by the actions of one or more units	Bakvis & Juillet, 2004, p. 8
End state	Characterized by minimal redundancy, incoherence and lacunae	Peters, 1998a, p. 296
The harmonious and effective "working together" of various parts of a system	The component parts of a system do not impede, frustrate or negate each other's activities	Metcalfe, 1994, p. 278
The articulation of elements in a service delivery system	The maximization of comprehensiveness, accessibility and compatibility among elements	Alter & Hage, 1993, p. 87
Process whereby two or more organizations create and/or use existing decision rules	To deal collectively with their shared task environment	Mulford & Rogers, 1982, p. 12
Mutual adjustment between actors or a more deliberate interaction	Produces positive outcomes to participants and avoids negative consequences	Lindblom, 1965, p. 23

Author's own compilation

to achieve fairly similar goals: to align tasks and efforts of organizations, to enhance coherence between different parts, and reduce redundancy, duplication and contradiction (Bakvis & Juillet, 2004; Bouckaert et al., 2010; Peters, 1998a) and to find ways for organizations to deal collectively with common tasks (Mulford & Rogers, 1982). What is more readily different, however, is what coordination consists of (column 1). Coordination consists of a variety of things: from mechanisms and instruments, to a practice of aligning structures and activities, an "end state," a harmonious and effective working together of different elements, a process through which organizations create or use decision rules to, finally, mutual adjustment between actors. This implies that the same goals could be achieved through different means.

Some authors distinguish between coordination as a process and coordination as an "outcome" or goal (Bouckaert et al., 2010). It is important to note that the use of the term "outcome" to mean goal can be confusing as outcomes have a specific, standard meaning in public policy and evaluation. They mean effects in the "real world" such as improved health or education (Pollitt & Dan, 2011, 2013). For this reason, and to enhance clarity, we prefer the term coordination as goal to coordination as outcome. Coordination as process involves the study of coordination mechanisms and instruments across time and place—the structures and processes of coordination. Coordination as goal focuses on the goals that coordination activities are supposed to achieve. It is clear from Table 2.1 that coordination activities are designed to achieve certain goals, such as improving policy coherence, reducing contradictions in service delivery or policy making among various organizations. The two approaches are intertwined: to achieve the goals of coordination, one needs to understand the processes and structures of coordination. Similarly, to investigate coordination problems it is important to understand the structures and processes designed to facilitate coordination and mitigate the effects of coordination problems. However, while acknowledging the close relationship between the processes and goals of coordination, there can be differences in focus, with some authors focusing on the processes of coordination while others focusing on the goals of coordination and their broader effects and implications. In the public policy and administration literature, researchers have proposed a series of dimensions of coordination. They specifically refer to coordination or to related concepts such as inter-organizational collaboration, cooperation, integration or to newer terms such as whole-of-government, joined-up government or holistic government (6, 2004; Bogdanor, 2005; Christensen & Lægreid, 2007; Pollitt, 2003). Table 2.2 provides a synthesis.

A reading of the literature has revealed different terms describing processes of coordination. Many of these come from the inter-organizational collaboration literature (e.g. Alexander, 1993, 1995; Fountain, 2013; Rico, Saltman, & Boerma, 2003). In the public policy and administration literature, this is commonly understood as horizontal coordination—coordination between central government agencies or between service delivery organizations operating at the same level. This type of coordination is different from vertical coordination which refers to central–local relationships or to the governance of agencies or service delivery organizations by a supra-body such as a central ministry or department. The focus of this book is on vertical coordination; that is, coordination performed by central healthcare institutions, primarily ministries of health, in order to coordinate the system of public hospitals. In this sense, our treatment of coordination is sector-specific (dimension one in Table 2.2). Likewise, we are interested in inter-organizational coordination—in how the ministry coordinates other institutions rather than coordination within the ministry itself. We treat coordination as an intermediate goal and are interested in problems of coordination rather than in the processes of coordination. We do not restrict our analysis to "compulsory" coordination, although this type is more readily connected to vertical coordination than voluntary forms of coordination. We are interested in both formal and informal coordination. The theoretical approaches, building on sociological institutionalism and principal-agent theory incorporate both types of coordination. On the one hand, we use the concept of hospital system culture, which consists of informal elements, and draw on conflicting interests and goals derived from principal-agent theory to explore how central institutions seek to achieve coordination in a context of hospital decentralization and autonomy.

Operationalizing coordination in empirical research is difficult to do and rare (Bouckaert et al., 2010, p. 63). Research on coordination, regardless

Table 2.2 Dimensions of coordination

Criterion	Range (from–to)	
Scope of goals	Sector-specific	Whole of government
Governmental span	Vertical	Horizontal
Organizational span	Intra-organizational	Inter-organizational
Policy cycle stage	Policy making	Policy implementation
Process/objective perspective	Coordination as process	Coordination as goal
Degree of compulsoriness	Central control	Voluntary action
Degree of formality	Formal	Informal
Predominant mechanism	Hierarchy	Networks/market
Type of goals	Positive	Negative
Level of abstraction	Coordination instruments	Coordination strategy

Author's own compilation. *Source*: Adapted from Beuselinck, 2008, p. 18

of sector, tends to be more descriptive rather than explanatory or predictive (Beuselinck, 2008). One salient approach is the study of coordination strategies, mechanisms and instruments and their change across countries, sectors or dynamically across time. This can range from a higher level of abstraction—coordination policy or strategy—to practical instruments. This approach can be termed coordination as a process. In this case, the operationalization of coordination consists of specifying and mapping coordination processes by means of various mechanisms and instruments. For instance, Bouckaert, Peters, and Verhoest (2010) systematically investigate the relationship between specialization and fragmentation in the public sector and mechanisms and instruments of coordination in seven OECD countries across time. In terms of the previous discussion of theories, they underline that it is necessary to use different types of theories such as neo-institutionalism, bounded rationality and cultural theories to understand coordination (Bouckaert et al., 2010, p. 270). They suggest that an important question for future research is the identification and use of relevant theories to explain coordination in the public sector. In another study, Beuselinck (2008) looks at initiatives aimed at improving coordination and possible explanations for these initiatives across various countries. Theoretically, the author uses neo-institutionalism in its three main forms: historical, rational choice and sociological, and develops an analytical framework to explain the drivers of new coordination initiatives. Another salient attempt to treat coordination in research can be termed a functional, goal-oriented approach. Central to this approach is a distinct interest in the benefits and costs (or problems) of coordination. For example, Walston, Kimberly, and Burns (1996) discuss the anticipated benefits of vertical integration in healthcare in a North-American context, with a focus on healthcare organizations. This paper uses DiMaggio and Powell's institutional isomorphism to explain why hospitals may choose a vertically integrated organizational form despite limited evidence of its benefits. The adoption of new organizational forms can be explained by the promise of efficiency and the drive to save as well as by pressure exerted from the institutional environment.

To attempt to operationalize coordination problems—a key component of this approach—it is necessary to clarify how they are different conceptually from other related concepts. Some studies of coordination do not use the term coordination problems, and prefer terms such as coordination needs, barriers or constraints. For instance, Fountain (2013) emphasizes four institutional constraints to effective cross-agency collaboration. These include: the presence of stovepipes, a legislative process that sends ambiguous messages, blurred lines of accountability and a budget process that inhibits shared resources. Beuselinck (2008) discusses the need for coordination and barriers to coordination (see also Hudson, Hardy, Henwood, & Wistow, 1999; Jennings & Krane, 1994). Some authors, however, refer specifically to coordination problems and distinguish between redundancies, lacunae and inconsistencies (Peters, 1998a). Huxham & Macdonald (1992) and Huxham (1993) use almost the same concepts, and distinguish between repetition, omission, divergence and counter-production. In their perspective, these are pitfalls that inhibit collaborative behavior. The new element in this classification is the inclusion of divergence. Divergence occurs when the actions of various individual actors or institutions follow their own goals rather than common goals. Counter-production (or inconsistencies or contradictions) is concerned with rules, laws, operating procedures or actions—both formal and informal—taken by certain organizations that contradict or negate the actions of other organizations. Repetition consists of partial or total overlap of efforts aimed at reaching a certain goal while omission is concerned with actions that are important to undertake in order to reach a specific goal, but are overlooked (Huxham, 1993; Huxham & Macdonald, 1992). The presence of coordination problems is neither new to the public sector nor easy to overcome. The extent to which these problems are a matter of concern to politicians and administrators varies geographically and temporally. The politics of coordination undergoes change (Peters, 1998a). A priori it is not entirely clear how severe these problems are at a given point in time, and in what ways they can pose difficulties to efficient and effective resource use and public service provision. The overarching argument in the battle for coordinated policy and implementation is that these problems can lead to sub-optimal effects, especially when we follow a systemic perspective.

Although in the past decade NPM as a managerial doctrine of change appears to have receded, it is still part of reform agendas across the world (Pollitt & Bouckaert, 2011, pp. 23–25; Pollitt & Dan, 2011, p. 5). While still on the agenda, scholars have increasingly noted that nowadays, NPM is no longer the only model put forward, but rather NPM-type reforms are combined with various post-NPM initiatives. These are known under a variety of labels such as digital-era governance (Dunleavy et al., 2006a), NWS, NPG (Pollitt & Bouckaert, 2011), public value (Moore, 1995), whole of government (Christensen & Lægreid, 2007), joined-up government (6,

2004; Hood, 2005; Pollitt, 2003), service integration or holistic government (Pollitt, 2003, p. 36). This new wave of reforms has been advanced and combined with business and management practices to address the challenges, contradictions and perceived or real unintended consequences of NPM (Dunleavy et al., 2006a; Van de Walle & Hammerschmid, 2011). While this argument is growing in popularity, it should be noted that most evaluations of NPM suffer from major methodological flaws which make any causal claims—in either sense, whether pro- or anti-NPM—quite local and/or fragile (Pollitt, 1995; Pollitt & Dan, 2013). In a recent paper, Van de Walle and Hammerschmid (2011, p. 4) state: "NPM's managerial reforms *may* (emphasis added) have led to public sector fragmentation and a decline in policy cohesion. Examples supporting this claim include extreme agencification, indicator- and target-driven short termism, pathological behaviors, or complaints about a break down in public sector ethos due to short-term employment practices, etc." However, they continue by concluding: "The evidence is scattered and far from straightforward." Similarly, other scholars emphasize the danger of fragmentation and coordination problems, but make qualified statements about the implications of these problems: "The principle of single-purpose organizations with many specialized and non-overlapping roles and functions *may* (emphasis added) have produced too much fragmentation, self-centered authorities and a lack of cooperation and coordination, hence hampering effectiveness and efficiency" (Christensen & Lægreid, 2007, p. 1060; see also Dan, 2014). Discussing administrative reform in Britain in the 1980s, Rhodes (1994) argued that the capacity of the British central government weakened, which led to a "hollowing out of the state" and possible problems such as fragmentation and accountability. Bouckaert and Peters (2004) reviewed "what is available and what is missing in the study of quangos" and discussed intended and unintended consequences of granting autonomy to service delivery organizations. They noted that these changes jeopardized systemic coordination and coherence, and new structures needed to be set in place to ensure that disaggregated bodies "all pull in the same direction" (p. 44). Furthermore, James (2004) discussed the UK government response to the creation of executive agencies under the New Labor joined-up government program. He argued that "NPM structures fragmented the public sector, provided incentive systems for individual organizations to focus on their own missions, partially to the exclusion of systemic effects, and created pressures for competition rather than collaboration" (p. 77). He usefully brought into the equation the difference between organizational performance versus systemic performance, and also the possibility that performance of some organizations may hamper the performance of other organizations. From a systemic standpoint, such a scenario can lead to null or even negative *systemic* performance. The author went on to mention that a focus on agency performance *can* (emphasis added) potentially hinder joint working, exchange of staff and a common development of policy and service delivery systems. The author concluded that these problems were confirmed in the case of the Benefits Agency—the UK's largest agency. However, he noted that whether similar problems occurred in other UK agencies rests on further empirical investigation. In conclusion, while the literature is clear about what the problems seem to be, it is far from straightforward as to how serious these problems are and to what effects they have given rise or what problems they have reinforced.

BIBLIOGRAPHY

6, Perry. (2004). Joined-up government in the Western world in comparative perspective: A preliminary literature review and exploration. *Journal of Public Administration Research and Theory, 14*(1), 103–138.

Alexander, E. R. (1993). Interorganizational coordination: Theory and practice. *Journal of Planning Literature, 7*(4), 328–343.

Alexander, E. R. (1995). *How organizations act together.* Amsterdam: Gordon and Breach Publishers.

Alonso, M. J., Clifton, J., & Diaz-Fuentes, D. (2013, October). *The impact of new public management on efficiency: An analysis of Madrid's hospitals.* COCOPS Working Paper No. 12. COCOPS Project.

Alter, C., & Hage, J. (1993). *Organizations working together.* London: Sage.

Askim, J., Christensen, T., Fimreite, A. L., & Lægreid, P. (2010). How to assess administrative reform? Investigating the adoption and preliminary impacts of the Norwegian welfare administration reform. *Public Administration, 88*(1), 232–246.

Atun, R. (2007). Privatization as decentralization strategy. In R. B. Saltman, V. Bankauskaite, & K. Vrangbæk (Eds.), *Decentralization in healthcare* (pp. 246–271). Berkshire: Open University Press.

Bakvis, H., & Juillet, L. (1994). *The horizontal challenge: Line departments, central agencies and leadership.* Ottawa: Canadian School of Public Services.

Bakvis, H., & Juillet, L. (2004). *The horizontal challenge: Line departments, central agencies and leadership.* Ottawa: Canadian School of Public Services.

Balle Hansen, M., Steen, T., & de Jong, M. (2013). New public management, public service bargains and the challenges of interdepartmental coordination: A comparative analysis of top civil servants in state administration. *International Review of Administrative Sciences, 79*(1), 29–48.

Bekker, R. (2013, December 9). *What was there new in public management?* Presentation at COCOPS High Level Conference, Brussels.

Beuselinck, E. (2008). Shifting public sector coordination and the underlying drivers of change: A neo-institutional perspective. KU Leuven, Faculty of Social Sciences. Ph.D. dissertation, Leuven.

Bevir, M. (2009). *Key concepts in governance*. London: Sage.

Bevir, M. (Ed.) (2011). *The Sage handbook of governance*. London: Sage.

Bloom, N., Homkes, R., Sadun, R., & Van Reenen, J. (2010). *Why good practices really matter in healthcare*. London: VoxEU.org, Centre for Economic Policy and Research.

Bogdanor, V. (Ed.) (2005). *Joined-up government*. Oxford: Oxford University Press.

Bossert, T. (1998). Analyzing the decentralization of health systems in developing countries: Decision space, innovation and performance. *Social Science Medicine, 47*(10), 1513–1527.

Bossert, T., & Beauvais, J. C. (2002). Decentralization of health systems in Ghana, Zambia, Uganda and the Philippines: A comparative analysis of decision space. *Health Policy and Planning, 17*(1), 14–31.

Bouckaert, G., Nemec, J., Nakrošis, V., Hajnal, G., & Tõnnisson, K. (Eds.) (2008). *Public management reforms in Central and Eastern Europe*. Bratislava: NISPAcee Press.

Bouckaert, G., Peters, B. G., & Verhoest, K. (2010). *The coordination of public sector organizations. Shifting patterns of public management*. Basingstoke: Palgrave Macmillan.

Boyne, G. (2003). Sources of public improvement: A critical review and research agenda. *Journal of Public Administration Research and Theory, 13*(3), 367–394.

Boyne, G. A., Farrell, C., Law, J., Powell, M., & Walker, R. M. (2003). *Evaluating public management reforms*. Buckingham: Open University Press.

Brans, M. (1997). Challenges to the practice and theory of public administration in Europe. *Journal of Theoretical Politics, 9*(3), 389–415.

Bryner, G. C. (1987). *Bureaucratic discretion: Law and policy in federal regulatory agencies*. New York: Pergamon Press.

Buchanan, A. (1988). Principle/agent theory and decision making in healthcare. *Bioethics, 2*(4), 317–333.

Busse, R., van der Grinten, T., & Svensson, P.-G. (2002). Regulating entrepreneurial behavior in hospitals: Theory and practice. In R. B. Saltman, R. Busse, & E. Mossialos (Eds.), *Regulating entrepreneurial behavior in European healthcare systems*. Buckingham: Open University Press.

Calvert, R. L. (1995). *Rational choice theory of social institutions: Cooperation, coordination, and communication*. In J. S. Banks & E. A. Hanushek (Eds.), *Modern political economy* (pp. 216–267). Cambridge: Cambridge University Press.

Chawla, M., Govindaraj, R., Berman, P., & Needleman, J. (1996). *Improving hospital performance through policies to increase hospital autonomy: Methodological guidelines. Data for decision making project*. Cambridge, MA: Harvard School of Public Health.

Chhotray, V., & Stoker, G. (2009). *Governance theory and practice: A cross- disciplinary approach*. Basingstoke: Palgrave Macmillan.

Christensen, T., & Lægreid, P. (2007). The whole-of-government approach to public sector reform. *Public Administration Review, 67*(6), 1059–1066.

Coase, R. H. (1937). The nature of the firm. *Economica [new series], 4*, 386–405.

Collins, D., Njeru, G., Meme, J., & Newbrander, W. (1999). Hospital autonomy: The experience of Kenyatta National Hospital. *International Journal of Health Planning and Management, 14*, 129–153.

Dan, S. (2014). The effects of agency reform in Europe: A review of the evidence. *Public Policy and Administration, 29*(3), 221–240.

Dan, S., & Pollitt, C. (2015). NPM *can* work: An optimistic review of the impacts of new public management reforms in central and eastern Europe. *Public Management Review, 17*(9), 1305–1332.

Downs, A. (1967). *Inside bureaucracy.* Boston: Little, Brown.

Dunleavy, P., Margetts, H., Bastow, S., & Tinkler, J. (2006a). new public management is dead—long live digital-era governance. *Journal of Public Administration Research and Theory, 16*(3), 467–494.

Dunleavy, P., Margetts, H., Bastow, S., & Tinkler, J. (2006b). *Digital-era governance: IT corporations, the state and e-government.* Oxford: Oxford University Press.

Dunn, W. N., Staroňová, K., & Pushkarev, S. (Eds.) (2006). *Implementation: The missing link in public administration reform in Central and Eastern Europe.* Bratislava: NISPAcee Press.

Dunsire, A. (1993). Modes of governance. In J. Kooiman (Ed.), *Modern governance.* London: Sage.

Eisenhardt, K. M. (1989). Agency theory: An assessment and review. *The Academy of Management Review, 14*(1), 57–74.

Eliassen, K. A., & Kooiman, J. (Eds.) (1993). *Managing public organizations: Lessons from contemporary European experience* (2 ed.). London: Sage.

Fayol, H. (1916). (in French) *Administration industrielle et générale; prévoyance, organisation, commandement, coordination, controle.* Paris: H. Dunod et E. Pinat.

Ferlie, E., Pettigrew, A., Ashburner, L., & Fitzgerald, L. (1996). *The new public management in action.* Oxford: Oxford University Press.

Flood, A. B. (1994). The impact of organisational and managerial factors on the quality of care in health care organisations. *Medical Care Research and Review, 51*, 381–429.

Fountain, J. E. (2001). *Building the virtual state. Information technology and institutional change.* Washington, DC: Brookings Institution Press.

Fountain, J. E. (2013). *Implementing cross-agency collaboration: A guide for federal managers.* IBM Center for the Business of Government.

Frederickson, H. G., & Smith, K. B. (2003). *The public administration theory primer.* Boulder: Westview Press.

Freeman, R. (1999). Institutions, states and cultures: Health policy and politics in Europe. In J. Clasen (Ed.), *Comparative social policy: Concepts, theories and methods.* Oxford: Blackwell.

Govindaraj, R., & Chawla, M. (1996). *Recent experiences with hospital autonomy in developing countries: What can we learn? Data for decision making project.* Cambridge, MA: Harvard School of Public Health.

Granovetter, M. (1985). Economic action and social structure: The problem of embeddedness. *American Journal of Sociology, 91*(3), 481–510.

Gretschmann, K. (1986). Solidarity and markets. In F.-X. Kaufmann, G. Majone, & V. Ostrom (Eds.), *Guidance, control and evaluation in the public sector.* Berlin: de Gruyter.

Gulick, L. (1937). Notes on the theory of organization. In L. Gulick & L. F. Urwick (Eds.), *Papers on the science of administration* (pp. 1–45). New York: Institute for Public Administration.

Hagen, T. P., & Kaarboe, O. M. (2006). The Norwegian hospital reform of 2002: Central government takes over ownership of public hospitals. *Health Policy, 76,* 320–333.

Hall, P. A., & Taylor, R. (1996). Political science and the three new institutionalisms. *Political Studies, XLIV,* 936–957.

Hall, R. A., Clark, J. C., Giordano, P. V., & Rockel, M. V. (1976). Patterns of inter-organizational relationships. *Administrative Science Quarterly, 22*(3), 457–474.

Hay, C. (2004). Theory, stylized heuristic or self-fulfilling prophecy? The status of rational choice theory in public administration. *Public Administration, 82*(1), 39–62.

Hollingsworth, R. J., Schmitter, P. C., & Streeck, W. (Eds.) (1994). *Governing capitalist economies.* Oxford: Oxford University Press.

Hood, C. (1991). A public management for all seasons. *Public Administration, 69*(1), 3–19.

Hood, C. (1995). The new public management in the 1980s: Variations on a theme. *Accounting, Organizations and Society, 20*(2/3), 93–109.

Hood, C. (2005). The idea of joined-up government: A historical perspective. In *Joined-up government* (pp. 19–42). Oxford: Oxford University Press.

Hood, C. (2011). Book review. The Ashgate research companion to new public management. *Governance, 24*(4), 737–739.

Hood, C., & Dixon, R. (2012). A model of cost cutting in government? The great management revolution in UK central government. *Public Administration* (pre-publication version). Accessed October 23, 2012.

Hood, C., & Peters, B. G. (2004). The middle aging of new public management: Into the age of paradox? *Journal of Public Administration Research and Theory, 14*(3), 267–282.

Hudson, B., Hardy, B., Henwood, M., & Wistow, G. (1999). In pursuit of inter-agency collaboration in the public sector. *Public Management, 1*(2), 235–260.

Huxham, C. (1993). Pursuing collaborative advantage. *The Journal of the Operational Research Society, 44*(6), 599–611.

Huxham, C., & Macdonald, D. (1992). Introducing collaborative advantage: Achieving inter-organizational effectiveness through meta-strategy. *Management Decision, 30*(3), 50–56.

James, O. (2003). *The executive agency revolution in Whitehall: Public interest versus bureau shaping perspectives.* Basingstoke: Palgrave Macmillan.

James, O. (2004). Executive agencies and joined-up government in the UK. In C. Pollitt & C. Talbot (Eds.), *Unbundled government. A critical analysis of the global trend to agencies, quangos and contractualisation* (pp. 75–93). London: Routledge.

Jennings, E. T., & Krane, D. (1994). Coordination and welfare reform: The quest for the philosopher's stone. *Public Administration Review, 54*(4), 341–348.

Jensen, M., & Meckling, W. H. (1976). Theory of the firm: Managerial behavior, agency costs and ownership structure. *Journal of Financial Economics, 3,* 305–360.

Kaufmann, F. X., Majone, G., & Ostrom, V. (Eds.) (1986). *Guidance, control and evaluation in the public sector.* Berlin: De Gruyter.

Kilmann, R. H., Saxton, M. J., Serpa, R., & Associates (Eds.). (1985). *Gaining control of the corporate culture.* San Francisco: Jossey-Bass.

Lindblom, C. E. (1965). *The intelligence of democracy.* New York: Free Press.

Malone, T. W., & Crowston, K. (1990). *What is coordination theory and how can it help design cooperative work systems?* Center for Coordination Science. Cambridge: MIT.

Malone, T. W., & Crowston, K. (1994). The interdisciplinary study of coordination. *ACM Computing Surveys, 26*(1), 87–119.

March, J. G., & Simon, H. A. (1993). *Organizations* (2 ed.). Cambridge: Blackwell.

McLaughlin, K., Osborne, S. P., & Ferlie, E. (Eds.) (2002). *New public management, current trends and future prospects.* London and New York: Routledge.

Metcalfe, L. (1994). International policy co-ordination and public management reform. *International Review of Administrative Sciences, 60,* 271–290.

Micheli, P., & Neely, A. (2010, July/August). Performance measurement in the public sector in England: Searching for the golden thread. *Public Administration Review, 70,* 591–600.

Mills, A., Vaughan, J. P., Smith, D. L., & Tabibzadeh, I. (1990). *Health system decentralization: Concepts, issues and country experience.* Geneva: World Health Organization.

Ministry of Health and Care Services. (2009). *The Coordination Reform: Proper treatment at the right place and right time.* Summary in English Report No. 47 (2008–2009) to the Storting. Oslo: Ministry of Health and Care Services.

Moore, M. H. (1995). *Creating public value: Strategic management in government.* Cambridge: Harvard University Press.

Moynihan, D. P., & Pandey, S. K. (2005). Testing how management matters in an era of government by performance management. *Journal of Public Administration Research and Theory, 15*(3), 421–439.

Mulford, C. L. (1984). *Interorganizational relations: Implications for community development.* New York: Human Sciences Press.

Mulford, C. L., & Rogers, D. L. (1982). Definitions and models. In D. L. Rogers & D. A. Whetten (Eds.), *Interorganizational coordination: Theory, research and implementation*. Iowa State University Press.

Nemec, J. (2007). Decentralization reforms and their relations to local democracy and efficiency: CEE lessons. *Uprava V, 3*, 7–40.

Nemec, J. (2008). Public management reforms in CEE: Lessons learned. In G. Bouckaert, J. Nemec, V. Nakrošis, G. Hajnal, & K. Tõnnisson (Eds.), *Public management reforms in Central and Eastern Europe*. Bratislava: NISPAcee Press.

Niskanen, W. A. (1968). The peculiar economics of bureaucracy. *American Economic Review, 58*, 293–305.

Niskanen, W. A. (1971). *Bureaucracy and representative government*. Chicago: Aldine-Atherton.

NISPAcee Journal of Public Administration and Policy, V(2), 2012/2013. The Politics of Agency Governance.

Osborne, S. P. (2006). The new public governance? *Public Management Review, 8*(3), 377–387.

Osborne, S. P. (Ed.) (2010). *The new public governance? Emerging perspectives on the theory and practice of public governance*. New York: Routledge.

Perrow, C. (1986). *Complex organizations: A critical essay* (3 ed.). New York: Random House.

Peters, G. B. (1998a). Managing horizontal government: The politics of co-ordination. *Public Administration, 76*, 295–311.

Peters, G. B. (1999). *Institutional theory in political science, the 'new institutionalism'*. London and New York: Continuum.

Pierre, J., & Peters, B. G. (2000). *Governance, politics and the state*. Basingstoke: Macmillan.

Pollitt, C. (1995). Justification by works or by faith? Evaluating the new public management. *Evaluation, 1*(2), 133–154.

Pollitt, C. (2003). Joined-up government: A survey. *Political Studies Review, 1*, 34–49.

Pollitt, C. (2005). Decentralization. In E. Ferlie, L. E. Lynn Jr., & C. Pollitt (Eds.), *The Oxford handbook of public management*. Oxford: Oxford University Press.

Pollitt, C. (2013). *What do we know about public management reform? Concepts, models and some approximate guidelines*. Unpublished paper supporting a presentation to the conference and workshop 'Towards a comprehensive reform of public governance', 28–30 January, Lisbon.

Pollitt, C., & Bouckaert, G. (2011). *Public management reform: A comparative analysis—new public management, governance and the Neo-Weberian state* (3 ed.). Oxford: Oxford University Press.

Pollitt, C., & Dan, S. (2011). *The impacts of the new public management in europe: A meta-analysis*. [Deliverable 1.1]. COCOPS Project.

Pollitt, C., & Dan, S. (2013). Searching for impacts in performance-oriented management reform: A review of the European literature. *Public Performance & Management Review, 37*(1), 7–32.

Pollitt, C., Birchall, J., & Putman, R. (1998). *Decentralising public service management*. Basingstoke: Palgrave Macmillan.

Pollitt, C., Talbot, C., Caulfield, J., & Smullen, A. (2004). *Agencies: How governments do things through semi-autonomous organizations*. Basingstoke: Macmillan.

Powell, W. W. (1990). Neither market nor hierarchy: Network forms of organization. In B. Staw & L. L. Cummings (Eds.), *Research in organizational behavior*. Greenwich: JAI Press.

Powell, W. W., & DiMaggio, P. J. (Eds.) (1991). *The new institutionalism in organizational analysis*. Chicago: University of Chicago Press.

Powell, W. W., Koput, K. W., & Smith-Doerr, L. (1996). Inter-organizational collaboration and the locus of innovation. *Administrative Science Quarterly, 41*(1), 116–145.

Preker, A. S., & Harding, A. (Eds.) (2003). *Innovations in health service delivery: The corporatization of public hospitals*. Washington, DC: World Bank.

Randma-Liiv, T., Nakrošis, V., & Hajnal, G. (2011). Public sector organization in Central and Eastern Europe: From agencification to de-agencification. *Transylvanian Review of Administrative Sciences* (Special Issue), 160–175.

Rhodes, R. A. W. (1994). The hollowing out of the state: The changing nature of the public service in Britain. *The Political Quarterly, 65*(2), 138–151.

Rico, A., Saltman, R. B., & Boerma, W. G. W. (2003). Organizational restructuring in European health systems: The role of primary care. *Social Policy & Administration, 37*(6), 592–608.

Ringard, Å., Sagan, A., Sperre Saunes, I., & Lindahl, A. K. (2013). Norway: Health system review. *Health Systems in Transition, 15*(8), 1–162.

Roberts, A. (1997). Performance-based organizations: Assessing the Gore plan. *Public Administration Review, 57*(6), 465–478.

Rondinelli, D., & Cheema, G. S. (1983). Implementing decentralization policies: An introduction. In G. S. Cheema & D. Rondinelli (Eds.), *Decentralization and development: Policy implementation in developing countries* (pp. 9–34). Beverly Hills: Sage.

Saltman, R. B., Busse, R., & Mossialos, E. (Eds.) (2002). *Regulating entrepreneurial behavior in European healthcare systems*. Buckingham: Open University Press on behalf of the European Observatory on Health Care Systems.

Saltman, R. B., Durán, A., & Dubois, H. F. W. (Eds.) (2011). *Governing public hospitals. Reform strategies and the movement towards institutional autonomy*. Copenhagen: World Health Organization and the European Observatory on Health Systems and Policies.

Schedler, K., & Proeller, I. (Eds.) (2007). *Cultural aspects of public management reform*. Amsterdam: Elsevier.

Schick, A. (1996, August). The spirit of reform: Managing the New Zealand state sector in a time of change. A report prepared for the State Services Commission and the Treasury, New Zealand.

Schneider, V. (2004). State theory, governance and the logic of regulation and administrative control. In A. Warntjen & A. Wonka (Eds.), *Governance in Europe: The role of interest groups* (pp. 25–41). Baden Baden: Nomos Verlagsgesellschaft.

Shafritz, J. M., & Ott, J. S. (2001). *Classics of organization theory* (5 ed.). Fort Worth: Harcourt College Publishers.

Shumavon, D. H., & Hibbeln, H. K. (Eds.) (1986). *Administrative discretion and public policy implementation.* New York: Praeger.

Smith, P. C., Mossialos, E., Papanicolas, I., & Leatherman, S. (Eds.) (2009). *Performance measurement for health system improvement. Experiences, challenges and prospects.* WHO Europe, European Observatory on Health Systems and Policies. Cambridge: Cambridge University Press.

Taylor, F. (1911). *Principles of scientific management.* New York and London: Harper & Brothers.

Tsoukas, H. (2003). New times, fresh challenges: Reflections on the past and the future of organization theory. In H. Tsoukas & C. Knudsen (Eds.), *The Oxford handbook of organization theory* (pp. 607–622). Oxford: Oxford University Press.

Van de Walle, S., & Hammerschmid, G. (2011). *Coordinating for cohesion in the public sector of the future; COCOPS project background paper.* COCOPS Working Paper No. 1.

Van Thiel, S. (2011). Comparing agencification in Central Eastern European and Western European countries: Fundamentally alike in unimportant respects? *Transylvanian Review of Administrative Sciences* (Special Issue), 15–32.

Verhoest, K. (2005). Effects of autonomy, performance contracting, and competition on the performance of a public agency: A case study. *The Policy Studies Journal, 33*(2), 235–258.

Verhoest, K., Peters, B. G., Bouckaert, G., & Verschuere, B. (2004). The study of organizational autonomy: A conceptual review. *Public Administration and Development, 24*(2), 101–118.

Verhoest, K., Van Thiel, S., Bouckaert, G., & Lægreid, P. (Eds.) (2012). *Government agencies: Practices and lessons from 30 countries.* Palgrave Macmillan: Basingstoke.

Vrangbæk, K. (2007). Key factors in assessing decentralization and recentralization in health systems. In R. B. Saltman (Ed.), *Decentralization in healthcare. Strategies and outcomes, Vanda Bankauskaite and Karsten Vrangbæk* (pp. 63–77). Buckingham: Open University Press for the European Observatory on Health Systems and Policies.

Walston, S. L., Kimberly, J. R., & Burns, L. R. (1996). Owned vertical integration and healthcare: Promise and performance. *Health Care Management Review, 21*(1), 83–92.

West, E. (2001). Management matters: The link between hospital organization and the quality of patient care. *Quality in Healthcare, 10,* 40–48.

Williamson, O. E. (1975). *Markets and hierarchies.* New York: Free Press.

CHAPTER 3

Theoretical Framework

The previous chapter surveyed the theoretical discourse on coordination and revealed a number of key points. On the basis of these points, we build a theoretical framework drawing on principal-agent theory and sociological institutionalism and, subsequently, apply it to the specific cases. First, cultural approaches have gained in importance in public policy and administration, but they have been used less frequently in the field of coordination in the public sector. Second, we have seen how group explanations through epistemic communities and their underlying culture can enhance understanding of what facilitates or hampers coordination. Third, we argue that sociological institutionalism provides a useful theoretical lens to understand the influence of cultural factors on coordination and possible coordination problems. Fourth, we argue that principal-agent theory provides key insights into conflicting interests and goals between principals and agents, positive and negative incentives, information asymmetry and imperfect monitoring. The theoretical framework, composed of selected insights from the two theories, is depicted in Fig. 3.1.

"Hospital System Culture"

The new institutionalism does not address coordination in any great detail (Peters, 1998a, p. 298). This means that this paradigm (and its various forms including the cultural perspective in sociological institutionalism) does not put forward clearly defined propositions about coordination. We

© The Author(s) 2017

S. Dan, *The Coordination of European Public Hospital Systems,*
DOI 10.1007/978-3-319-43428-5_3

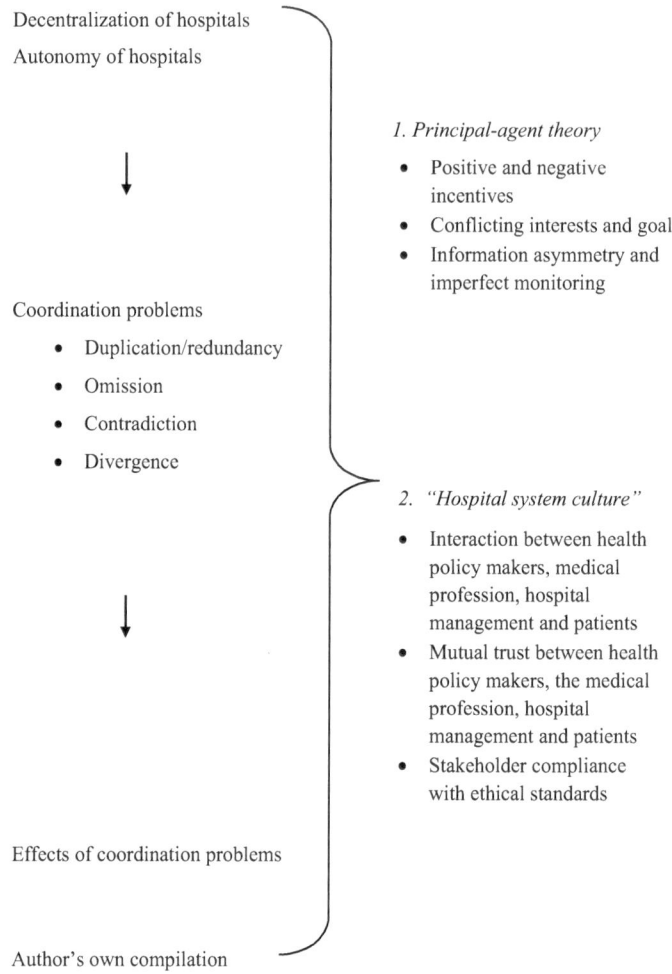

Decentralization of hospitals
Autonomy of hospitals

1. Principal-agent theory

- Positive and negative incentives
- Conflicting interests and goals
- Information asymmetry and imperfect monitoring

Coordination problems

- Duplication/redundancy
- Omission
- Contradiction
- Divergence

2. "Hospital system culture"

- Interaction between health policy makers, medical profession, hospital management and patients
- Mutual trust between health policy makers, the medical profession, hospital management and patients
- Stakeholder compliance with ethical standards

Effects of coordination problems

Author's own compilation

Fig. 3.1 Theoretical framework of coordination of public hospitals

therefore need to distill indirectly how cultural factors—which are a central component of the sociological version of new institutionalism—could impact coordination. Of all three variations of new institutionalism—historical, sociological and rational choice—sociological institutionalism has the most to say about how culture influences political and administrative processes (DiMaggio, 1997; Peters, 1999). Although we derive our concept of the hospital system culture from the sociological version of the new institutionalism, in this book, we do not treat the other interesting set of ideas that are part of sociological institutionalism, such as institutional isomorphism (DiMaggio & Powell, 1983). Therefore, we recognize that we do not assess the merit of sociological institutionalism as a whole by means of our explanation of central hospital coordination in selected European public hospital systems. We focus on the role of the hospital system culture which is *derived from* sociological institutionalism, but is only one aspect, though an important one, of the theory. The hospital system culture does not equal sociological institutionalism, and the theory may contain other important aspects relevant for public hospital coordination, which other researchers may choose to incorporate in their theoretical frameworks. Culture can presumably have an impact on coordination as it does on other social, political and administrative phenomena which have been more thoroughly documented than hospital coordination.

Although the traditional understanding of culture sees culture as shared values and norms only, a different view understands culture as "a repertoire or toolkit of habits, skills and styles from which people construct 'strategies of action'" (Swidler, 1986, p. 273). In line with this alternative view, we see culture not only as shared norms and values, but also as behavior patterns that are shared by a certain group or community. These are values in action. The underlying assumption is that public hospitals are not only producers and providers of healthcare services, but are also, intentionally or inadvertently, culture-producing systems. This does not necessarily imply that there is only one specific culture across a hospital system or that it is unanimously shared or accepted by all its different members. Different healthcare professions contribute different elements to the hospital system culture, and professional socialization is an important shaper of norms and attitudes (Oberfield, 2014; Wanberg, 2012). Although different groups to some extent share a certain culture that is supposed to bind them together, there may be different sub-groups within a larger stakeholder group that do not necessarily share the same values and norms. Furthermore, though there may be agreement on general principles, the different sub-groups may have different priorities at a certain point in time or they may have different views or approaches to achieving certain goals. Sharing a similar culture does not necessarily guarantee that the action and behavior of sub-groups and individuals are all moving in the same direction. The hospital system culture is not necessarily optimistic, positive and consistent with the law—or with healthcare policy goals. The cultural orientations of the different actors may support or inhibit central coordination—some may support it, say the local politicians' cultural elements, while others, say, the elite medical profession's culture may hinder it. There is already sufficient literature that has documented a complicated relationship between the medical profession and managerialism in some welfare states where traditional professional norms have been challenged (e.g. Clarke, Gewirtz, & McLaughlin, 2000; Harrison, Hunter, Marnoch, & Pollitt, 1992). Nevertheless, the concept of the hospital system culture does imply that there may be certain characteristics that are to some extent common within a specific hospital system but vary across different hospital systems and affect central coordination by hindering it, facilitating it or both.

To study the possible relationship between culture and central coordination in public hospital systems specifically, we therefore propose the concept of *"hospital system culture."* We derive this concept from sociological institutionalism and therefore see culture as an institutional element. By this concept, we mean, on the one hand, the interaction between four main stakeholders—the medical profession, patients, health policy makers and hospital management. This understanding of culture does not restrict itself to, for example, the norms of the medical profession or those of hospital managers or politicians governing public hospitals. It does not only consist of the values that these professions share, but also in the ways in which these different groups use the values that they have resulting in patterns of behavior that characterize each of these different professional communities. The hospital system culture thus encompasses the inner, specific world of the medical profession, but goes beyond it to include hospital managers, patients and politicians involved in hospital governance at the central, regional or local level or as members of hospital boards. It is the dynamic interaction of these different institutions—with their own values, norms and behavior patterns—that constitute the culture of a certain public hospital system. On the other hand, the hospital system culture is also imbued with some more general values, drawn from the wider society. We emphasize two such cultural factors: the mutual trust between the medical profession, health policy makers, patients and hospital management, and the compliance of these stakeholders with ethical standards and existing regulation. The following observations about this characterization of the hospital system culture are in order. First, our understanding of the term includes the patient as a stakeholder, and we thus acknowledge the increasing interest in putting the patient in the center in many healthcare systems across the world. Patients are encouraged to be proactive contributors to healthcare service organization and treatment. At the same time, it does not only include policy makers and the medical profession, but also hospital management considering the growth of managerial ideas in the healthcare sector in the recent decades. Therefore, the culture is diverse and incorporates the values and norms of each of its members. These values and norms are consistent with each other in some respects, but conflicting in other respects. Similarly, within the different groups, there may be differences of values, norms, interests and goals that make joint action difficult. Second, the result of the interaction between these stakeholders is expected to influence the effectiveness of central coordination of public hospitals. Third, mutual trust between the actors influences the problems of coordination. In a high-trust environment, coordination is expected to be easier to enact than in an environment characterized by low mutual trust between the various actors of the public hospital system. Fourth, compliance with ethical standards can play an important role in the effectiveness of central coordination by facilitating it (in case of compliance) or effectively resisting it (in case of low compliance with ethical standards and regulation).

We set forth the following propositions derived from this theory, and later in the country chapters we investigate the mechanisms through which these cultural factors affect public hospital coordination:

1. The interaction between health policy makers, medical profession, hospital management and patients influences central coordination of public hospitals
2. Mutual trust between health policy makers, medical profession, hospital management and patients is helpful to central coordination of public hospitals
3. Stakeholder compliance with ethical standards affects central public hospital coordination. Usually, high levels of compliance with declared standards will assist in the implementation of official attempts at coordination
4. Hospital system culture is one reason for the differences in coordination across the selected hospital systems.

Taking into account these four specific elements of the hospital system culture, we distinguish between the three cases, as shown in Table 3.1.

Table 3.1 Characterization of hospital system culture

Case	Estonia	Norway	Romania
Dimension			
Interaction between key stakeholders			
Mutual trust between stakeholders	Medium	High	Low
Stakeholder compliance with ethical standards	Medium	High	Low

Author's own compilation

Although there is no comparative data available for all three countries on the exact dimensions of hospital system culture included in this research, general data available on trust in the public sector from the Eurobarometer surveys and corruption from the Corruption Perception Index of Transparency International support the characterization in Table 3.1. Norway is widely accepted as a high-trust society in which compliance with ethical standards is high, whereas Romania is characterized by low trust in public sector institutions and a culture of limited compliance with ethical standards. Estonia is a case in between the other two and is characterized by a medium level of trust in public institutions and compliance with ethical standards.

PRINCIPAL-AGENT THEORY

An actor-oriented theory, principal agent proposes an intentional role for actors in enabling coordination through the design and implementation of positive and negative incentives. It is expected that these incentives can steer behavior in a specific direction to align to certain predefined goals. The theory assumes that regardless of the type of hospital system culture, central coordination can be enacted if organizational actors so desire and if they develop and implement the proper coordination mechanisms and instruments. These positive and negative incentives are needed to address the agency problem which arises due to conflicting interests and goals between the principal and the agent and the limited information that the principal has at his disposal to monitor the agent's behavior to ensure that it aligns with the principal's interests and goals. Conflicting interests and goals and information asymmetry are essential components—conditions—of the theory—they explain the need for the principal to develop incentives. The theory is thus complex in that it posits that all these three main components affect the relationship between the principal and the agent. For the purposes of our research, a dyadic, one-to-one relation between one principal and one agent is unsatisfactory. We need a one-to-many relation at least or, even better, a many-to-many relationship. Although principal-agent theory has primarily been applied to dyadic relationships in business settings, it can also be applied, and it has been applied, to reflect more complex relations in other sectors including healthcare (e.g. Bossert, 1998; Bossert & Beauvais, 2002; Eisenhardt, 1989). In our context, on the one hand, there are multiple agents, represented by public hospitals in a specific hospital system. On the other hand, there is a primary principal which sets the public hospital policy in each country—typically the ministry of health. However, this is not the only "coordinator," though it can be the most instrumental one. Another important institution with a coordinating role in social health insurance systems is the central purchasing agency—the national health insurance fund which collects social contributions and reimburses hospital service providers. These institutions do not have an official policy role, but nevertheless play an important coordinating role through their central function of channeling financial resources into the system. They do not only collect and reimburse, but they may also create incentives to steer provider behavior. For these reasons, we treat them as a principal in the principal-agent relationship. In a context of decentralization involving a transfer of hospital ownership from the ministry of health to counties or municipalities, new local owners can also acquire coordinating functions within their jurisdiction. This change does not totally cancel the role of central coordinators as these can still maintain important coordinating functions within their purview. However, it does mean that regional and/or local public authorities can also be given the role of principal. For this reason and in these situations when this does happen, we consider them as principals. All of this implies that a more realistic principal-agent picture for our purposes includes multiple principals and multiple agents. These are depicted in Fig. 3.2.

We set forth the following propositions derived from principal-agent theory:

1. Positive incentives designed by central institutions with a coordinating role enable hospital system coordination

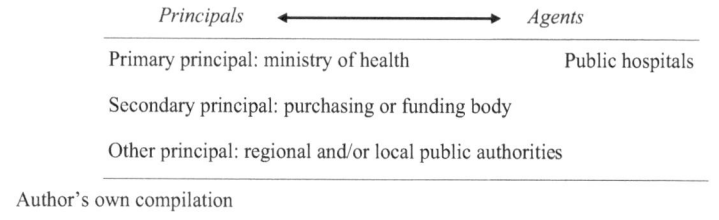

Author's own compilation

Fig. 3.2   Principal-agent relations in public hospital systems

2. Negative incentives (in the sense of sanctions or penalties) designed by central institutions with a coordinating role enable hospital system coordination
3. Conflicting interests and goals between principals and agents hinder central hospital system coordination
4. Information asymmetry and imperfect monitoring hinder central hospital system coordination.

BIBLIOGRAPHY

Bossert, T. (1998). Analyzing the decentralization of health systems in developing countries: Decision space, innovation and performance. *Social Science Medicine, 47*(10), 1513–1527.

Bossert, T., & Beauvais, J. C. (2002). Decentralization of health systems in Ghana, Zambia, Uganda and the Philippines: A comparative analysis of decision space. *Health Policy and Planning, 17*(1), 14–31.

Clarke, J., Gewirtz, S., & McLaughlin, E. (Eds.) (2000). *New managerialism, new welfare?* London: Sage.

DiMaggio, P. J. (1997). Culture and cognition. *Annual Review of Sociology, 23*, 263–287.

DiMaggio, P. J., & Powell, W. W. (1983). The iron cage revisited: Institutional isomorphism and collective rationality in organizational fields. *American Sociological Review, 48*(2), 147–160.

Eisenhardt, K. M. (1989). Agency theory: An assessment and review. *The Academy of Management Review, 14*(1), 57–74.

Harrison, S., Hunter, D. J., Marnoch, G., & Pollitt, C. (1992). *Just managing: Power and culture in the National Health Service.* London: Macmillan.

Oberfield, Z. W. (2014). *Becoming bureaucrats: Socialization at the front lines of government service.* Philadelphia: University of Pennsylvania Press.

Peters, G. B. (1998a). Managing horizontal government: The politics of co-ordination. *Public Administration, 76*, 295–311.

Peters, G. B. (1999). *Institutional theory in political science, the 'new institutionalism'*. London and New York: Continuum.

Swidler, A. (1986). Culture in action: Symbols and strategies. *American Sociological Review, 51*(2), 273–286.

Wanberg, C. (Ed.) (2012). *The Oxford handbook of organizational socialization*. Oxford: Oxford University Press.

CHAPTER 4

Research Design

Case Selection

Public hospitals in Estonia, Norway and Romania exhibit differences in the degree of autonomy and centralization/decentralization. Four types can be distinguished, which we define in the following way (Fig. 4.1). The Estonian hospital system is characterized by decentralized ownership and a high level of hospital autonomy. We name this an NPM case. The Romanian public hospital system can be divided into two subtypes depending on the type of hospitals. This is the case since not all public hospitals have been decentralized, although most of them have. A small part of the public hospital system in Romania, which we label non-NPM, includes centralized ownership and low hospital autonomy. Third, we have two mixed types. One is in Romania and includes decentralized ownership and low hospital autonomy and another mixed type in Norway which exhibits centralized ownership and a high degree of hospital autonomy. Despite differences between the three hospital systems, policy makers in all three cases have grappled with the same set of reform ideas: decentralization versus recentralization and hospital autonomy versus central ownership. Tension and conflict have been part of these relations, which implies that a theory that incorporates differing interests and conflicting goals is likely to be relevant in this context. The use of principal-agent theory is thus expected to helpfully inform our

© The Author(s) 2017
S. Dan, *The Coordination of European Public Hospital Systems*,
DOI 10.1007/978-3-319-43428-5_4

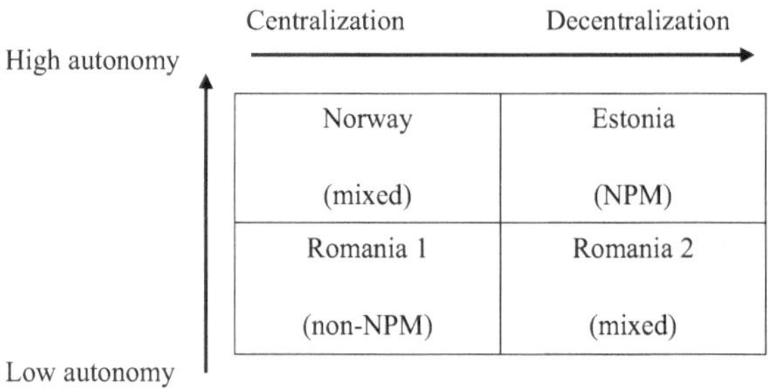

Centralization   Decentralization

High autonomy

Norway	Estonia
(mixed)	(NPM)
Romania 1	Romania 2
(non-NPM)	(mixed)

Low autonomy

Author's own compilation

Fig. 4.1   Type of public hospital systems
Author's own compilation. *Note: Romania 1 includes those public hospitals of regional and national importance which have not been decentralized and are still owned by the Ministry of Health. Romania 2 refers to most hospitals in the country and includes county and local hospitals which have been decentralized and are owned by local public authorities as a result of the decentralization reform.*

understanding of central coordination. For these reasons, these three cases are good examples of central hospital coordination in a context of NPM-type reform. These cases are different culturally, which is a good ingredient for a cultural perspective which we adopt on the basis of sociological institutionalism. As shown in Fig. 4.1, the cases reflect different arrangements in terms of hospital autonomy and decentralization. This further informed the case selection theoretically, and the decision to use three cases (rather than more or fewer) proved sufficient for this purpose. Practical concerns also had to be taken into account considering the time and financial constraints of a doctoral project. These countries, however, share characteristics of other similar countries and are examples of larger families of states: Nordic, Baltic and Central and Eastern European, respectively. In this sense, the implications of this research may apply beyond the borders of the three cases.

This classification of cases puts us in a position to analyze the relation between organizational reform, on the one hand, and coordination, on the other hand. The three hospital systems enable research on coordination problems in a context characterized by different hospital system arrangements (decentralization and level of hospital autonomy). This has a number of useful research implications. First, it allows us to compare different systems and to observe how central coordination is achieved in systems which exhibit different arrangements. Second, it is closely related to our overarching goal which is to investigate the relation between NPM reforms and coordination. This is relevant since, as we saw earlier, one of the major concerns in the post-NPM (and anti-NPM) literature is the lack of coordination as a result of NPM-type reform. The expectation therefore is that coordination problems are a bigger issue in strongly NPM systems (i.e. Estonia) than in mildly (Norway and part of the Romanian system) or non-NPM system (the other part of the hospital system in Romania). All other things equal, if we find more evidence of coordination problems in strongly NPM systems than in the other systems, then that evidence may support the assumption that NPM leads to or reinforces coordination problems. But if no convincing relation can be established between reform and coordination problems, then we are in a position to question this claim. Conversely, if coordination problems are identified in centralized and/or in systems with low hospital autonomy, then we can begin to question whether autonomy and decentralization are in fact the main drivers of coordination problems. This approach provides a framework in which the debate over NPM and coordination can be placed and discussed. Specific as well as broad—and interesting implications—could be drawn. Finding evidence that there are other important factors that explain why the center fails to properly coordinate the periphery may challenge some of the current arguments in our field. On the other hand, if we indeed find convincing evidence linking decentralization and autonomy with coordination problems, then these arguments will be reinforced.

METHODS OF PRIMARY DATA COLLECTION

The main source of empirical data consists of a program of in-depth, in-person semi-structured interviews conducted in each of the three country cases with both experts from ministries of health and other central healthcare institutions (i.e. national health insurance funds and audit offices) and from hospitals. The collection of data through interviews took place in two main phases: a preliminary phase and a main phase spread across three years during 2012–2014. The choice of in-person, in-depth interviews as the main data collection method reflected the challenges discussed earlier, some of which had been foreseen prior to field work. Difficulties with the internal validity of hard-to-define concepts had to be taken into account. It is difficult to ask a question about coordination, or coordination problems or hospital system culture or conflicting interests and goals, and expect that respondents are all thinking about the same thing. The main advantage of in-person, in-depth interviews lies precisely in the ability of the researcher to probe for further explanation and clarification on the spot, whenever necessary. We believe that this method considerably improved the internal validity of the research. An additional advantage of the method concerns the possibility to explore causal mechanisms connecting reform, on the one hand, with both coordination and coordination problems, on the other hand. The causal chain between these phenomena is not simple to spell out, and it involves intermediary layers and factors which could more easily be explored qualitatively than by using quantitative methods. The method did not allow the quantification of coordination and the control of variables. The use of complementary data sources can help to triangulate the perceptions obtained through interviewing. Overall, for these reasons, the choice of methods fitted best with our purposes, subject matter and setting of the research in different countries.

Preliminary Interviews

In the summer of 2012, the researcher conducted a series of preliminary open-ended interviews in Estonia and Romania in the attempt to gain direct contact with the larger debates on hospital reform in each country. He conducted in-depth face-to-face interviews with ten health experts in Romania and five in Estonia. In Estonia, the interviews were in English and in Romania in Romanian. The experts represented different types of organizations such as central government, health insurance funds, public hospitals, academia and local offices of international organizations. The principal criterion for selection was their direct experience with hospital reform in the past 20 years and their diverse organizational settings. It was important to assess the perception of different actors to understand the possibly different perspectives on hospital reform. In addition to insights on recent developments in hospital reform, many of the interviewees provided a list of helpful contacts and sources of secondary data, such as relevant legislation, policy and evaluation studies and statistical data.

The goals of these interviews were:

- to identify relevant sources of data on issues critical for the success of the research such as relevant legislation on decentralization and management autonomy;
- to discuss recent developments (legislative or of other nature, if they existed) concerning decentralization/recentralization and governance of public hospitals;

- to discuss the best approach to conducting field research, to be performed later in the course of the project.

PROGRAM OF SEMI-STRUCTURED INTERVIEWS

The main source of empirical data consists of a program of structured interviews with relevant actors in hospital reform and coordination in each country. Underlying this approach was the expectation that coordination problems are perceived and interpreted differently at various levels of the healthcare system. One can expect that national policy makers will emphasize the need for systemic coordination and performance, whereas representatives of hospitals might be more concerned about the need for local autonomy and organizational performance. This is particularly the case in the countries selected, considering that in each of these cases there have been intense discussions about the role of each level and the degree and type of autonomy that hospitals ought to enjoy. For this reason, it was important to select potential interviewees both from central institutions and hospitals. In selecting the population and the sample, we did not aim at representativeness. Other methods (e.g. survey-based) are in a better position to aspire for this than in-person, in-depth interviews. Case study-based research following a co-variational approach may seek sample representativeness, whereas in congruence analysis this is not a primary concern. Researchers using a congruence analysis are not interested in generalizing their findings from a sample to a population but in generalizing from empirical observations to theoretical concepts and theories. In this sense, our methodological approach is consistent with a case study approach based on congruence analysis. Nevertheless, we selected hospitals and individual interviewees guided by a set of criteria. First, centrally, we chose a pool of potential interviewees that were directly involved in hospital reform and governance. We aimed not for one but a plurality of interviewees assuming that they might have different views, whether they were part or not of the same organizational unit in the ministry or purchasing/funding agency. Second, in terms of hospitals the situation differed from one country to another. In Estonia, where the current hospital master plan includes 19 acute care hospitals, we sent a request to each hospital and finally conducted interviews in almost half of them (eight different hospitals). As the Appendix shows, these were of different types in terms of competence and complexity, size and geographic location. In Romania, where the population of hospitals is significantly greater, this approach was not possible. In this case, we chose hospitals of different types following the same criteria (size, competence and complexity, and region) as well as decentralization status (i.e. decentralized: owned by local administration, or centralized: owned by the Ministry of Health). In the end, we were able to conduct interviews in different types of Romanian public hospitals (Appendix). Another decision needed to be made about individual interviewees. We wanted to interview at least one representative of each hospital. Whenever possible this was the hospital manager, but in some cases when this was not possible, we interviewed another member of the executive or governing board. The decision reflected the assumption (which proved true) that hospital management would be in the best position to gauge the relation with central institutions and give informed answers about how the hospital as an entity works with other hospitals in the system. Other members of staff may have usefully provided relevant insights but those may have not reflected the situation of the hospital as a whole. The questions were aimed at assessing perception from the perspective of the hospital leadership rather than individual perception of hospital board members.

We designed two different interview questionnaires: one for central healthcare institutions and one for hospitals. Some introductory questions were identical while most questions were different—geared to the specific organizational setting of the interviewee. The researcher conducted the interviews in person. The Appendix includes the questionnaires in both English and Romanian. We conducted a total number of 57 interviews distributed as follows across country and organizational setting (Table 4.1). We either recorded or took detailed notes of all interviews, which were then analyzed following this standard process of qualitative data analysis:

Table 4.1 Interviews by country and organizational setting

Organizational setting Country	Central healthcare institutions	Public hospitals	Other	Total
Estonia	11	9	2	22
Norway	4	6	6	16
Romania	3	10	6	19
Total	18	25	14	57

Author's own compilation

Repeating ideas = > Themes = > Findings = > Conclusions

METHODS OF SECONDARY DATA COLLECTION

The findings chapters draw on empirical data collected in the course of the research and on relevant legislation, policy documents, evaluations and relevant published academic research. There are several reasons why it is advantageous to integrate secondary data with the primary research, although each source needs to be handled with care. First, it is important to look at academic studies for reasons of scholarly rigor and impartiality. However, the boundaries between what is academic and what is official policy are not always clear cut. This is particularly the case in the Estonian context in which a small number of experts work for central government or other national healthcare institutions and at the same time conduct academic research. The Health Systems in Transition (HiT) series of the European Observatory on Health Systems and Policies is a helpful source in this category. Two Estonian HiT reports (Koppel et al., 2008; Lai et al., 2013) have been used in this chapter. Using the same format, similar reports have been written for Romania and Norway. Another useful recent Estonian study is Habicht, Habicht, and Jesse (2011) which investigates hospital governance in great detail. Habicht, Aaviksoo, and Koppel (2006) evaluate hospital sector reform drawing upon a survey of hospital management and supervisory boards and interviews with key stakeholders. These are two studies in Estonia which specifically deal with a detailed evaluation of hospital governance in a context of hospital autonomy. They do not cover decentralization, but other studies treat decentralization to some extent (e.g. Koppel et al., 2008; Lai et al., 2013). A number of consultancy reports were produced that had an important impact on the development of the hospital system in Estonia. These influenced the adopted legislation and significantly shaped the reform model such as the Hospital Master Plan 2015 report (Hellers et al., 2000, see also Bakler, 2003). We have also consulted studies by international organizations which in part dealt with hospital governance (World Health Organization, 2005, 2010, 2011). Importantly, two evaluations by the National Audit Office of Estonia investigated the purchase and use of expensive medical equipment in hospitals (National Audit Office, 2008, 2011) and the sustainability of the hospital network in a context of changing socio-demographics (National Audit Office, 2010).

Hospital management reforms in Romania are more recent than in Estonia and Norway. This means, *inter alia*, that they have so far been under-researched. The public hospital system has continued to undergo change since 2010, when the decentralization reform occurred, and some structural and organizational change is expected to continue in the coming years. The empirical chapter draws on existing material and acknowledges that hardly any academic studies have been carried out so far focusing specifically on hospital decentralization and autonomy. One of the exceptions is Popa (2014) which studied the various stakeholders' perceptions on the decentralization reform as recorded in the newsprint media. Most sources, however, consist of legal acts, substantiation notes to the legal acts, official policy documents and technical reports conducted by different international experts to assist the World Bank's healthcare projects in Romania. As it will become clear in the empirical chapter, these technical reports, and the international organizations more generally, have been instrumental to both the launch and the content of the reform. Fortunately, these two main types of material have covered the reform in great detail, and the overall process, rationale, content and expected changes and benefits were easy to pin down. The interviews with key policy makers and hospital managers cast further light on the perceptions of reform. What is needed now, a few years after the adoption of the decentralization legislation, is an evaluation of the actual change on the ground and an assessment of the impact of the reform.

As in the case of Estonia, and unlike the Romanian case, there is considerable material available on the 2002 Norwegian hospital reform, which is the main hospital policy in Norway investigated in this research. The empirical chapter on Norway (Chap. 7) first introduces the idea of coordination of public hospitals in Norway, and draws upon various sources that document the rationale and content of the changes entered into force in 2002. In addition to secondary evidence, it makes use of the interviews conducted in Norway to evaluate the relationship between the 2002 hospital reform and coordination. We studied the official policy documents that introduced the reform proposal, particularly Proposition 66 (2000–2001) from the Ministry of Health and Care Services to the Parliament. The document includes detailed information about the rationale and need for reform and a discussion of expected impacts. We also looked at audit reports, evaluations and academic studies to complement the policy documents and concluded that hospital reform has received considerable attention in the past decade (e.g. Office of the Auditor General, 2009, 2012, 2013a, 2013b, 2014). The academic literature has investigated, for example, the economic effects of the reform (e.g. Magnussen, Hagen, & Kaarboe, 2007), the balance between central control and hospital autonomy (e.g. Lægreid, Opedal, & Stigen, 2005) and the governance of public hospitals (e.g. Magnussen, 2013). We have found less research on coordination of hospitals and more on hospital governance more broadly, although more generally coordination is a recurring theme in health policy and public policy in Norway. Importantly, the more recent coordination reform of 2012 aimed primarily at improving coordination between specialist and primary care, rather than at coordination of hospitals or between hospitals.

Intertwined with thinking about theories, that determined the choice of methods from the outset, the following theoretical challenges emerged in the course of the empirical research: conceptualization of coordination and coordination problems, thinking in before and after terms, and gathering data on both perception and "hard" evidence.

ADDRESSING SPECIFIC THEORETICAL AND PRACTICAL ISSUES

The Concept of Coordination

First, operationalizing coordination and distinguishing it from other similar and partially overlapping concepts, such as governance, collaboration and cooperation, was not easy. Coordination is not fully distinct from the other similar concepts referred to above—it presents some different facets and "borrows" from these concepts. Understood as a function of governance (but not the same as governance), the concept of coordination embraces the idea of working together which in the daily practitioner language is commonly referred to as collaboration or cooperation. In this sense, coordination includes key aspects from all these other concepts and is likely to be mistaken for one or more of them. Making sure that interviewees understood that it was systemic coordination that we were interested in was equally challenging. We addressed this problem by explaining the definition of coordination that we employed which is "the activity taken by national policy institutions such as ministries of health to ensure that public hospitals work as a whole system." Some hospital managers thought about this definition in terms of governance or the role of the ministry of health in governing their specific hospital. This was not a problem in itself since we were interested in the experience of their specific hospital. This did not imply a need on their part to take an integral view of the hospital system. Interviewees based in central institutions tended to approach the questions from a systemic perspective by virtue of their institutional affiliation. Some, however, took a more functional stand depending on their daily responsibilities but additionally were probed to think of the hospital system as a whole.

Defining Coordination Problems

Second, defining and explaining coordination problems also posed some challenges, though less so than the concept of coordination itself. To address this problem, we first made sure that the definitions used for each of these coordination problems were as practical as possible. For instance, in the interview questionnaire, sent out in advance, we used the following types and definitions of coordination problems:

- *Duplication or redundancy* which occurs when for example two different hospitals perform the same task that could be performed more efficiently and effectively in one place only
- *Omission or lacunae* involving gaps in performing a needed task so that a task ultimately ends up not being performed by any hospital
- *Contradiction* defined as differences in policy, legislation or regulations governing hospitals that contradict one another
- *Divergence* in the sense of self-interested action by a specific hospital that affects the system of hospitals as a whole.

In those situations when these definitions were not well understood, we provided examples of possible situations and asked if respondents were confronted with one or more of these situations. In-person interviews were helpful since they allowed the clarification of any misunderstandings on the spot. Sending a questionnaire or a survey would have not helped in this case, and it would have likely created much confusion about the meaning of these terms. Consequently, responses would probably have suffered from internal validity problems and therefore ultimately been of little help.

Thinking in Before and After Terms

Third, thinking in before and after terms was not easy for a number of reasons. It was difficult for some interviewees to remember what coordination had been like before the reforms. This was especially true in the case of Estonia which had undergone hospital reform much earlier than, for instance, Romania. Likewise, Norway reshaped its hospital system configuration a decade ago, but in this case, coordination has been a major policy concern in recent years and it was to be expected that thinking about the relation between reform and coordination would be easier under these circumstances. Relatedly, connecting reform with coordination and specifically with coordination problems was not always straightforward. Thinking causally on complex relations was expected to be hard. At the same time, it needed discretion on the part of the researcher to ensure objectivity and avoiding the pitfall of suggesting a certain response or line of thinking. We consciously sought to avoid this pitfall by giving respondents time to reflect on the likely causal chain between reform and coordination, and probed for additional elaboration and explanation when a certain causal pattern emerged. Probing interviewees to reflect on before and after terms facilitated causal thinking to some extent. Some respondents elaborated on the likely mechanism linking reform with coordination and were asked to provide specific examples based on their experience. Although interviews are not designed quantitatively to measure and assess the effect of reform on coordination, they proved helpful in revealing possible causal paths and mechanisms. This brought to light not one but quite a few mechanisms connecting reform with coordination.

Perception versus Evidence

Fourth, interviews in the three countries facilitated the collection of in-depth perceptions about hospital coordination. Perception, although useful, is likely to show only one "cut" of the story and leave out other possibly important facets. Perceptions, as useful as they are, are not the same as direct, concrete evidence. This was the case in this research, and in addressing this pitfall, we took the following preventive measures. First, we made sure to interview different actors to understand the problem more holistically than it would have been the case had we focused on specific cases or one group of respondents only. Considering the subject matter of vertical coordination of public hospitals, it was important to make sure that the interviewees represented both central and local institutions. It was to be expected that these different actors coming from different positions would likely have different views about the kind and extent of coordination that was needed. Second, we asked for hard evidence in addition to perceptions on the main claims that interviewees made. In-person, on the spot interviews again proved useful in this sense. The other type of evidence collected consisted of documentary and statistical data and research results that we had not been aware of beforehand. Others provided specific examples and referred to sources where these situations could be studied in greater detail. This was especially true in the case of coordination problems which were more amenable to exemplification. In this way, we learned for example about "diverging" hospitals or cases of policy contradiction and duplication.

Access, Cultural Differences and Language

Having access to the right people and needed data was to some extent a practical challenge but varied across countries. The challenge took two forms: no response and, in some cases, insufficient time to cover each question in the needed detail. Overall, it was easier to gain access to people and data in Estonia and Norway than in Romania. One explanation may be that there is simply less research on this topic in Romania than in the other countries, which in turn can be explained by the relatively recent hospital reforms in Romania. We believe, however, that there is more to it than this, and cultural factors have a role to play. This is manifested in a developing research culture or lack of experience or interest in participating in research. Issues of political sensitivity and transparency also seemed more problematic in Romania than in the other two cases. Healthcare and specifically hospital care, in which the stake is the greatest, are politically delicate issues. Under growing public and political scrutiny, both hospitals and central institutions found reform, organizational relationships, coordination problems and results to be highly sensitive issues. It was to be expected—and it turned out to be so—that these aspects would stir discomfort. Another reason that made research in Romania more challenging was the difficulty in some cases to find the necessary contact information for potential interviewees and plan interviews ahead in those cases where contact information was readily accessible. We believe that this can again best be culturally explained. It is common for professionals in Romania, due in part to low salaries, to have two, three or more different jobs at the same time. This was likely to make them less able to participate in academic research. We conducted the interviews in English in Estonia and Norway and in Romanian in Romania, after translating the original English version of the interview questions. We did not see in language itself a major barrier, although some potential interviewees in Estonia and Norway may have not replied to the request to participate in the research due to lack of sufficient English skills. Similarly, a small number of interviews were more difficult to conduct due to limited English proficiency. However, in these few cases, we sought to ensure mutual comprehension by adjusting speaking pace and rephrasing certain questions or words that were difficult to understand. The translation of the questions into Romanian was performed by the doctoral researcher with a view to limiting any differences arising from the translation process. The researcher translated the questions in such a way as to preserve the meaning of the original version. The Romanian word for coordination "coordonarea" resembles the English word, and both originate from the prefix "co" meaning together and the Latin word "ordinare" which means to place in the same order or rank. Whenever needed, the researcher defined, both for the English and Romanian interviews, the concept of coordination as conceptualized in this book.

These factors (i.e. culture, language) in some cases posed difficulties to a smooth empirical work and to some extent restricted access. To address these issues, we extended the original population of potential interviewees in all countries, especially in Romania where there was greater need to do so than in the other two cases. This was possible because the population of hospitals in Romania is much greater than in the other countries. In Estonia, the current hospital master plan includes 19 acute care hospitals, and almost half of them (eight) responded to the request to participate in the research. In those cases when the hospital manager was not available, we interviewed another member of the executive board. The same approach was taken in the case of central institutions. This enabled us to still be able to interview at least one representative from relevant institutions, be they hospitals or directorates in the ministry of health or the health insurance fund. In all countries, we selected and interviewed different types of hospitals according to different criteria: organizational status when relevant (i.e. centralized or decentralized), size, county, geographic region, and the competence and complexity of the hospital. In the Romanian case, due to the large number of hospitals and problems with access, the data collected through interviews need to be supplemented to address the research questions in the needed depth. To this end, in all three cases, we also draw on other sources such as official legislation, hospital system databases, statistical sources and published research on hospital reforms. These sources were used to complement the interview material.

BIBLIOGRAPHY

Bakler, T. (2003). "Hospital Master Plan'ist" haiglavõrgu arengukavani. [From "Hospital Master Plan" towards hospital network development plan] [In Estonian]. *Eesti Arst, 2003*(Special Issue for Health Forum), 23–27.

Habicht, T., Aaviksoo, A., & Koppel, A. (2006). *Hospital sector reform in Estonia. Summary.* Tallinn: Praxis Center for Policy Studies.

Habicht, T., Habicht, J., & Maris, J. (2011). Estonia. In R. B. Saltman, A. Durán, & H. F. W. Dubois (Eds.), *Governing public hospitals. Reform strategies and the movement towards institutional autonomy*, Hospital governance in eight countries (chap. 7, pp. 141–161). Copenhagen: World Health Organization and the European Observatory on Health Systems and Policies.

Hellers, G., et al. (2000). *The Estonian hospital master plan 2015.* Stockholm: SC Scandinavian Care Consultants and SWECO International on behalf of the Ministry of Social Affairs.

Koppel, A., Kahur, K., Habicht, T., Saar, P., Habicht, J., & van Ginneken, E. (2008). Estonia: Health system review. *Health Systems in Transition, 10*(1), 1–230.

Lægreid, P., Opedal, S., & Stigen, I. M. (2005). The Norwegian hospital reform: Balancing political control and enterprise autonomy. *Journal of Health Politics, Policy and Law, 30*(6), 1027–1064.

Lai, T., Habicht, T., Kahur, K., Reinap, M., Kiivet, R., & van Ginneken, E. (2013). Estonia: Health system review. *Health Systems in Transition, 15*(6), 1–196.

Magnussen, J. (2013). Hospital sector governance in Norway: Decentralization and the distribution of tasks. *Eurohealth Observer, 19*(1), 19–22.

Magnussen, J., Hagen, T. P., & Kaarbøe, O. M. (2007). Centralized or decentralized? A case study of Norwegian hospital reform. *Social Science and Medicine, 64*, 2129–2137.

National Audit Office of Estonia. (2008). *Meditsiiniseadmete soetamine ja kasutamine tervishoiuasutustes.* (Purchase and use of medical equipment in medical institutions). Tallinn: National Audit Office.

National Audit Office of Estonia. (2010). *Haiglavõrgu jätkusuutlikkus.* (Hospital network sustainability). Tallinn: National Audit Office.

National Audit Office of Estonia. (2011). *Järelaudit meditsiiniseadmete soetamisest ja kasutamisest meditsiiniasutustes.* (Follow up audit of purchase and use of medical equipment in medical institutions). Tallinn: National Audit Office.

Office of the Auditor General. (2009). *Investigation into the financial management of the regional health authorities and health trusts.* [Document 3:3 (2009–2010)]. Oslo: Office of the Auditor General.

Office of the Auditor General. (2012). *Efficiency and financial performance in state-owned companies should be followed up more closely.* [Press release]. Oslo: Office of the Auditor General.

Office of the Auditor General. (2013a). *An audit investigation of efficiency in hospitals.* [Document 3:4 (2013–2014)]. Oslo: Office of the Auditor General.

Office of the Auditor General. (2013b). *Execution of state ownership must be bolstered.* [Press release]. Oslo: Office of the Auditor General.

Office of the Auditor General. (2014). *Investigation of electronic messaging in the health and care sector.* [Document 3:6 (2013–2014)]. Oslo: Office of the Auditor General.

Popa, A. E. (2014). Hospital decentralisation in Romania: Stakeholders' perspective in the newsprint media. *International Journal of Health Planning and Management, 29*, 70–89.

World Health Organization. (2005). *Assessment of hospital reforms.* [Full report. World Health Organization Mission to Estonia]. Copenhagen: World Health Organization Regional Office for Europe.

World Health Organization. (2010). *Responding to the challenge of financial sustainability in Estonia's health system.* Copenhagen: World Health Organization Regional Office for Europe.

World Health Organization. (2011). *Responding to the challenge of financial sustainability in Estonia's health system: One year on.* Copenhagen: World Health Organization Regional Office for Europe.

CHAPTER 5

Coordination of Public Hospitals in Estonia

This first of the three case studies is structured as follows (the other two chapters follow a similar structure): It begins with description, continues with evaluation and ends with explanation. We first describe changes in public hospital policy and hospital trends and then move on to describe the specifics of hospital reforms analyzed in this book as they pertain to the decentralization and autonomy of public hospitals. Following this first part, we evaluate the relationship between public hospital reforms and coordination problems drawing on primary and secondary data sources. Finally, using the theoretical framework introduced earlier in the book, we seek to explain the effectiveness, or lack thereof, of central coordination.

OVERVIEW OF HEALTHCARE POLICIES AND HOSPITAL TRENDS (1991–2013)

The Estonian healthcare system has undergone major change since the country obtained its independence from the Soviet Union in 1991. Healthcare in Estonia is now organized, financed and coordinated in very different ways than it used to be in Soviet times. Soon after independence, policy makers took radical steps to reform the Soviet system and establish it on different grounds. The process had started in late 1980s with the new approach within the Soviet Union, which enabled the beginning of a

© The Author(s) 2017
S. Dan, *The Coordination of European Public Hospital Systems*,
DOI 10.1007/978-3-319-43428-5_5

process of reform in the member states of the union. Estonian authorities used this possibility and began planning for a new healthcare system based on a decentralized Bismarck-type health insurance arrangement. A main concern at that time was to do away with what was considered inefficient and low quality and realign the system to reflect Western developments and trends. This approach was part of a larger shift that affected not only health policy but also politics, the economy and society at large. The shift included a move from centralization to decentralization, planned economy to market economy and a single-party political system to multiple-party system. Some of the premises were laid out before independence, but it was after the independence that de facto change started to occur. Importantly, these changes had direct consequences on the organization, funding, provision and regulation of healthcare. Soon after independence, the Health Insurance Act established a health insurance system through which funds were collected through an earmarked social tax rather than channeled from the state budget as used to be the case before. One of the main principles of healthcare organization in those early stages was decentralization—which took different forms. It involved devolution of certain planning functions to municipalities, the creation of county-based sickness funds and de-concentration of planning and control to the county level (Lai et al., 2013, p. 33). In 1992, the status of medical staff changed from civil servant to employees subject to private labor contracting. After these decentralization initiatives, however, policy makers decided to integrate and recentralize certain functions to improve national coordination. This has been a trend that has persisted throughout the past 20 years. A recent example includes the centralization of primary healthcare management from county governors to the national Health Board. This change includes human resource planning which aims to cover possible shortages in primary care staff across the country (Lai et al., 2013, p. 152). Table 5.1 includes a list of the main changes since 1991–2013.

The number of hospitals in Estonia has decreased significantly compared to Soviet times. In 1991, there were 120 public hospitals with approximately 18,000 beds, but by 2001, the numbers fell to 67 and 9100 beds only. Many hospitals were either closed or turned into nursing homes because they did not meet new licensing requirements (National Institute for Health Development, 2014). This was especially the case in small localities and less so in urban areas. The declining trend continued well into the early 2000s, specifically 2003 when major organizational and planning reform led to a new configuration of the system consisting of a much

Table 5.1 Healthcare policy initiatives in Estonia, 1991–2013

Year	Policy initiative
1991	– Establishment of Health Insurance system and regional sickness funds through adoption of the Health Insurance Act (renewed) – Improving the provider licensing system – Beginning of primary care reform: introduction of the respecialization training for family doctors
1992	– Medical staff moved from a civil service status and began to work under private labor regulations – Development of the first essential drug list – Adoption of the National HIV/AIDS Program 1992–1997 (finished) – Established the Public Health Department in the University of Tartu by reorganization
1993	– Establishment of the Ministry of Social Affairs – Establishment of the State Agency of Medicine and the Centre for Health Promotion (the latter became the National Institute for Health Development in 2003) – Primary care reform: introduction of family medicine as a separate medical specialty and starting of postgraduate training – Introduction of the reimbursement system for the prescription of pharmaceuticals
1994	– Adoption of the Health Service Organization Act (renewed in 2001) – Establishment of the Central Sickness Fund with the subordinate regional sickness funds (centralized)
1995	– Adoption of the Medicinal Products Act (renewed) – Patient co-payments for primary care and specialist visits introduced – Adoption of the Public Health Act – Health Policy Document approved by the government (canceled in 2008)
1997	– Primary care financing reform and establishing requirement for family doctors to be registered – Adoption of the Mental Health Act – Adoption of the Artificial Insemination and Embryo Protection Act – National Program on the Prevention of HIV/AIDS and Other Sexually Transmitted Diseases 1997–2001 (finished) – Adoption of the National Tuberculosis Program 1998–2003 (finished)
1999	– Adoption of the Occupational Health Act
2001	– Adoption of the Estonian Health Insurance Fund Act – Renewal of the Health Services Organization Act (1994) – Adoption of the Law of Obligations Act
2002	– Establishment of Health Care Board (which became the Health Board in 2010 through merger of different agencies) – Renewal of the Health Insurance Act (1991) – Adoption of the National HIV/AIDS Prevention Program 2002–2006

(continued)

Table 5.1   (continued)

Year	Policy initiative
2003	– Adoption of the Hospital Master Plan 2015 – Adoption of the Communicable Diseases Prevention and Control Act – Establishment of National Institute for Health Development – Adoption of the first inter-sectoral health strategy: National Strategy for Drug Use Prevention until 2012 (finished)
2004	– Renewal of the updated Medicinal Products Act (1995) – Adoption of the National Tuberculosis Program 2004–2007 (finished) – Implementation of diagnosis-related groups as payment system
2005	– Adoption of the Blood Act – Adoption of the National Strategy for the Prevention of Cardiovascular Diseases 2005–2020 (abolished in 2012) – Adoption of the National HIV and AIDS Strategy 2006–2015 – Establishment of Estonian eHealth Foundation
2006	Updating of the Hospital Master Plan 2015
2007	Adoption of the National Cancer Strategy 2007–2015
2008	– Adoption of the National Tuberculosis Strategy 2008–2012 – Adoption of the NHP – Establishment of the health information system (nationwide e-health system)
2010	– Establishment of the Health Board as a result of merger of the Health Care Board, Health Protection Inspectorate, the Chemicals Notification Center and medical devices department of the State Agency of Medicine
2012	– Centralization of primary care organization

Source: Adapted from Lai et al. (2013, pp. 23–24).

smaller number of hospitals (Fig. 5.1). This has particularly been the case for acute hospitals, the number of which decreased to just over 20 by 2013. The process of reducing hospital capacity at that time involved mergers and integration of facilities and organizational forms. Despite this drastic decrease, which followed broader international and European de-hospitalization trends, compared to EU levels Estonia had more hospitals than average per 100,000 inhabitants throughout this period. The relatively low population density and decreasing population affected this trend, which however has not been characteristic of Estonia alone. The number of acute hospital beds (usually regarded as a better capacity indicator) has followed similar trends. Before the structural reform of the network, the number of hospital beds in Estonia was higher than the EU average, but by 2013, it was lower than both in the EU overall and in the EU 10 and approximately similar to EU 15 (Fig. 5.2).

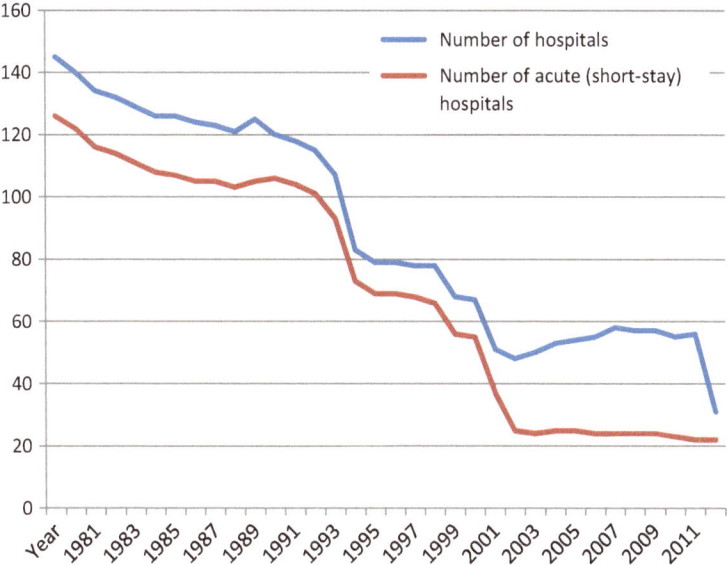

Fig. 5.1   Change in the number of hospitals in Estonia, 1981–2013
Author's own compilation. *Source*: World Health Organization, European Health
for All database, updated December 2015

The Reform Model: Hospital Management Autonomy and Political Decentralization

The Health Services Organization Act of 2001 came into effect in 2002 and proposed a new configuration of the publicly owned hospital network. Together with the Hospital Master Plan 2015 (HMP 2015), which was adapted to become the Hospital Network Development Plan (HNDP), it had the most significant impact on hospital organization and provision in the recent history of the country. For this reason, we divide the discussion on hospital reform into two major phases: before and after the adoption of the Health Services Organization Act of 2011 and the HNDP. These two phases are nearly equal in duration, each spanning circa a decade: 1991–2000 for the first phase and 2001–2014 for the second phase.

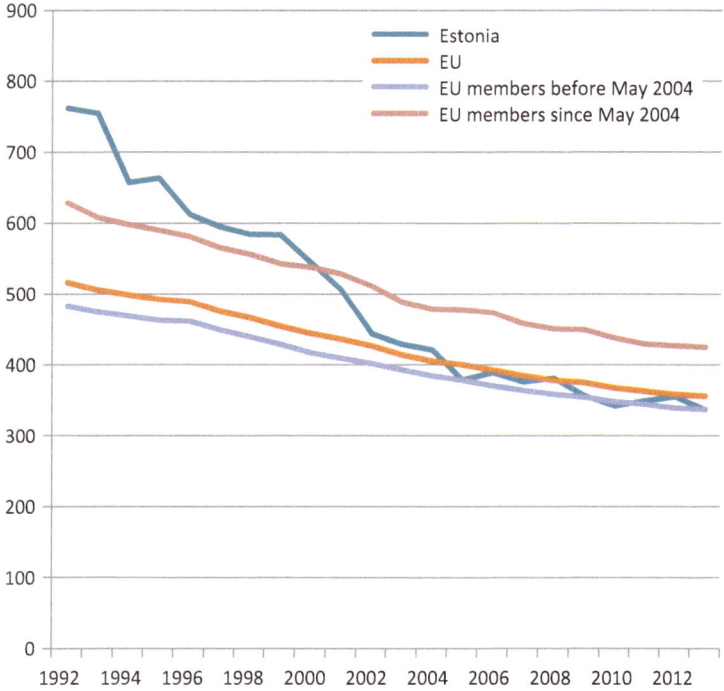

Fig. 5.2 Number of acute hospital beds per 100,000 inhabitants in Estonia, 1992–2013

Author's own compilation *Source*: World Health Organization, European Health for All database, updated December 2015

1991–2000

In the early 1990s, healthcare decentralization was one of the main policy goals, and it took different forms (Lai et al., 2013, p. 33). First, planning was devolved to municipalities. Second, through de-concentration, healthcare administrator positions were established in governors' offices in each county to ensure local planning and control. Third, 22 independent, non-competing sickness funds were set up in each county and a few main cities with the aim of contracting with hospital providers which were granted managerial autonomy to decide on staff and investment plans. These bold measures, however, proved problematic due to a number of factors (Lai et al., 2013, p. 33). First, counties lacked sufficient capacity to manage the new responsibilities and financial resources were limited so that in practice the new roles and functions could not be adequately exercised. Policy makers concluded that the setup of the regional sickness funds lacked coordination, and in 1994, they created a Central Sickness Fund under the supervision of the Ministry of Social Affairs. This decision was also motivated by regional inequalities since some regions fared better economically than others and there was no central pooling of funds (Koppel et al., 2008, p. 181, 184). The Central Sickness Fund was tasked with ensuring coordination and improving efficiency in resource utilization through central pooling and capitation-based allocation. The number of regional funds was reduced to 17 from 22. In the second half of the 1990s, the planning role of the Ministry of Social Affairs was enhanced, and increasingly the Ministry was expected to "lead the way" and provide an integrated approach to the healthcare and hospital system as well as overall leadership. Concurrently, counties and municipalities gradually decreased their planning role (Lai et al., 2013, p. 34).

The legislation in the 1990s had little regulatory power and did not regulate the form of hospital ownership. In a context of high decentralization, there was no comprehensive legislation regulating the entire system. Healthcare was regulated through ministerial directives pertaining to different types of healthcare services. The line item budget was replaced with a payment system based on services that were actually provided. The status of hospitals at that time was characterized in the following way (World Health Organization, 2005, p. 7):

- There was a mix of possible forms, which were not regulated by law, which is believed to have led to unclear roles, responsibility and accountability;
- The planning followed a decentralized model with significant decision making granted to local authorities;
- The management structure, despite early efforts to increase organizational autonomy, was thought to be limited and characterized by little coordination.

Hospitals at that time were owned by the central government, municipalities or other public organizations and were of different types, that is, central, general or local. Many hospitals were mono profile and focused on specific medical conditions and specialties such as tuberculosis, oncology or psychiatry. Due to inpatient overcapacity, the bed occupancy rate was not sufficient to ensure either financial sustainability or good quality of care (Hellers et al., 2000). Local and organizational interests prevailed over the interests of the system as a whole (Koppel et al., 2008, p. 187). Following the 1994s Health Care Services Organization Act, the ownership of most hospitals was transferred from the central government to municipalities. Most tertiary care hospitals (a total of seven) were still directly subordinated to the Ministry, but general (local) and long-term care hospitals fell under the administration of municipalities (Habicht, Habicht, & Jesse, 2011, p. 143). However, during the 1990s, some municipalities refused the administration of the hospitals within their jurisdiction while others accepted the new tasks but were unable in practice to provide proper management and governance. As a result, the Ministry was responsible for the administration of these hospitals as state agencies. Although the hospital configuration at that time was not sustainable and system planning was necessary, it was not until the late 1990s that comprehensive legislation was drafted. Regional and hospital plans, it was believed, needed to be confronted with long-term systemic planning, taking into account the sustainability of the system, demographic change, financial predictions, human resources capacity and growing public expectations. During the 1990s, some initiatives to improve hospital planning and efficiency in urban areas, especially Tallinn, were met with resistance (Estonian Health Insurance Fund, 2012, p. 87). At that time, there were 17 hospitals in Tallinn (compared with only 4 acute hospitals after the implementation of the HNDP). Confronted with negative media opposition, and aggravated by the Russian financial crisis in 1998 and 1999, the Government had to develop a new approach to reform, which followed soon afterwards.

2000–2014

The Estonian hospital reform of the early 2000s had its origins in the efforts taken during the 1990s. The reform process in this sense was incremental. The World Bank's Estonia Health Project 1995–1999 made an important contribution in preparing the way for what was soon to follow (Koppel et al. 2008, p. 186). The project loan led to the creation of a general health sector reform framework, helped build needed capacity at the center of government and stimulated political commitment to push reform forward.

HOSPITAL MASTER PLAN 2015

The first step was the development of the Hospital Master Plan 2015 (HMP). The stated objective of the Ministry of Social Affairs was "to obtain savings and increase the efficiency of hospital care by easing constraints effecting the hospital system in Estonia including unused capacity, long length of stay, deficiencies in management, budget, accounting and facility design" (Hellers et al., 2000, p. 59). Following a World Bank competitive bidding process, arranged by the Ministry of Social Affairs, two consultancy companies based in Sweden won the contract to develop a hospital master plan with a projection for 2015. The final report, delivered in April 2000 (see Hellers et al., 2000), presented the status quo of the hospital sector and benchmarked it against the Swedish and Norwegian systems. The report included a list of recommendations for change including the development of a more efficient and sustainable hospital network structure (based on four main regions, i.e. north-east, north-west, south-east and south-west), improved hospital licensing, quality insurance and accreditation, hospital infrastructure and specific recommendations for hospital planning in the capital city Tallinn (Hellers et al., 2000, pp. 9–15). The analysts concluded that the Estonian system was still characterized by hospital overcapacity compared to the Swedish and Norwegian systems. Hospitals were deemed "too many and too big and often in an unsatisfactory condition" (p. 60). Recommendations included a sharp reduction in the number of acute care hospitals based on existing and projected catchment areas, a reduction in the average length of stay and in the use of "social beds" within the acute network, and improvements in the bed occupancy rate. The report included specific recommendations that proved instrumental in reconfiguring the hospital network and later in developing the HNDP. These included:

- most Estonians would live within 70 km (one-hour distance) from an acute hospital;
- in each of the four main catchment areas, there would be a regional or a central hospital providing both secondary and tertiary care;
- the number of acute hospitals will be reduced through mergers and restructuring by three quarters—from 68 to a total of 13 by 2015, that is one university hospital (Tartu), one regional (Mustamäe), four central hospitals (Kohtla-Järve/Jõhvi, Tallinn Central, Tallinn

West and Pärnu) and seven secondary hospitals (Haapsalu, Paide, Rakvere, Narva, Kuressaare, Viljandi and Võru).

Although the plan was criticized by some for being too radical, policy makers in the Ministry of Social Affairs used it as an important basis for further discussion and consultation, and many of the principles and recommendations were included in the Health Services Organization Act, adopted one year later. The HNDP, finalized in 2003, originated in the Hospital Master Plan 2015.

Self-Governed Hospitals and Political Decentralization

Structural reform was envisaged through the Hospital Master Plan 2015 and the ensuing HNDP, but it was the Health Services Organization Act of 2001 that established the governance of the healthcare system. The changes legislated through this important piece of legislation were not completely new—a first act bearing the same name had already been adopted in 1994—but it clarified the legal basis of the system and incorporated the lessons drawn from the 1990s. Among the provisions of the new act, we mention the following (Habicht et al., 2011, p. 145):

- recentralization of planning functions
- the introduction of a new licensing system for both doctors and healthcare providers
- clarification and definition of the legal status of all healthcare providers, regardless of type, as private entities
- definition of financing responsibilities of different sources of funding
- creation of the Health Care Board as a central state agency of the Ministry of Social Affairs tasked with licensing providers and supervising the healthcare system.

The act defined seven types of hospitals depending on size, catchment area and type of care: regional, central, general, local, special, rehabilitation and finally nursing hospitals. The first four types provide acute services, while the rest provide long-term and nursing care. The law mandated all healthcare providers to operate under private law as autonomous entities based on three different legal forms: private entrepreneurs (for primary care practices) and foundations or limited-liability companies for hospitals. Following this corporatization reform, hospitals were organized either as foundations or limited-liability companies (also known as joint-stock companies). The legal basis for hospital foundations is the Foundations Act, while for limited-liability companies, it is the Commercial Code. These legal acts apply equally to all organizations regardless of sector which means that they also apply to the public hospitals in the same way (Habicht et al., 2011, p. 147). By law, hospitals organized as limited-liability companies are profit-making, while hospital foundations are non-profit. This implies that legally there is nothing that could prevent joint-stock companies for making profit, although there is no evidence that this has taken place thus far. The profit made is more likely to be invested in the hospital rather than paid to external owners and investors (Habicht, Aaviksoo, & Koppel, 2006, p. 10). Despite this difference between the two legal forms, some have argued that in practice there are no major differences in how they are managed and how they operate (e.g. Habicht et al., 2011, p. 147).

More than 60 % of all acute hospitals (12 out of 19) that are part of the HNDP are foundations, including the two largest regional hospitals in Tallinn and Tartu, respectively. Seven hospitals, most of which are small general and local hospitals, adopted the joint-stock company form. There are two notable exceptions to this pattern, however. The two relatively large central hospitals in Tallinn (East Tallinn and West Tallinn) also operate as limited-liability companies. Whether foundations or joint-stock companies, publicly owned hospitals can make decisions concerning staff management and compensation, equipment, infrastructure and financial matters. They also enjoy full residual claimant status which gives them the possibility to develop further based on hospital strategies, but they are also required to cover any debt they may incur. To the extent that the legislation and hospital statutes allow, each hospital has the freedom to decide on a wide range of organizational and governance issues including (Habicht et al., 2011, pp. 151–157):

- internal hospital structures with certain large hospitals adopting a decentralized organizational structure (while others a more integrated one) with the possibility of different units to retain earnings within that unit and pay staff accordingly
- clinical specialties, which are regulated by the Health Services Organization Act of 2001 depending on hospital type and through the licensing process, but hospitals still have some degree of freedom to choose which specialties to develop further;

- investment plans in equipment and infrastructure including the possibility to take out loans and use other financial instruments;
- co-payments for ambulatory care and individual bed days according to the law;
- remuneration policy, including the payment of performance-related pay and other bonuses.

The 19 acute care hospitals that were eventually included in the HNDP include three regional hospitals, four central hospitals, nine general hospitals and three local hospitals (Table 5.2). These publicly owned hospitals operating under private law were stimulated to become more professional and managerial—organizationally responsible for decisions made within a regulatory and financial framework. When asked to characterize the autonomy of their hospital management, most hospital managers have responded affirmatively stating that they enjoy sufficient autonomy to make both tactical and strategic decisions. Hospital managers in Estonia have experienced the discretion to make decisions and have learned to make use of this granted discretion. For example, one hospital manager emphasized that "within the budget framework, we are free to decide on

Table 5.2 Type of hospitals in the HNDP, Estonia

Regional	*North Estonia Medical Center Foundation*
	Tallinn Children Hospital Foundation
	Tartu University Hospital Foundation
Central	East Talinn Central Hospital Ltd
	West Tallinn Central Hospital Ltd
	East-Viru Central Hospital Foundation
	Pärnu Hospital Foundation
General	Järvamaa Hospital Ltd
	Kuressaare Hospital Foundation
	Läänemaa Hospital Foundation
	Rakvere Hospital Ltd
	South Estonia Hospital Ltd
	Narva Hospital Foundation
	Viljandi Hospital Foundation
	Valga Hospital Ltd
	Hiiumaa Hospital Foundation
Local	Jõgeva Hospital Foundation
	Põlva Hospital Ltd
	Rapla Hospital Foundation

Author's own compilation

a wide range of issues" (Interviewee 1). Another underlined the financial responsibility derived from the status of the hospital:

> "We can say that the hospital management is quite autonomous: we can make our own budget and have responsibility for economic management and the responsibility to hire doctors or nurses." (Interviewee 2)

Although hospital managers perceive their autonomy to be significant, the autonomy is not boundless. There are a number of legal provisions that regulate the activity of hospitals. In what follows, we discuss these in turn and will return to them later in the chapter when analyzing specific cases of central coordination.

First, according to the master plan, the type of hospital (i.e. regional, central, general and local) regulates what services each hospital can provide. The exceptions are the two largest regional hospitals (Tartu University Hospital Foundation and North Estonian Regional Hospital Foundation in Tallinn) which need to cover a wide range of tertiary care specialties. The second layer consists of four central hospitals. Although they can provide a wide range of services, their coverage is more limited than that of regional hospitals. Further down, general (county) and local hospitals are only allowed to provide a limited range of services. In short, this structural framework should in theory provide some limitation to hospital behavior in terms of the type of services hospitals are legally entitled to provide. Second, a financial framework, worked out by the Estonian Health Insurance Fund in consultation with the hospitals and medical specialties, regulates the number of cases that the insurance fund will purchase from hospitals. Hospitals may choose to treat more cases but will not be reimbursed if they exceed the limit or if they provide services that they are not legally allowed to provide. Third, hospital management is accountable to a hospital supervisory board which in most cases consists of local politicians. The exception is the regional hospitals where the central government is represented along with other societal stakeholders. Major decisions as well as the annual budget need the supervisory board's approval. A fourth category of central regulation includes licensing and approvals as, for instance, in the case of the construction of new facilities. Hospital managers, however, do not experience these limitations in the same way, and in some cases, it is debatable whether some of the regulation actually limits hospital decision making at all. Some of the managers have argued that the main restrictions to their autonomy are limited financial resources and/or medical staff rather than specific government regulation:

> "We report to the supervisory board and have to submit the budget annually. The main limit is finance; we have to make sure that finances are balanced. Also we need to make sure we have enough means for investment in technology. There are some formal things, bureaucratic mechanisms. For instance, concerning new buildings we need to provide information to the Ministry of Social Affairs concerning the number and type of beds; it's a kind of bureaucracy through which you still finally get what you want; sometimes you just have to do some stupid paperwork." (Interviewee 1)

Another manager made the same point while characterizing autonomy to be balanced—neither too much nor too little:

> "To me the system is quite balanced, we can't say we have too many restrictions or too free hands [...]. We still feel that the lack of resources or the lack of doctors affects managers' will more than other elements. It's about pure money because actually hospital managers have to make decisions based on the availability of resources and the number of doctors working in Estonia and the money available give quite clear borders for hospital managers to make decisions. We are not or cannot act in a way like we have unlimited resources, we just have to accept the realities." (Interviewee 3)

When it comes to the relationship with supervisory boards, this does not seem to restrict the possibility for management to make decisions, but it does mean that those decisions need to align with the vision of the supervisory board. Whether the views align depends on who is on the boards. The interviewed hospital managers have different backgrounds: Some have medical studies and later became hospital managers, but the majority of them have a business background, but have worked in healthcare for a number of years. Those with a business background were more likely to think managerially and use business language—words such as market, company, competition and quality—when referring to their activity. The possibility to make a wide range of decisions under the existing reform model is seen as empowering and motivational:

> "I think that before the reform there was no special motivation to the hospital management to do something or develop because before there was a fixed budget and the budget structure was also fixed. But now my budget structure is not fixed; I offer to the council and we negotiate; nobody else

can write the structure I should have and where I should invest... there is also bigger responsibility for me and motivation to think or do something. I am manager and would like to make good decisions and proposals to the owners so I am motivated to think." (Interviewee 2)

This empowerment, as we shall see in greater detail later in this chapter, can be channeled in different directions—it does not necessarily exclude unwise decision making. The intention of the reform model was to leave room for "self-regulation" and organizational financial responsibility. There is considerable evidence that this has occurred in practice, as expressed by this member of a hospital executive board:

"If you are under private law then principally you can decide, but if you make foolish decisions then you have fewer possibilities the next year. If you have surplus then you can implement your ideas but if you have minuses then you can't do it because banks are not going to help. If a hospital is state owned and you want a loan from a bank you need to go to the government or the Ministry of Finance." (Interviewee 6)

Considering that the reform was implemented in 2002, it was important to assess whether the autonomy of hospital management has changed in the meantime. Interviewees considered that the autonomy and the model of the system more generally had not changed much since 2002. This general opinion was echoed by a member of the executive board of one of the hospitals in Tallinn who drew a parallel between hospital autonomy, entrepreneurship and central and local governance:

"My opinion is that autonomy is the same as in 2002 when the biggest reform was made and that meant that we are for example a limited stock company. That means that our shares are owned by the municipality 100 % and the form of entrepreneurship, or how do you call it, that automatically, by the law, means that the Ministry of Social Affairs or the local government cannot act like an administrative body of the organization and their influence is minimized." (Interviewee 5)

Hospital managers, many of whom have business training, have been stimulated and have learned "the trade of doing healthcare business." They understood that the reform model is management oriented rather than government centered. In terms of hospital decentralization, there are a number of features that characterize the publicly owned hospitals.

The hospital system is largely decentralized in the sense that most hospitals are owned or founded by local authorities rather than the central government. The exception is regional hospitals that provide tertiary care. This local ownership means in practice that hospital supervisory boards consist of local politicians. In the case of regional hospitals, there is more variation in the structure of the supervisory boards. That structure also includes the central government in these few cases only. Some interviewees have expressed concerns about the implications of this situation. These include concerns about the professionalism and decision-making capacity of supervisory boards as well as the role of local politics and local interests. While local politicians might act in such a way as to promote the interests of their local constituencies—and hence promote democracy locally—interviewees have tended to perceive the role of politicians as being "political" *par excellence*. This means that hospital managers perceive politicians to act for political purposes, which may change regularly, and do not have the capacity to help develop the hospital on a long-term and sustainable basis. One interviewee has captured this aspect in the following way:

> "Members of the supervisory boards are mostly politicians, so they come and go and don't have time to learn about healthcare management. Only for a few of them is this something in which they have specialized knowledge." (Interviewee 6)

Especially in a context of pressure for the reorganization of small hospitals, local politicians have attempted to preserve the status quo and fought for the survival of the small hospitals in their jurisdiction. One interviewee stressed that this had been a major struggle:

> "A second issue is the struggle for survival of the small county hospitals. According to the hospital master plan and common sense they should have changed their profile because they have too few patients but it is not competition in the medical field but political fight because politicians in each county are trying to defend the status quo to have the hospital because it's one of the biggest employers. Nevertheless, there are issues with three things: patients, doctors and money." (Interviewee 1)

Fighting to keep the local hospital network unchanged may affect the ability of central policy institutions to enact change to the system as a whole. The local interest contradicts the national interest. Furthermore, the governance structure appears to impede central policy-making as long as the state is not represented in the governance structures of small hospitals and hospitals themselves are autonomous entities. As one concerned interviewee argued:

> "It's a concern maybe even a problem… if you think you have a strategic state level hospital network, from the health insurance fund point of view you have to give them contracts. They have a huge advantage compared to other providers. If you know the governance structure, the state is represented only in the supervisory boards due to state ownership but stays away from local hospitals supervisory boards which I think is nonsense because they have state-level priorities. So decisions are made without any kind of influence or any kind of say from the state." (Interviewee 8)

Do Self-Governed Hospitals Compete or Collaborate?

The reform model characterized by limited central coordination is expected to stimulate competition between hospitals. This is especially so in a context of limited financial resources, a limited number of specialized medical personnel and changing socio-demographics. We first discuss whether hospitals in Estonia compete and, if so, we ask if this competition is systemic or specific to some regions, hospitals or types of care only. We then discuss what hospitals are competing for, followed by an explanation of the reasons why hospitals compete. We are particularly interested in whether there is a relation between the type of hospital system and competition. We then turn to how interviewees assess competition, and find that competition has both advantages and disadvantages. We then present findings on the relationship between competition versus collaboration and end this section with a discussion of findings on alternatives to competition. Our research shows that competition only partially crowds out collaboration. Conversely, from a cultural perspective, collaboration only partly crowds out competition. Competition between hospitals was not entirely a product of the reform, but our research shows that the reform model created an impetus for competition.

A first finding concerning competition is that publicly owned hospitals in Estonia do compete with one another. The majority of interviewees, whether members of hospital management, central policy makers or auditors, have shown that competition is an important feature of the system. Some interviewees have argued that competition is widespread, while others think that competition occurs mostly between the large hospitals, that is Tallinn versus Tartu, on the one hand, and Tallinn versus Tallinn, on the other hand. The fact that there are three main hospitals in Tallinn that to some extent provide similar services in the same specialties leads to competition between them. Tallinn, though a large city by Estonian standards, is a small city by European standards. The three main hospitals in Tallinn share the same "market," as one interviewee emphatically put it:

> "We are acting on the Tallinn market; we have 400,000 citizens [...]. The hospitals want to develop their activity and that's why we have to compete for contracts. All depends on contracts, on the number of patients and the amount of money. If you lose patients, you lose money and you can't develop that particular area of your organization; that's the problem. If the government says that there are too many hospitals in Estonia, then why doesn't the government do something?" (Interviewee 5)

There is also competition between the two main regional hospitals providing tertiary care in Tallinn and Tartu respectively, though some have been reluctant to call this competition in a market sense. They have considered the nature of the healthcare market, which does not follow the textbook rules of a competitive economic market as well as existing friendly agreements between these two top medical centers. Although there are different autonomous players on the market and some of them provide similar services, there is only one purchaser of services, the health insurance fund. While this is true, patients are free to choose a provider of their choice. Assuming that hospitals they choose are entitled to provide that service, the health insurance fund is expected to purchase the service. Since hospitals have the capacity to provide more services than they currently do, they are interested in increasing the volume of service. Hospitals, under these conditions, compete for patients and money from the insurance fund, which means that some elements of an economic market really do exist. Other voices, however, do not consider that competition is so prevalent, and, if it exists, believe it is concentrated in Tallinn and between Tallinn and Tartu. Small hospitals do not compete because they serve different catchment areas:

> "There is competition for patients but it is not so rough because of geographic limitations. Sometimes there is competition for tertiary hospital services between the major hospitals. The big fight, in fact, is for health workers due to emigration. There is a lot of tension in the system because professionals have to work harder due to emigration of part of the workforce, hence the strike last year." (Interviewee 6)

This interviewee—who had an instrumental role in the adoption of the healthcare reform—argued that there is no hospital-free market in Estonia. The system is planned according to the HNDP, and it is in effect a kind of planned, rather than free market:

"Concerning competition I can see it in two places only: in Tallinn and in Tartu; in all other places it doesn't work. [...] I don't see too much competition in this system; it is some kind of mixed system between planning and free development..." (Interviewee 11)

Although competition exists, it is not systemic: It only concerns certain hospitals and services that are better paid than others. As a result, hospitals are interested in providing more of what is profitable, and there is evidence that they have the tools and information needed to assess which services are profitable and which are not, as this quotation shows:

"Of course, as in other countries where financial resources are limited, hospitals have more capacity to provide services than we have money to pay them. We have not had such kind of a systemic problem, but we have time after time some problems in some specialties that are very well paid by the insurance fund and we have some services that are more profitable. And hospital managers are very smart people and they know every year which services are more profitable and then all hospitals are interested in those specialties and services." (Interviewee 10)

Hospitals compete for patients, type and volume of service, contracts with the health insurance fund and medical personnel:

"This competition issue, there is interest in providing more expensive services and buying equipment to provide these services more and more and to compete for getting patients. Competition for good specialists who can provide these services is also an issue. Sometimes looking at waiting lists; in some hospitals they are bigger than in others but it's hard to evaluate them. There may be pressure for funds to get more money because of these lists." (Interviewee 9)

There is disagreement about the causes and effects of competition and about whether the setup of the system is intrinsically prone to favoring competition. Whether competition crowds out collaboration is also controversial. One line of thought is that the reform model comprised of autonomous and decentralized hospitals triggers or reinforces competition. When asked about the relation between the reform model and competition as compared to the situation before the hospital reform was implemented, interviewees were more likely to think of the current system as more prone to competition than was the case before. Some hospital managers, in particular, feel empowered and incentivized to compete:

> "One of the advantages of the current system is that there is more competition in the system. We are acting on the market like other enterprises. I will describe this as a positive thing. [...] We are ready to compete to obtain some agreement and we are ready to compete with the other Tallinn hospitals." (Interviewee 5)

Another interviewee who drew a clear connection between the setup of the system and the inclination to compete put it this way:

> "There is a link with the system because hospital management is interested in providing more services, more expensive services to get more money because they want to develop so it's their decision... but this was maybe one of the goals of the system: to make hospital managers interested in the activity and they have become interested, and now we have to manage it in the opposite way." (Interviewee 9)

Speaking from a policy-making position, this person observed how the reform reached one of its intended goals, but this has also become part of the problem. It is important to note that without the autonomy to decide on service organization and provision, hospitals might not have developed the interest in developing their activities. The autonomy granted to hospitals was instrumental in this respect. The healthcare system is embedded into the larger pro-market and pro-business socio-economic context of post-independence Estonia. It is consequential that in a country of the size of Estonia, inter-sectoral labor mobility is common, and, once the system was set up, business managers to a significant extent started to populate hospital executive boards. Since independence, there has been openness for private managers and ideas, which helped shape the system on a quasi-private basis and which later stimulated openness to private management practices. The attitude of the hospital leadership drives competition. This leadership can derive from general management, as we have seen earlier, or from professionals, particularly chief doctors in certain specialties who desire the latest equipment and are interested in medical innovation:

> "In hospitals the level of competition is mostly determined by the attitude of the so-called chief doctors and that's it, chief doctors who are concerned

with the hospital they are working in, with the highest level of service or with services which maybe are not needed by the population at that level that hospitals are trying to offer..." (Interviewee 3)

We have not identified hospital management as a group as always having the same attitude to competition. Among the respondents included in the research, there are both hospital executives and representatives of central institutions who think competition has both positive and negative effects. Variation in perception depends on belief in the role of competition in healthcare or the nature of the healthcare "product"—public good and subject to no competition whatsoever, public but subject to competition and private good subject to competition on the market. A first group of interviewees consists of those who are against competition. They think that healthcare is a public good, and competition is likely to make things worse. For example, they argue that as a result of competition, hospitals fight with one another for contracts, medical personnel and patients. Some interviewees are, however, quite ambivalent about the mechanism through which competition is likely to make things worse and the specific deteriorations resulting from competition. For example, this interviewee seems to believe that competition between corporatized hospitals leads to hospitals "fighting" with one another. However, she also believes that competition is "power for development" and therefore a good thing:

> "I think that in some ways the previous centralized system was better. In a centralized system there is not such a big fight between hospitals as it is now. It is said that this is power for development, so competition is good." (Interviewee 12)

As long as healthcare is different from a business market, competition in the hospital sector may not work. A middle-ground view sees the corporatized hospital system as a complex system that is difficult to control and, as a result, it leads to different effects—some positive and others negative. Due to the high degree of autonomy, hospitals have developed a certain organizational identity that is distinct from that of other hospitals. This means in practice that they are interested in developing their own "business":

> "The system has its pros and cons, I cannot say that it's completely good or completely bad [...] Hospitals try very hard to be the best compared to other hospitals and it may sometimes be good for the patient. But it all comes with very ridiculous waste of resources in developing several health

or hospital information systems with wasting medical staff working hours in different hospitals so… it's hard to say if it's completely black or white but for me it does not make much sense…" (Interviewee 3)

There is a third view which sees competition as positive overall. This does not mean that there are no issues stemming from hospitals competing with one another, but overall, despite these possible issues, the benefits exceed the costs. An important benefit of competition is the drive toward quality improvement. In a country once characterized by basic socialist healthcare services with little innovation, this benefit should not be underestimated. The competitive pressure can be a remedy against organizational sloth:

"If we don't have competition at all and only one hospital for all patients, then I think the quality at least the client quality goes down, so we should have some competition between hospitals. But I think that 19 hospitals today are too much. If we look to the future I think that for Estonia six hospitals are enough." (Interviewee 2)

"Hospitals are first of all competing for patients; if you want to get more patients you need to provide very good services and it means that you must work with the staff, you must have qualified staff, you must give them good salaries; you can hire doctors from other hospitals. […] I think competition helps in this respect… I think it leads to better quality in Estonia. I would assess it as positive. […] In terms of disadvantages, I can't say that if a hospital takes our patients, that that is a problem; it means that we need to improve…I cannot say that a centralized system is better, nowadays medicine is so quickly developing; nobody wants to be at the same level of staff; staff want to develop, to do more. If they see something elsewhere they want to develop that too. […] I think that competition has been a key element to develop quality in Estonian hospitals; I don't see any major problems with it. From a patient perspective, it is also good." (Interviewee 12)

Furthermore, there is also a sense in which competition makes hospitals more patient-focused. It is, nevertheless, debatable if this resembles client-focus in a business sense. It is questionable what the implications of patient-focus are, particularly from a clinical perspective. Patients may feel better in their interaction with the hospitals, but this does not necessarily mean that clinically they are better off. With many advanced medical services, patients are not easily able to assess the clinical quality of their treatment. There is, however, considerable evidence that the competitive pressure has at least contributed to a change of attitude in how hospitals interact with their patients. Again, this is a novel development in a post-communist context—as it is also the case in Romania and elsewhere in the post-socialist world. If we compare the current situation with the Soviet system where patients had little say and little to choose from, then this change in hospital-patient interaction is a major improvement in itself. Therefore, it can be considered a major step forward even if clinical quality may not have yet improved significantly. Ideally, the improvement in patient interaction should also lead to improved clinical outcomes, but clinical outcomes depend on many other factors including the quality of the treatment. Clinical outcomes matter the most ultimately, but we can think of patient-focus as an important step toward improved outcomes. For example, this interviewee specifically stresses this benefit:

"From a patient perspective I think that competition is a good thing. I can choose, I should be polite with my client; the patient is the client, it is very important. When I have to do nothing to obtain an agreement or contract I don't care about that. It helps the organizational culture…" (Interviewee 5)

Those interviewees who favor competition are more likely to think in market terms and compare the status quo with a situation in which there is no competition. They see monopoly in healthcare—the case in which only one hospital in the country provides a certain service—to raise a number of problems. These include an increase in prices through price making and the lack of a second opinion, which may be important for clinical purposes.

We now turn to the findings on the relation between competition and collaboration. The question is, given the competition in the system, do hospitals still work together? If yes, in what ways? Does competition crowd out collaboration? There is evidence that notwithstanding competition, hospitals do collaborate when need be. This collaboration, however, can best be described as purposeful. Hospitals tend to engage in it when they have an interest to do so. This is, for example, vividly described in this quote which critically assesses the behavior of hospitals:

"Hospitals have their own institution, speaking of networking, and they are coordinating their work quite a lot, but they definitely, for example, don't share the market there. If they want something against the doctors or against the health insurance fund, they are cooperating very well, but all the other times they think they are on the market." (Interviewee 13)

This collaboration takes different forms. For instance, hospitals refer patients to other hospitals for certain treatments that are not available in-house or purchase services from other medical institutions. The hospitals in Tallinn collaborate while still competing at the same time. They collaborate in some ways, when need be, but compete in other ways when money is at stake. Their natural penchant in Tallinn may be to compete rather than work together, but this does not mean they do not work together at all. Hospitals seem to collaborate because they have to and not because they want to:

> "We are also collaborating; if we don't have some technical system, we buy certain analyses from the North Estonia Regional Hospital, for example. If we don't have it, our patients go to other hospitals and they make that procedure and then patients come back to us. It's collaboration but the problem is for example with MRI; the price of the procedure is so good. So if you talk about collaboration, it's a problem. For us it is more profitable, it is good for us to have MRI on our own and not buy these services from other companies which are acting on this market." (Interviewee 5)

Overall, however, hospitals in Tallinn are perceived to compete rather than collaborate which is different from what happens in other parts of the country. This shows that despite the corporatized nature of the hospitals and the inclination to compete, hospitals do collaborate:

> "There is collaboration in the hospital system. In Estonia there is quite a different picture between what is going on in Tallinn and what is going on in other hospitals and I would say that cooperation is on the level of clinical pathways, and how doctors have their social ties with colleagues from other hospitals concerning treatment and how to move patients from one hospital to another... So I would say there are quite a lot of activities which you can say are about cooperation." (Interviewee 3)

Some non-Tallinn hospitals have also experienced a difference compared to the situation right after the reform. They are more inclined to collaborate now than was the case at that time. Hospitals have been under pressure to increasingly integrate their activities and look to the system and less to their own house, and there is some evidence that to some extent they have followed this direction:

> "From our perspective, at the beginning it was like a market and we were competitors, but now we cooperate more and more. We have quite a normal working network between the hospitals. Big hospitals are trying to connect

with small hospitals...these are voluntary connections, for instance doctors in big hospitals work partly in smaller hospitals. And from now on the connections will start to be official. So we are sitting and talking about how patients can have the best treatment. This means that patients don't have to be treated in my hospital, but they have to receive the best treatment." (Interviewee 7)

We specifically gathered evidence on the state of the hospital sector compared with the situation before the reform. We were interested in assessing the model of the reform compared to the previous system. We have found that interviewees—regardless of institutional affiliation—were overall positive about the reform. This does not mean that they thought the current system had arrived to where it should be. Throughout this chapter, we provide empirical evidence pointing to concerns and problems with the decentralized and autonomous hospitals coupled with weak central coordination. Nonetheless, not even a single interviewee advanced the idea of going back to the situation before the reform. They have clearly experienced improvements in the past 10 to 15 years. These improvements have included changes in standard measures of efficiency, financial discipline and the sustainability of the system considering that no other major organizational change has been adopted since the hospital reform. Had the system not worked, major change would have been expected. That, however, has not occurred, as the corporatized and decentralized arrangement is still operating today, years after the reform:

"Sometimes hospitals behave responsibly but sometimes there are problems. Let's say that all systems have their positive and negative aspects. During these ten years we have acknowledged what the negative aspects of this system are. Yes there are, but let's say that the ideal system does not exist... it's about how do you manage the disadvantages. [...] The previous state owned and funded system was obviously very inefficient, so this problem we have solved if you look at the common efficiency indicators: number of beds, bed occupancy rate, average length of stay in hospitals and so on." (Interviewee 9)

This same theme is also evident in the following assessment based on personal experience before and after the reform:

"The tricky thing is that I remember that time when the hospitals belonged to the structure of the ministry ... and it was a very bad situation because these hospitals had no financial discipline because they had no personal financial responsibility. They wasted the entire budget they received from the ministry until the summer and then they came to the ministry and asked for additional money and there wasn't any budgetary discipline. I think this is the biggest change: that now they are quite autonomous from the ministry and they feel they are responsible for all that happens in hospitals. If they were part of the ministry then they would not feel any responsibility. It is my personal experience; I had been here already since 1998 and I saw the end of the ministry hospitals and the start of the new system. For the system this means that we can control the costs better than 15 years ago..." (Interviewee 10)

What is also evident in these assessments is the perception that giving distinct financial responsibilities to hospitals through their own management and supervisory boards improved overall financial discipline. There are exceptions, as we document in this chapter, but overall the system has not succumbed to financial and fiscal pressure. Financial mismanagement was one of the main worries of the promoters of the reform, but so far no hospital has gone bankrupt:

"The main worry when we implemented these changes was how well they followed the financial rules and how disciplined they were with their budget, but our experience is that we follow up their budget situation: how much loans they have and how stable their budget and how sustainable they are. That was our main worry. And time and after we had some problems with the management of specific hospitals, but if we look at the hospital network as a whole there are no big financial problems." (Interviewee 10)

Politically, the policy position still favors the current model, as clearly expressed by this interviewee from the Ministry of Social Affairs:

"The system based on autonomous hospitals works; we are satisfied and have no plan to change it." (Interviewee 10)

Likewise, other stakeholders see that the problems with the system would not warrant fundamental change to the model, for instance centralizing the ownership or changing the legal form of hospitals:

"I think it was the best that could happen; nevertheless, there are many details that could be better but the scenario was the best. You can't make the state so thin that you can only see the skin." (Interviewee 1)

Improving collaboration between hospitals and increasing the level of inputs, especially financial resources and medical personnel, can help address some of the problems of the system today:

> "The system is working well but it can be improved. If we cooperate more now as part of these networks it will be better, I hope. Since five years ago when the head of the Tartu University Hospital, Urmas Siigur, said at a conference: stop the fighting and start cooperating. The system is working well given the level of inputs. We think that we cannot be more effective with the current level of resources. What we are missing is money and doctors and nurses. If we don't put more money into the system and raise salaries our doctors and nurses will continue to leave the country…"
> (Interviewee 7)

This problem with medical and nursing staff leaving the country is itself an effect of competition—international competition—because the job market for highly trained professionals is international. Strengthening central coordination could be achieved through developing and implementing a system of quality indicators. Improving and enforcing regulation could resolve the lack of coordination concerning the purchase and use of expensive medical equipment. The question remains if changes in this direction would alter the model—stronger central coordination is likely to mean less hospital autonomy in practice. While there is an inherent trade-off between central coordination and local autonomy, it may also be possible to improve central coordination in some sore areas while at the same time leaving hospitals the possibility to decide on a range of operational and tactical aspects. This means that the reform model could co-exist with stronger central coordination.

Mechanisms and Instruments of Coordination

The 2001 Health Services Organization Act stipulated the coordination mechanisms at the national, local and hospital level. Given the two possible legal forms, hospitals could either be "founded" in the case of foundations or "owned" in the case of limited-liability companies. The Act did not specify one founder or owner for each hospital only—more than one was possible. They could be the central government, municipalities, other public legal bodies or a combination of these. In this sense, Estonian hospitals, though autonomous entities grounded in private law, are publicly owned. All hospitals were required to operate following a governance model with both a management and supervisory board. Management boards are responsible for daily operations, whereas the supervisory boards appoint and supervise the management activity, and provide strategic planning. Founders or owners nominate the members of the supervisory board which in turn appoint the management board. It is the responsibility of the management board to decide on the internal hospital structure, activities and processes. Accountability follows the same vertical structure: The management board is accountable to the supervisory board which is in turn accountable to the founders or owners (Habicht et al., 2011, p. 148). The lines of accountability are designed to ensure that hospitals operate in the public interest. The model thus consists of three governance layers. However, national actors (i.e. the state) are only part of the structure in those few cases in which the central government is a founder or owner. There does not seem to be greater competition in hospitals with government representatives in the hospital supervisory boards than in hospitals without government representatives in the hospital boards. This may mean, as we have seen, that in practice through this model, national actors cannot hold supervisory and management boards accountable, nor directly coordinate their activity. This is expected to fall under the purview of the other owners or founders (i.e. municipalities, the University of Tartu) which may or may not share the vision or the interests of national policy makers.

Hospitals in the HNDP derive most of their revenue from public sources through contracts with the Estonian Health Insurance Fund, which are negotiated by the management board. Owners or founders may not have an important role to play in this process, nor is there any guarantee that they (or the supervisory board) have the capacity or the interest to get involved in the details of this process. The steward of the hospital network is the Ministry of Social Affairs and its central agencies, which together are responsible for planning, regulation, supervision and policy development. These various functions, along with more specific provisions, are stipulated in the Health Services Organization Act 2001 with subsequent amendments. The Health Board, a central agency, is expected to play a key role in protecting health, enforcement of regulation and hospital licensing. By law, the Ministry of Social Affairs is expected to coordinate:

- the requirements for the preparation of reports on healthcare statistics and economic activities in the field of healthcare, the composition of the data and the submission procedure;
- the functional development plans of hospitals, the approval procedure, medical technology and building design documentation;
- access to healthcare and maintaining waiting lists;
- quality assurance requirements

The hospitals in the HNDP—the government network—are entitled to preferentially sign contractual agreements with the insurance fund and were included in national development plans for infrastructure renovation and development. The different categories reflect the spectrum of medical services that each type is expected to provide and the catchment area it is expected to serve. First, North Estonia Medical Center and Tartu University Hospital are the two largest medical institutions in the country, and each covers a population of 500,000. Tartu University Hospital, however, provides a wider range of services, including pediatric care, whereas the North Estonia Medical Center has a more limited coverage. Some specialties are historically covered by the three other main hospitals in Tallinn, especially by the West Tallinn and East Tallinn central hospitals (Koppel et al., 2008, p. 111). This situation sets Tallinn apart from the rest of the country. The Tallinn Children Hospital is likewise classified as regional, is smaller in size and provides pediatric services for the Northern part of the country. Altogether, the three regional hospitals provide more than a third of total bed capacity (Habicht et al., 2011, p. 146). The plan also envisaged four so-called "central hospitals" (two of which are based in the city of Tallinn), each serving a catchment area of 200,000 population. These are different from the three regional hospitals, and these "central hospitals" provide 23 % of the total number of beds. Unlike the regional hospitals, by law, these four central hospitals were expected to provide primarily secondary care along with a narrower range of tertiary services. General hospitals are usually county hospitals with the exception of the counties where a regional or central hospital was already envisaged. The general and local hospitals are smaller than the rest and in total provide close to a third of the total bed capacity (Habicht et al., 2011, p. 146). The hospital network is thus an important mechanism of coordination of the organization and provision of hospital care.

CASES AND PROBLEMS OF COORDINATION

Coordination of Medical Personnel: A Problem of Contradiction

In a context of worries about the international mobility of doctors and nurses, an important question concerns the response of central government to what has increasingly become a crisis of medical personnel. This is a wider concern internationally as professional mobility raises questions about who loses and who wins. Within Europe, two of the main patterns of professional mobility have been from the East to the West and from the South to the North (Buchan, Wismar, Glinos, & Bremner, 2014). There are also major flows from outside of Europe into Europe. Each medical institution in Estonia, by virtue of its autonomous status rooted in private law, is free to make decisions on the employment and remuneration of medical personnel. There is the provision that each category of medical personnel needs to register according to specific criteria and there are minimum salary requirements as well as the regulation on the maximum number of hours per week. To respond to international mobility, especially to Finland, the aging of the medical staff and internal mobility from rural areas to the cities, the Ministry of Social Affairs has taken a number of initiatives. These, however, have only enjoyed partial success and concerns remain about the shortage of medical personnel, especially in small localities. First, the Ministry of Social Affairs initiated a program and created incentives for young doctors to work in small hospitals, but according to official data, this program has yet to have an impact in practice. So far few doctors have applied to join the program, but it is hoped that in the coming years, young doctors will find the program more appealing. Second, health policy makers have increased the number of medical and nursing students, but this is considered insufficient to cover the expected need for medical personnel, and the number will need to continue to increase. The challenge, however, is that this falls under the competence of the Ministry of Education and decisions on the number of students need to be made by the state. These need to reflect the priorities of the state policy and the constraints of the state budget. The higher education financing system has changed and universities receive a lump sum depending on the number of students, but it does not differentiate between types of education. Since medical studies are among the most expensive, universities have a negative incentive to admit and educate medical doctors. This, in fact, is an example of contradiction and lack of coordination in government policy. One interviewee from the Ministry of Social Affairs, for example, has voiced this concern in the following way and set the problem in a broad context:

> "I think we should go further, we should increase the number of young doctors in universities and of course nurses, but it's a big, big debate with the Ministry of Education because the Ministry of Education has changed the financing system of higher education institutions just this year. Before it was a bit easier because then the Ministry of Education defined exactly in the contract with universities... but starting this year they give lump sums to universities... and universities can decide what type of students they admit. We managed to get into university contracts with universities teaching doctors and now we want to increase this number but I am not very sure that the Ministry of Education is happy about it. [...] (Interviewee 15)

The stock of medical doctors trained in Estonia who practice their profession in the EU15 increased considerably since the accession to the EU which facilitated the international movement of health professionals. Available statistics indicate that in 2003, 30 medical doctors worked in the EU15 compared to 175 in 2005—almost a six time increase (Buchan et al., 2014, p. 73). Most of the doctors preferred Finland (94 doctors) followed by the UK (45) and Germany (27). Though less significant in absolute terms than in other new EU member states, such as Poland, Romania or Bulgaria, this outflow of medical personnel puts strain on the limited resources of a small country as Estonia. Small fluctuations can make a big impact. Estonian health professionals choose Finland as a result of better salary and work conditions, active recruitment policies, similar languages, geographical and cultural proximity and close ties between medical institutions in the two countries (Buchan et al., 2014, p. 78). Interviewees perceive that the Ministry of Social Affairs is taking action, but they acknowledge that so far it has only been effective in part:

> "Central policy institutions should understand that they are the only body able to regulate the number of doctors working in Estonia [...]. Publicly it's already some months or a year that we know that the number of admissions for medical faculty is growing. Maybe it's late but at least they have been reacting." (Interviewee 3)

"There should be more central coordination of medical personnel and the number of medical students should increase, but the Ministry of Education says that Estonia is producing doctors for Europe. There should be some regulation saying that they must work a number of years in Estonia or some other kind of arrangement but at least in part they should be encouraged to work at home. We as a hospital in a big city don't have problems with medical staff shortage." (Interviewee 5)

The movement within the country also takes the form of sectorial mobility between the hospitals in the government network and private medical centers. Due to higher co-payments in private centers, and possible higher income, doctors can decide to work, for instance, only half time in a hospital and the other half in a private institution putting pressure on the publicly owned system and raising concerns about waiting times, accessibility as well as ethical issues.

Coordination of the Hospital Network

Restructuring the ten-year-old hospital network has received increasing attention in the past years in the face of socio-demographic change. The purchase of expensive medical equipment has convinced some that the hospital sector in Estonia needs a new hospital structure. We discuss the approach taken by the Ministry of Social Affairs to coordinate the hospital network and look at stakeholder perceptions concerning the purchase of expensive medical equipment. The Ministry of Social Affairs has thus far only indirectly and timidly attempted to make changes to the hospital network. This is contrasted with the strong position central policy makers took when implementing the hospital reform in the early 2000s. The Ministry of Social Affairs has preferred to postpone radical change and convene discussions rather than take action:

"The Ministry is just whispering to hospitals and to supervisory boards: you should discuss it and that's all." (Interviewee 15)
"The hospital system is quite static; we hear different thoughts from the Ministry about how to develop it, about how many hospitals Estonia really needs, but where decisions are I don't know. It has been five years or more since these have started. [...] The impact should be clearer or maybe I will use the word aggressive." (Interviewee 5)

What is interesting is that this view is shared by different stakeholders: hospital management, the insurance fund, the audit office and representatives of the Ministry of Social Affairs itself. The Ministry has developed and discussed ideas to improve the configuration of the hospital network, but these are perceived to lack real action. In reality, little has changed. This hesitation is effectively captured by this quote stemming from a representative of the Ministry of Social Affairs itself:

"Hospital reform is not completely finished, it is not midway, it is actually more than midway, but there are some issues which were not done and, yes, the Ministry has changed its mind and decided that we don't finish the reform as it was intended exactly. It concerns two more hospitals to turn into local hospitals and so on and actually we started two years ago an attempt to do it some other way. All medical specialties had to rewrite their development plans and all specialties had to define which kind of services they want to keep in county levels and which ones in tertiary level or central hospital level." (Interviewee 15)

One main idea has been to support administrative mergers hoping that hospitals themselves will decide what service ought to be provided and where. It is hoped that in this way, hospitals will be easier to coordinate. Presumably if the network includes fewer administrative entities, they will function more as a network, and this network would be easier to govern than it is the case today. As far as central coordination is concerned, this comes as a surprise if we consider the small size of the hospital system in Estonia—only 19 publicly owned hospitals. One representative of the Ministry of Social Affairs has explained this plan in this way:

"What we see is that we want to reduce the number of hospitals; it is now in works, we try to merge hospitals. It's easier to manage the system if we have fewer hospitals. We try to merge the hospitals to have less management; we don't deal with human resources, finance, and service organization. Now we are just trying to merge hospitals to have less management to which we give very direct rules and guidelines with what we are expecting from them: which kind of services at which quality level. This is the main idea of what we are now doing and trying to implement in our system…but we have no idea to take over some hospitals from the municipalities or change our foundation system." (Interviewee 10)

Duplication: A Coordination Problem or an Administrative Glitch?

Duplication, a situation in which two or more hospitals provide services that could be provided more efficiently and effectively in fewer places, is related to the current configuration of the acute care hospital network. Interviewees agree that the 19 acute care hospitals included in the HNDP are too many for the current and future needs of the nation. The hospital network emerged more than 10 years ago, and it was a product of much political compromising. Faced with a declining population, changing demographics and mobility inside the country, the number of small hospitals is considered unrealistic. The same is the case for the situation in Tallinn where there are major concerns with duplication and divergence. The underlying ideas are converging toward reorganization, integration and the creation of networks locally between central and regional hospitals, on the one hand, and the general and local hospitals, on the other hand. For example, an interviewee from the Ministry of Social Affairs has phrased these ideas in this way:

> "This is one way to reorganize: to make hospital networks and then if they have the same management they define the same aims and purposes for these organizations. In these hospital networks they discuss and agree which services and in which places to provide the services in the network. We have very clear plan: we have now seven big hospitals (regional and central) but overall we have 19 hospitals in the government hospital network, and we want to reduce from 19 to at least seven. The phase of the project has advanced in some cases like the case of Tartu University Hospital and South Estonia Hospital; they are now preparing for the merger." (Interviewee 10)

We see thus that policy makers' aim, in a first phase, is to reduce the number of legal entities through administrative mergers. This is also expected to involve physical mergers and a reduction in the number of hospital facilities located in different places. It is assumed that this approach is more managerially and politically feasible than closing down or substantially changing the status quo by means of a central policy decision. This is not a phenomenon that is unique to Estonia. It is politically difficult to close down hospitals, but ultimately the same purpose can be obtained but through a different, and less politically costly means. The first step is to merge legal entities, but later on the management of those legal entities, under cost pressure, finds it necessary to close or greatly diminish actual sites—because multiple sites cost more money. It is the politics of the trajectory that causes the authorities to move in incremental steps rather than just doing what is obviously rational to most hospital planners.

Though the hospitals included in the government plan are targeted as a whole there is no evidence indicating that duplication is a systemic problem. It does not concern all hospitals, medical specialties and types of procedures. The evidence collected indicates that there is a concern in the case of expensive medical equipment and procedures such as MRI and high-level services, but less so in the case of common hospital care. For example, this interviewee stresses this point and provides insights into the issues at stake:

> "On the one hand this is related to this big number of small hospitals; we cannot say that this happens in all hospitals and for all services. This happens more in the case of high-profile services…the incentive is very clear: doctors are interested in doing something interesting and the problem is that Estonia is a small country and there are only a few interesting places. Hospitals want to have good doctors so I think hospitals very much compete for good doctors and to be attractive for the doctors you have to enable the doctors to innovate their services. So it very much generates ineffective care organization. If it's a very narrow service then it's up to hospital management to decide and invest. We as a health insurance fund cannot say: no, you're not allowed to because there is no commission supervising this certification in Estonia. So it exists; it definitely happens." (Interviewee 8)

There is agreement, both among the management of hospitals in Tallinn, and hospitals elsewhere in the country, that Tallinn again constitutes a special case. The current configuration of Tallinn hospitals is prone to duplication. This is especially so in the case of the two central, limited-liability hospitals, East Tallinn and West Tallinn. A National Audit Office report concluded that the hospital network is too big and unsustainable given the resources that the state can afford to spend on healthcare. The report criticized the lack of political leadership and held the Ministry of Social Affairs responsible for "damaging the interests of the state and hospital managers" (National Audit Office of Estonia, 2010). Moreover, improving governance and strengthening performance through better resource allocation and purchasing were two of the four main recommendations of a World Health Organization study assessing the financial sustainability of the healthcare system (World Health Organization, 2010,

2011). The report challenged decision makers to take action and improve the financial sustainability of the system as a whole.

Coordination of Expensive Medical Equipment in the Face of Divergence: The Case of East Tallinn Central Hospital

The purchase of expensive medical equipment in Estonia lacks effective central coordination. Hospitals can decide what equipment to purchase, and no approval is needed as long as the device meets international quality standards. The insurance fund regulates the number of cases and the average price per case, but not the type of equipment that hospitals ought to purchase. The existing hospital plan is supposed to regulate what services each type of hospital may provide, but as we make clear in this section, this is not always followed in practice:

> "The state cannot decide if hospitals should buy equipment or not. There is no regulation, no policy, the equipment just needs to meet EU requirements and that's all […] Personally I think we should have some kind of policy and influence but the Ministry of Social Affairs thinks we have freedom, everybody can decide and make reasonable decisions and if it's calculated as a reasonable decision then it's their responsibility to decide and so on…" (Interviewee 15)

Using the typology of coordination problems introduced earlier, we show that the purchase of expensive medical equipment is characterized by divergence—decision and action taken by a hospital or group of hospitals that affects the system of hospitals as a whole. Unlike duplication, divergence is more specific and case centered. The most salient example of divergence is the case of East Tallinn Central Hospital Ltd. (henceforth East Tallinn). We show how decisions made by the leadership of East Tallinn have resisted central coordination. The effects of these decisions on the system are analyzed in the following section. East Tallinn is one of the two central hospitals in Tallinn, legally a limited-liability company, and is owned by the city of Tallinn. It is thus a decentralized and autonomous entity and one of the 19 acute hospitals included in the HNDP. According to its status of central hospital, East Tallinn can provide and be reimbursed by the insurance fund for a wide range of services, but unlike regional hospitals, it may not offer tertiary cancer treatment. The two cancer centers in Estonia recognized by the government are Tartu University Hospital and

North Estonia Regional Hospital in Tallinn, and it is only these two medical centers that are supposed to provide chemotherapy and radiotherapy. Central hospitals may provide *some* oncological services, but not chemotherapy and radiotherapy. Despite the regulation, East Tallinn decided to borrow money and purchase expensive medical equipment in order to start providing these services and boasts being a center of oncology. Cancer treatment was implemented in 2007, and 3000 patients are treated annually in the center (East Tallinn, 2014). The hospital actively promotes its cancer center:

> "At East-Tallinn Central Hospital we are treating all types of tumors, except hematological malignancies. The Center of Oncology offers modern and complex care for cancer patients with different treatment options at outpatient's clinic, daycare clinic and inpatient departments." (East Tallinn, 2014)

The cancer center specifically states that treatment methods may consist of chemotherapy, including "severe complications of chemotherapy in the inpatient department," oncological surgery or radiation oncology. However, the health insurance fund, by law, may only purchase these services from the two recognized cancer centers, and this has led to tension and lobbying in the system as well as financial risk, as this interviewee emphasized:

> "This year we are very carefully looking and following what happens with the financial status of one big Tallinn hospital. There are some problems there but we know that the supervisory board had setup very strict financial rules in this hospital and they try to minimize their loans and other financial responsibilities." (Interviewee 10)

Despite this financial monitoring, East Tallinn eschewed coordination and the reaction of central authorities has proved insufficient thus far. There are voices which claimed that East Tallinn does not comply with existing regulation in other respects also such as organizing public tendering. This quote vividly depicts how some interviewees perceive this hospital:

> "I think that managers...it's like an effort to be the best and get the most of the market but I still think that they are well aware of what they are

providing; that they are providing a public good; that they are the providers and that healthcare and the patients are the most important. I think that for the East Tallinn Hospital it is totally different… I don't know what is going on there. For example, years ago they had an audit for public tendering… The law says that hospitals have to do the tendering as well, but East Tallinn doesn't do the public tendering because they are not providing public goods. […] All the other hospitals are doing the public tendering and we know. I think this is a unique problem in this sense, but I think in other hospitals they might show a higher cost than the real cost, but I don't have the evidence." (Interviewee 13)

Omission to provide a service due to lack of coordination between hospitals is not a concern in the case of Estonia. There are medical treatments that are unavailable in Estonia, but this situation is not due to lack of coordination, but to absence of the service, lack of proper medical devices or the needed competence. In these cases, patients are referred to treatment abroad, especially in Finland. Not only is omission not a problem, but it is sometimes desirable for a healthcare system not to provide every service for both economic and clinical reasons. It may not be safe to provide some services since the level of quality would not warrant it:

"We have some gaps, i.e. lack of services that are not done in Estonia but this is normal. From a patient safety and efficiency perspective I think it is good that we are not doing everything, but from the perspective of doctors they want to do something or learn; this is not good." (Interviewee 14)

"I don't think that anything remains undone due to lack of coordination…There are some specific cases when we send patients abroad but these are not due to lack of coordination but to common sense." (Interviewee 1)

Explaining Coordination

In this section, we return to the theoretical propositions introduced in Chap. 3. We seek to explain the empirical findings in light of the propositions derived from principal-agent theory and sociological institutionalism. We take each proposition in turn and confront it with the empirical evidence gathered in the course of the research. We begin with the propositions derived from principal-agent theory and continue with the role of hospital system culture.

Positive and Negative Incentives

Proposition 1: Positive incentives designed by central institutions with a coordinating role enable hospital system coordination

Proposition 2: Negative incentives (or sanctions) designed by central institutions with a coordinating role enable hospital system coordination

Principal-agent theory posits that the principal can make use of positive incentives, such as for example financial stimuli, or negative incentives, such as various types of punishment, to coordinate the behavior of the agents. The theory postulates that these incentives are effectively aligning the agents' behavior according to the interests of the principal. For our purposes, this means that the coordinating agencies effectively employ incentives for the purpose of improving coordination and addressing coordination problems. This research found that positive financial incentives embedded in the current financing system are instrumental to hospital decision making. However, they are ineffective in addressing the coordination problems identified in this research. They may well serve other purposes, but they do not address the reorganization of the hospital network and the purchase of expensive medical equipment. Therefore, the positive financial incentives are not effective instruments to deal with duplication and divergence. In the case of Estonia, the health insurance fund signs contracts with each hospital, and it prioritizes the purchase of services from the 19 hospitals included in the government network. Contracts are capped in the sense that the insurance fund only purchases a pre-defined number of cases for a certain average price each. This leads to a capped budget consisting of the number of cases and the average price per case. Hospitals may decide to treat more cases than budgeted, but they are not reimbursed for those extra cases. If there is a need to treat more cases and no money or personnel are available from other sources, then hospitals need to put patients on the waiting list. Contract volumes are agreed with each provider starting from the standard contract conditions which apply to all providers. The financial appendices to the contracts are agreed every year between the insurance fund and the management of each hospital. The price lists are a result of negotiations between hospitals, the insurance fund and medical specialties which, as we discovered, can have an important influence in the process. Some specialties—most notably oncology and radiology—have managed to negotiate advantageous prices for hospitals providing services in those specialties more than in other specialties. This gives hospitals a bigger margin over their costs, and as a result, they have been incentivized to develop services in those generously priced specialties. The positive financial incentives have played an important role in decisions concerning the purchase of expensive medical equipment, as in the case of East Tallinn Central Hospital. This next quote usefully illustrates this process:

> "The prices are done by the health insurance fund together with hospitals and specialties. They are negotiated twice. It means that it very much depends on the activity of the people in the specialty unions and usually they are coming from big hospitals, from Tallinn or Tartu, and of course they want equipment and then they describe how it looks like, what has to be done… It means they actually have very big impact to advise the health insurance fund […] It happened that all radiology, oncology are very beneficial to do because they have very good prices […]. The people in these specialty unions managed to negotiate it better, to explain better why everything has to be inside this average price." (Interviewee 15)

The capped budget is a means through which the insurance fund attempts to control costs and protect the financial sustainability of the system, and there is evidence that this has proven effective in this sense:

> "We have strongly capped budgets; it is hard to explain to our Finnish friends how we are running this hospital… You need to keep within the budgeted amount, so if you as a hospital are running out of money by October it's your problem… You will not be reimbursed if you produce more cases. It does create a problem because every year we have more cases but on the other hand with limited resources it is the only way… we as a multi-profile hospital need to provide everything whereas other smaller units and hospitals can choose what to provide." (Interviewee 1)

Hospital managers experience this coordination tool through the pricing system the most, and they wish that the financing tools were clearer and financial incentives less influential. Some perceive a lack of fairness and transparency concerning the major differences in the pricing system between different specialties:

> "The biggest problem is that for some specialties and procedures, e.g. radiology, MRI, the prices are very good. These medical specialties have a very big influence in negotiating all those prices. They have a stronger voice, better connections; that's the explanation for these price differences. It's sad to say but it's true. That's why I say that clarity is very important.

There are specialties that are very well priced and specialties where we are losing money, for example intensive care. We are losing money; every patient is non-profitable if I can say like this. This is more a managerial problem than a medical one... This pricing has incentives for doctors to open private practices in those areas or in the case of hospitals to offer treatments that are well priced compared to those that are not so well priced." (Interviewee 5)

A second main thread concerns the focus on hospital autonomy, or in the words of many interviewees, hospital responsibility. This includes finance, but goes beyond it and encompasses an emphasis on hospital identity and a new attitude of "seeking out" and engaging with patients. This has taken different forms, and not all are perceived positively. In becoming more financially disciplined, hospitals have also become more financially interested than before. If they see themselves as possessing a certain identity, then it is not surprising that they want to promote and develop that identity further. One hospital manager explained the thinking—and doing—behind this new organizational identity:

"We know that through the financial incentives a lot of things can be changed from the health insurance fund first and then from hospital managers. Now we are all the time thinking: how this policy, what kind of motivation it offers; what kind of cases we can do more. This I think is a major change compared to the previous system and also clients or patients are important; if you don't have patients you can't sell the cases to the health insurance. [...] The main change is that now we are more client-oriented than it was in the Soviet period... A possible side effect is that sometimes we want to make more investigations because there is motivation for that. We know that money comes through patients not through asking politicians." (Interviewee 2)

What this research shows is that positive financial incentives influence hospital behavior along with the status of hospitals as self-managed organizations operating under private law. The reform fostered the interest and pursuit of the financial stimuli and has made central coordination more difficult than before. However, there is no convincing evidence to support the proposition that the use of incentives—whether positive or negative—enables hospital system coordination. Negative incentives (sanctions or penalties) have not yet been applied in those cases where divergent hospital behavior might have warranted their application. As shown in this chapter, the weakness of the state institutions, coupled with a high degree of hospital autonomy, can explain why sanctions have not been used.

Information Asymmetry and Imperfect Monitoring

Proposition 3: Information asymmetry and imperfect monitoring hinder central hospital system coordination

Principal-agent theory further postulates that information asymmetry between the principal and the agent along with imperfect monitoring of the agent hinder coordination. The principal does not have enough information, or the quality of the information is inadequate, to monitor the agent's behavior. Moreover, the tools that the principal uses to monitor the activity of the agent are inadequate and ineffective. In the case of hospital coordination in Estonia, we suggest that information asymmetry plays a minor role. The issue, we suggest, is not the lack of information about the problems of coordination but the political will of the principal to enact coordination. For example, policy makers are well familiar with the divergent behavior of East Tallinn Central. Moreover, they are also well aware of the duplication in the system and the need for reorganization of the hospital network. What is missing is the goodwill and political ability to act on these realizations. Information asymmetry would postulate that it is precisely the lack of information that prevents the principal from enacting coordination, whereas our research suggests that this is not the case. Reliable information on the quality of hospital care is scarce, as shown below, but it is still questionable if the lack of reliable information on quality hinders coordination. The central government may possess adequate information on service quality, but the fact of having that information does not suffice to improve coordination of the quality of care. Having the needed information, important though it is, does not guarantee decision making that reflects that information. It is not enough for decision makers to know what decision to make—they also need to be able and willing to make that decision. The Ministry of Social Affairs is bound to "stick to the law"—it can only coordinate the activity of hospitals on the basis of the existing legislation, which needs to be changed should the Ministry of Social Affairs wish to strengthen its coordination. This is, however, static as the legislation can neither easily nor rapidly be changed. At the same time, the nature of the reform model allowed hospitals significant decision-making authority within the financial and structural framework. This was helpfully captured in the interviews with representatives of the Ministry of Social Affairs:

> "We can govern hospitals through legal acts; if we want to change something we have to do it through laws. Another tool is that some hospitals

are partly state foundations, so founded in part by the state as well as by municipalities and other institutions as in the case of Tartu whereas the North Estonia Hospital is a 100 % state foundation...so we can also govern them through the supervisory boards because we have our representatives there. But to change something we have to change the rules which are in legal acts and we cannot tell them to do that or to not do that; to not develop these services. If it isn't in legal acts then it doesn't mean anything. [...] It is quite tricky and difficult to govern in this way; it is quite difficult in some situations; everything has to be written in the legal acts..." (Interviewee 9)

The health insurance fund, on the other hand, though a key player in the system is not a policy institution and hence its primary role is not to coordinate the provision of healthcare. This is where the conundrum lies: The Ministry of Social Affairs has the policy, but does not have the real power; the insurance fund has the power, but does not have the policy. The health insurance fund is an independent agency with its own supervisory and management boards. It is not a policy institution, but it has the minister of social affairs as chair of the supervisory board. There is evidence, however, suggesting that the Ministry of Social Affairs and the insurance fund coordinate their activities and agree on strategic matters such as the annual budget or the importance of quality assessment—a growing interest in Estonia as in other countries. This means that although not a policy institution, the fund can have an important say in major policy decisions. It is debatable, however, what kind and how much of an influence the insurance fund actually has:

"The insurance fund can't coordinate the hospitals; it has no right to do this. They have to manage themselves—this is official, but since the insurance fund is the single purchaser, it coordinates hospitals anyhow. I am not sure how soft this is, but it is in a non-direct way." (Interviewee 14)

"The Ministry of Social Affairs has weakened its position during the years and has become weaker and weaker and the hospitals are growing stronger and I think the health insurance fund is in a bad position in the sense that if they had a lot of money they would be king of course but as they have limited resources and are really struggling, they keep the status quo, nothing changes... so we can manage until the next year. That has weakened its position and it can't really make decisions anymore. If we look, for example, at the list of services and how it has changed, nothing has changed for years in inpatient care." (Interviewee 13)

Though this above statement is more extreme than most other evidence found, it does align with the well-documented idea that central coordination is yet to be strengthened and improved. The interest in the governance of quality, both in the Ministry of Social Affairs and in the health insurance fund, has grown, but the use of performance information for coordination purposes is still in its infancy and has been rather passive up to this moment. For example, one representative of the insurance fund argued:

> "Hospitals are independent and they know this very well and the Ministry and under the Ministry the partners are not strong enough to put something into law; the only one who has some kind of power is the health insurance fund. We don't have official power, however, and in my opinion we are formally quite weak, but now we are discussing with our people from the law department if we can put in contracts requirements about what hospitals should do. And now we are renewing the contracts but the quality part; our new chairman thinks that the quality topic is very important so he wants to put it in contracts; much stronger and clearer conditions about quality. But our law people say that this is not possible because there is nothing about this in our law... currently what is in the law is that hospitals must do their best, not in specific ways." (Interviewee 14)

In the context of managing quality, ensuring a proper volume of service is seen as important, but in a country as small as Estonia, it is difficult to ensure the right volume. From a policy perspective, it is challenging to manage quality in this context: If some services are no longer accepted or financed in Estonia, then doctors are likely to leave the country where they can perform their specialty and it thus creates a vicious circle especially in a context when there is a shortage of medical personnel. Managing quality becomes part of the problem rather than the solution. One of the functions of the health insurance fund is to "examine the quality and necessity of services partially or fully compensated by the insurance fund" (Estonian Health Insurance Fund, 2014). Policy makers recognize that quality management is still weak:

> "Our task in the future is to work out more standards and guidelines for hospitals; we think they know what we want to do, but we need to put in written form what our expectations are... for example how to assess quality, what quality indicators to use to assess their own work and to compare different hospitals. This is the main need: to compare and to try to standardize

quality...I see a very big role for the Ministry to coordinate; it is one weak point in our system..." (Interviewee 10)

If coordination problems have indeed been problematic, then it can be expected that they have led to certain negative effects. We have openly asked interviewees about what impacts they have perceived as a result of poor central coordination and specifically asked for evidence that could substantiate their claims. Opinions vary among both policy makers and hospital management boards. There are some who consider that the efficiency, financial sustainability and quality of hospital care depend on dealing with these problems. For example, this quote explains how in a hospital system characterized by competition, the purchase of expensive medical equipment that remains under-used can affect both the financial situation of the hospital and the quality of treatment and patient safety:

"There are certain requirements which are regulated by the Ministry of Social Affairs. I think this is very important, but what happens inside this regulation is of course very much about how all these autonomous hospitals act and what they start to do, so theoretically the situation is that if they are autonomous they should act like a private company and make economically wise decisions. [...] There is requirement about what they have to provide but...in real life it might not go in that way because to provide the minimum level they need doctors but to keep doctors you need to be able to expand your package of services, so it's difficult." (Interviewee 8)

Concerns about patient safety and quality are also mirrored by this interviewee who, from the position of the health insurance fund, has experienced the challenge of purchasing services from hospitals that are licensed to perform a certain procedure, although the quality may be lower than in other hospitals:

"The insurance fund, we understand this but the law obligates us because they have license and so we have to buy also from them. [...] I think this is very important because it's about resources and patient safety. Let's talk about hip replacement: all these three hospitals provide this procedure. So if there is a decision by one doctor not to operate a patient, the patient can go to another hospital and may receive the operation there though it may not be wise to have the operation. If there is variation in treatment and lack of understanding; sometimes if you pay you can go faster. So this is definitely a problem." (Interviewee 14)

Speaking of effects, one interviewee discusses the case of East Tallinn Hospital and sees no positive effects of having a third oncology center and is concerned about quality and the efficient use of resources in the Tallinn catchment area:

> "The effects are many. First, on the workforce, the two oncology centers have agreed about salary levels but if a third one comes in it may disrupt the existing agreements given that there are not so many oncologists in Estonia. A second effect concerns the purchase of expensive medical equipment and a possible effect on quality if the third hospital does not have all the necessary qualifications and does not use needed protocols. [...] I don't see almost any positive effects because one explanation could be that we bring the services closer to the patient geographically but in the same case when these two parties are in the same city competing, it is nonsense." (Interviewee 1)

Nonetheless, there are other respondents who think that these are concerns that need to be addressed, but are "normal" administrative glitches that may create or reinforce inefficiency, but do not threaten the quality of care and the financial sustainability of the system. Other factors, they believe, are more problematic than these organizational problems of coordination. Speaking from a central policy role, this quote usefully reflects the policy conundrum in dealing with duplication and divergent hospital behavior:

> "I can't say that this is the biggest problem, but sometimes it appears and we discuss it and ask our partners to go and discuss and try to find good solutions and make agreements not to develop these services... so we have to find the proper balance between access and economically-efficient use of resources. To assess this you can look at the numbers compared to other OECD countries and sometimes it's also a legend about every hospital buying very expensive and not necessary equipment; I think in some sense it's overestimated, I think. Since we are a little nation perhaps economic efficiency is not the most important thing maybe. But in some very expensive cases it's a good idea to keep this idea of competence center and in two places sometimes it's already too much. Experts coming from outside say that you only need one large hospital and that's all, but inside Estonia the picture is a little bit different if you live here." (Interviewee 9)

Perceptions differ but we have found little evidence on the negative effects of problems of coordination. These problems are generally perceived negatively, but there is variation in how serious they are thought to be in reality. Some have also questioned whether reducing duplication is always a desirable goal. In some cases, it may be important to have different medical centers providing the same type of service in order to allow the option of a second opinion, if need be. In this sense, it can be argued that patient choice is equally important. It brings into discussion the many competing values that need to be considered and balances that need to be weighed. Having more of one value may involve having less of an equally important one. This arrangement may also improve accountability as professionals in different institutions could hold each other accountable for the quality of healthcare. These considerations, however, need to be balanced with the size and changing demographics of Estonia as well as with ensuring a certain volume of service that is deemed essential for patient quality and safety purposes.

Conflicting Interests and the Hospital System Culture: Where Politics, the Elite Medical Profession and Management Meet

Proposition 4: Conflicting interests and goals between principals and agents hinder central hospital system coordination

The propositions related to the hospital system culture introduced in Chap. 3 are as follows:

1. The interaction between health policy makers, medical profession, hospital management and patients influences central coordination of public hospitals
2. Mutual trust between health policy makers, medical profession, hospital management and patients is helpful to central coordination of public hospitals
3. Stakeholder compliance with ethical standards affects central public hospital coordination. Usually, high levels of compliance with declared standards will assist in the implementation of official attempts at coordination
4. Hospital system culture is one reason for the differences in coordination across the selected hospital systems.

A fourth proposition of principal-agent theory concerns conflicting interests and goals between the principal and the agent. If the interests and goals of the agents are different from those of the principal, then it will be difficult for the principal to determine the agents to act on his behalf. In the case of hospital coordination, it is expected that differing interests and goals will hinder coordination. The hospital system culture, derived from sociological institutionalism, suggests that cultural factors would affect coordination—either by facilitating or hindering it. The Hospital Association groups together the acute care hospitals included in the HNDP and a few other private clinics. Hospital managers play a key role in this association as representatives of their hospitals. This in theory should be a means through which collaboration can be fostered, but there are mixed views whether this in fact works in practice. There is evidence that it works for some purposes but not for others. For instance, the Hospital Association has been successful in negotiating the minimum salary as well as in carrying out negotiations with the health insurance fund concerning the standard contract conditions, but it has failed to come up with one voice on issues concerning the reorganization of the hospital network and service provision:

> "We have this hospital association but there are different groups within it, and I think that we have strong competition between hospitals: competition for patients, for doctors, nurses…I think that from some points of view this is good, but only for some level of competition. If we don't have the possibility to agree in most of the issues, then it's not good. Here should come the role of the Ministry. One example is oncological services: at the moment we have three oncological centers but in a normal European regional hospital they have patient capacity around 2 million patients, but we have right now only 1.3 million people. If regulations worked well then we could do good cooperation. I think it's not economical; it's not good for professionals because we don't have patients for everybody to do." (Interviewee 4)

The decision to maintain the status quo, however, has been political, and there has not been enough political will to change what is considered as needing change:

> "Tallinn hospitals could be reorganized, for instance one hospital has buildings in different places, which is not efficient… We have the same owner so it should be easy but the decision is political and does not concern efficiency. Politicians have connections—doctors, managers—and they may say to keep them separately and they will get votes in exchange. It's sad but politicians don't see the big picture." (Interviewee 5)

We thus clearly see at play the interaction between three of the four key stakeholders (politics, the medical profession and hospital management) and the mechanism through which the result of this interaction hinders central coordination. Local politicians collaborate with key hospital stakeholders to preserve the status quo and resist initiatives from the center to consolidate the public hospital network. Patients appear to play a minor role as an active and organized stakeholder in this interaction which has implications not only on the organization of hospital services, but also on service delivery and patient treatment. This is a weak element of the Estonian hospital culture.

An alternative idea explaining the effectiveness of central coordination is that insufficient administrative capacity hinders central coordination—not the political will. For example, this idea is reflected in this following quote which captures the perspective of the Ministry of Social Affairs:

> "I don't know; our state structure is not so big. Estonia is a small country and we have a shortage of personnel everywhere, and we have to be quite rational about our work: what we do and how we do it, but today we have to consider that our population has learned what democracy is and how to use it and how to take part in making decisions and we have to involve all our partners for all decisions and it makes processes slow and also needs more human resources from our side and therefore during the 1990s it was possible to make the legal acts and develop the plan quite quickly. Now we have to consider that it takes time; some decisions need years to work out good solutions and regulate." (Interviewee 9)

Although adequate administrative capacity is an important ingredient of effective coordination in any hospital and administrative system, we argue that hospital coordination in Estonia is primarily hindered by lack of political will. The structural and financial frameworks are in place, but decisions to renew the existing frameworks, though well-motivated economically and medically, have been postponed. Furthermore, the society as a whole has changed compared to 15 years ago when the hospital reform was implemented. At that time, a small group of enthusiastic reformers were able to push reform forward more easily than in the current political and social context. While at that time reform was radical and to a considerable extent top-down, today reform needs to be incremental and sensitive to the various interests and goals populating both the political and medical world. Because of these differing perspectives, it is difficult to find an agreement that would satisfy all stakeholders. These stakeholders have learned to make their voice heard. Though the state has the legal authority to implement reform, it has avoided the political risk that would affect the interests of important local and hospital stakeholders. If these stakeholders all agreed, then central coordination would be much easier to enact in practice and would probably not even be necessary. Making changes to the system would be politically costly especially during electoral times. This has been and continues to be a barrier to reform:

> "Specialty unions were consulted at the end of last year and then we organized some common seminars and we tried and listed all kind of services which should be here or there and discussed it with hospitals, with counties, with specialties and actually in October we have local municipality elections and now it is very quiet. But hopefully when it is over we can discuss it a little bit again because in 2015 we will have new elections. It means that the time span is first half of next year to really do something…" (Interviewee 15)

The delicacy of closing down hospitals or discontinuing a certain specialty is particularly acute in Estonia. Since supervisory boards of most hospitals consist of local politicians, politics is intertwined with management decisions. As a result, decisions do not necessarily reflect the efficiency and quality of hospital care, but rather national or local preferences:

> "We want to merge different hospitals which have different owners and it is very difficult to negotiate with municipalities. I don't know why; there are political reasons and especially some municipalities they are very interested in keeping hospitals in their own ownership. Perhaps there are no rational reasons, but just how to divide power among the politicians. But I think it would be easier to implement changes if all these autonomous hospitals were state owned. This is the only area where I feel I want to change it. But this doesn't mean that I want all hospitals in state ownership because municipalities are also quite autonomous from the state." (Interviewee 10)

This same person speaking from a policy position provides further insight into the dynamics of hospital consolidation:

> "Hospital managers have very good relationships with each other and with supervisory boards, whose members are mainly politicians. And there are some tricky relationships between the party from which the minister is and this party which governs the Tallinn municipality and then among politicians there is competition which influences hospital management and then it is very difficult. I see a big role for the Ministry to regulate this problem

with law, decree or to try to lead these negotiations and find a compromise with the hospitals in this question. There is a need for national coordination; we may say that in such questions. To prevent or solve this problem, we need more national coordination, and it's on our agenda today to do it." (Interviewee 10)

In this context, the central political actors have decided to sit in the background and develop policy documents which in reality have little impact. Central coordination efforts have also been faced with pressure from both politicians and certain medical specialties, and these, as in the case of oncology, have run against existing regulation:

"But there has been pressure to allow central hospitals to provide this and that which is not allowed today; and all this pressure comes through politicians sometimes or from specialists which are our advisers. So sometimes it's quite difficult to govern this kind of system..." (Interviewee 9)

Central and local politics are intertwined with the hospital management and certain elite medical specialties. On the one hand, this finding is surprising since the creation of autonomous hospitals operating under private law sought to keep politics out and invite professional managers in. On the other hand, it is helpful to bear in mind that politicians populate the supervisory boards of the hospitals, and although they may not know much about healthcare and management, they know what their political mandate is. They have learned to lobby and resist what would undermine the realization of their political agenda. This is to be expected in a decentralized administrative and hospital system in which the locals have experienced the continual growth of the center and have tried to counteract that growth.

Politics, regardless of political orientation, has been influential in resisting change, but the post-independence Estonia has been characterized by a preference for center-right political and economic ideas which remain influential 20 years later. Though a planned market—implemented under a social-democratic social affairs minister—the system has been endorsed by ministers across the political spectrum and has undergone little change since adoption:

"From the very beginning there has been a policy of thin state—the state should not interfere into businesses that can be run like a business except for instance defense, foreign relations, some of the social security. At that time we had the youngest prime minister in Europe, he was 28 or something like that; they were really radical guys and they followed the understanding that businesses run best and healthcare is part of a business. Healthcare is a specific branch of business…so from the beginning there were revolutionary changes in all aspects." (Interviewee 1)

We have discovered that, in addition to politics and the medical profession, hospital management is an important stakeholder and has proved influential in fostering entrepreneurship in the hospital sector, as shown in these two quotes, as expressed by central policy makers:

"I think that the managers of these seven or ten big hospitals have very big influence and are important stakeholders for the Ministry and they have very big influence if we are planning changes in our system." (Interviewee 10)

It is common practice in Estonia, due to the inclination toward the market and toward business and the small number of specialists, for business professionals to work in the public sector. This cross-sector professional mobility has been encouraged, and in practice, it has led to a growth of business managers who run public sector organizations, including public hospitals. As a result, hospital management has become a key proactive stakeholder that has sought, and to some extent has succeeded in following an organizational agenda that has made central coordination difficult. However, this management agenda has not been supported by hospital managers alone, but as shown throughout this chapter, also by the other key stakeholders—local politicians and the medical profession. Informal coordination between these stakeholders can work effectively to resist central coordination efforts in a context of a weak center and generous hospital autonomy. In the case of Estonia, the small size of the hospital sector and informal coordination are factors that are expected to improve coordination. "Everybody knows everybody" is often put forward as an element of the culture of a small hospital sector. Since all physicians trained in Estonia are educated in the same one medical school, Tartu University, we would expect that they become part of an epistemic community which later, through socialization, would foster informal coordination. If everybody knows everybody, then coordination ought to be made easy, but we have discovered that in fact despite the small size of the hospital sector, central coordination has proved painfully difficult. The explanation lies in the influence of organizational and individual conflicting interests and goals. Everybody may know everybody, but it does not necessarily mean that everybody agrees with everybody. Local politicians may agree with key doctors and hospital managers in their jurisdiction, but they do not necessarily agree with the interests of central policy makers. In this case, the size of the sector loses its relevance—it does not necessarily lead to effective coordination. We have seen, however, that coordination between the different actors (national politicians, local politicians and hospital supervisory and management boards) can be fostered through political means. In this sense, informal coordination becomes instrumental, but it does not necessarily lead to policy change nationally. Local politicians and hospital boards have been effective in influencing national policy rather than the other way around. National policy makers aim for the efficiency and sustainability of the system as a whole, whereas local politicians and hospital boards follow a decentralized and organizational logic and aim for local interests and the realization of local and organizational goals. If these actors shared the same interests and goals, as unrealistic as that may be in practice, we would expect central coordination to be easy. We have also seen how different interests and goals between the hospitals hinder central coordination. In some aspects, they also make inter-organizational coordination difficult. Hospitals work with one another effectively on shared goals, such as negotiations of employment conditions or other similar agreements but fail to work together on matters that endanger their existence or position in the system, such as changes to the hospital network and service provision. In this chapter, we have seen how other key elements of the principal-agent theory, specifically the role of financial incentives, affect coordination. The financial incentives embedded in the pricing system favor certain specialties over others, and this led to investment decisions that reinforced duplication and divergence. We have also shown that information asymmetry plays a minor role with the exception of information on quality. Other than quality, central policy makers possess sufficient information on the activity of the hospitals, but this has not facilitated central coordination. In terms of the hospital system culture, we have shown how certain cultural elements have played a key role, particularly the role of politics and political and economic ideas, the role of entrepreneurship in the hospital sector and the influence of certain elite medical specialties.

We have argued that the result of the dynamic interaction between these key stakeholders has posed challenges to central coordination. Non-compliance with ethical standards is not a systemic problem in the case of the public hospital sector of Estonia, but we have provided evidence of isolated cases in which non-compliance with existing regulation has resisted central coordination. Mutual trust between key stakeholders has been an important element of the hospital reform, which granted hospitals considerable autonomy, but we have shown that in some cases, this trust has not been reciprocated. While this is true for some specific cases, most notably East Tallinn Hospital, we have not found evidence of a major systemic trust "gap" in the case of Estonia.

BIBLIOGRAPHY

Buchan, J., Wismar, M., Glinos, I. A., & Bremner, J. (Eds.) (2014). *Health professional mobility in a changing Europe, European observatory on health systems and policies.* Copenhagen: World Health Organization Regional Office for Europe.

East Tallinn. (2014). Center of Oncology, East Tallinn website. Accessed November 03, 2014.

Estonian Health Insurance Fund. (2012). *The story of the Estonian health insurance fund. 20 years of treatment and insurance.* Tallinn: Estonian Health Insurance Fund

Estonian Health Insurance Fund. (2014). *Estonian health insurance fund functions.* Available online. Tallinn: Estonian Health Insurance Fund.

Habicht, T., Aaviksoo, A., & Koppel, A. (2006). *Hospital sector reform in Estonia. Summary.* Tallinn: Praxis Center for Policy Studies.

Habicht, T., Habicht, J., & Maris, J. (2011). Estonia. In R. B. Saltman, A. Durán, & H. F. W. Dubois (Eds.), *Governing public hospitals. Reform strategies and the movement towards institutional autonomy*, Hospital governance in eight countries (chap. 7, pp. 141–161). Copenhagen: World Health Organization and the European Observatory on Health Systems and Policies.

Hellers, G., et al. (2000). *The Estonian hospital master plan 2015.* Stockholm: SC Scandinavian Care Consultants and SWECO International on behalf of the Ministry of Social Affairs.

Koppel, A., Kahur, K., Habicht, T., Saar, P., Habicht, J., & van Ginneken, E. (2008). Estonia: Health system review. *Health Systems in Transition, 10*(1), 1–230.

Lai, T., Habicht, T., Kahur, K., Reinap, M., Kiivet, R., & van Ginneken, E. (2013). Estonia: Health system review. *Health Systems in Transition, 15*(6), 1–196.

National Audit Office of Estonia. (2010). *Haiglavõrgu jätkusuutlikkus.* (Hospital network sustainability). Tallinn: National Audit Office.

National Institute for Health Development. (2014). *Health statistics database.* Tallinn, National Institute for Health Development. Accessed March 26, 2014.

World Health Organization. (2005). *Assessment of hospital reforms.* [Full report. World Health Organization Mission to Estonia]. Copenhagen: World Health Organization Regional Office for Europe.

World Health Organization. (2010). *Responding to the challenge of financial sustainability in Estonia's health system.* Copenhagen: World Health Organization Regional Office for Europe.
World Health Organization. (2011). *Responding to the challenge of financial sustainability in Estonia's health system: One year on.* Copenhagen: World Health Organization Regional Office for Europe.

CHAPTER 6

Coordination of Public Hospitals in Romania

As in the previous chapter, this second empirical chapter begins with description, continues with evaluation and ends with explanation. We first describe changes in public hospital policy and hospital trends and then move on to describe the specifics of the hospital reforms analyzed in this book as they pertain to the decentralization and autonomy of public hospitals. Following this first part, we evaluate the relationship between public hospital reforms and coordination problems drawing on the primary and secondary data sources. Finally, using the theoretical framework introduced earlier in the book, we seek to explain the effectiveness, or lack thereof, of central coordination.

OVERVIEW OF HEALTHCARE POLICIES (1991–2014)

The Romanian healthcare system has undergone major change since the end of communism at the end of 1989. Healthcare in Romania is organized, financed, delivered, governed and coordinated in very different ways than it used to be in the communist times. As in the case of Estonia, the starting point is the state of the healthcare system under communism. This can easily be described nowadays in a simplistic—and negative—manner which may do justice if we compare it to the situation today, but may also leave out important aspects. These include access to care which was free at the point of delivery at that time. Although it was

© The Author(s) 2017

S. Dan, *The Coordination of European Public Hospital Systems*,

DOI 10.1007/978-3-319-43428-5_6

free at the point of delivery and every patient (or citizen) could have access to it, it consisted mostly of basic services delivered in inpatient settings, polyclinics and so-called dispensaries (small health centers) in rural areas. There is wide agreement over the main characteristics—and problems— of the Semashko-type Soviet system which was adopted throughout the Soviet Union and the former communist countries in Central and Eastern Europe. These characteristics include overemphasis on inpatient, hospital-based treatment at the expense of primary care, which, unlike today, was hardly recognized as a distinct medical specialty. Funding was tax-based and centralized. Informal payments and various forms of corruption, however, were common and designed to lead to better care and hospitalization conditions. Healthcare providers were budgetary institutions, directly funded through the state budget.

Whereas Estonian policy makers took radical steps to reform the Soviet system and establish it on different grounds soon after independence, Romanian policy makers adopted a gradual, incremental approach. Some commentators have argued that this approach, permeating the society and economy more generally, can be attributed to the different context of the Romanian society and economy in the 1980s and furthermore to the type of communist regime in Romania which in some ways differed from that in other countries in the region (Boia, 2012; Boia, 2013; Molnar, 2000). According to this view, the Romanian communist system diverged from the directions of the Soviet Union and became more intense in the decade preceding its collapse. While others were considering opening up, the Romanian state was closing in. The political will to adopt "tough" measures also fluctuated during transition so that major reform had to wait long before adoption. Whereas Estonia rebuilt its public service on completely different grounds after independence, Romania did not. The Romanian approach relied to a large extent on the same civil service apparatus as before 1989. In public administration more generally, the first attempt to develop an accelerated, comprehensive public administration reform was in 2001, followed by a second major program in 2005 after negotiations with the European Commission. In 2005, the European Commission recommended three main areas for improvement: civil service, local public administration reform through accelerating the decentralization process and changes in public policy formulation (e.g. Dan, 2015). This broader approach and public sector context had an impact on healthcare reform which was and has remained predominantly a public sector responsibility. Healthcare reform reflected larger trends in public administration, management and policy. Table 6.1 includes a list of the main changes from 1989 to 2014.

From a structural, systemic perspective, we can distinguish four main areas of reform:

- building a social health insurance system;
- establishing a significant role for primary healthcare;
- rationalization of hospital facilities and hospital care;
- hospital decentralization and hospital management autonomy.

Efforts in all these main areas were initiated in the 1990s, and have continued throughout transition and Europeanization and to some extent continue today. An exception is the Social Insurance Law which had been approved by Parliament in 1994 and 1997, respectively, and became effective in 1999. The status of the National Health Insurance House has also changed—until 2005 it was subordinated to the Ministry of Public Health, but became quasi-independent in 2005 through a government ordinance (Table 6.1). Initiatives to establish a more prominent role for primary care (which was limited during communism) were taken early after the revolution and took the form of pilot projects in a number of selected counties. Later in the late 1990s as the system transitioned to social insurance, primary care reform was implemented across the country, and family doctors were tasked with a gate-keeping role in the system. This trend of greater emphasis on the use of primary care has continued recently and is considered a key goal of current healthcare reform plans (e.g. Dan & Savi, 2013). As stated in official policy documents, such as the National Strategy for Hospital Rationalization (Ministry of Health, 2010), a key current goal of reform is to "remodel" the demand for health services. According to this strategy, this involves a greater use of primary care and a reduction in the use of hospital care. The underlying objective is to increase savings and efficiency of the healthcare system as a whole starting from the observation that a greater reliance on primary care can reduce referral rate to higher and presumably more expensive types of care (Substantiation note to Government Decision 303/2011). In proposing this shift, central policy makers argued that hospital care is still considered in Romania by some as the "foremost method of intervention," a legacy of the communist regime (Ministry of Health, 2010). Although recent financial stringency measures are driving this wave of reforms, quality considerations are presented as complementary (Ministry of Health,

Table 6.1 Healthcare policy initiatives in Romania, 1992–2014

Year	Reform or policy initiative
1992–1994	Simulation testing of primary care reform in four districts
1993	A Healthy Romania, produced by a team of experts, funded by World Bank
1994	Social Health Insurance Law approved by the Senate
1994	Government Decision no. 370/1994 to pilot primary care reform in eight districts (ended in 1997)
1995	Legislation to establish the College of Physicians
1997	Social Health Insurance Law approved by the Chamber of Deputies with implementation starting in 1999
1998	Public Health Law no. 100/1998—which regulated public health and the responsibilities of different actors along with a list of national public health programs
1999	Ministerial Order no. 201/1999 placed restrictions on the number and distribution of pharmacies (amended in 2005)
2002	Emergency Ordinance no. 70/2002 decentralized ownership of public healthcare facilities from central to local government (not implemented in practice)
2002	Emergency Ordinance no. 150/2002 modified initial National Health Insurance Law
2002	Law on Mental Health Promotion and protection of persons with mental challenges
2002	National Anti-Poverty and Social Inclusion Plan, Government Decision no. 829/2002
2005	Government Ordinance removed National Health Insurance Fund from the direct coordination by Ministry of Public Health
2006	Health Reform Law no. 95/2006—a first comprehensive healthcare law encompassing various levels of care
2007	Ministry of Public Health strategic plan for 2008–2010
2008	Report of the presidential commission for healthcare. Set the priority of an integrated approach to reform and placed further emphasis on the key role of primary care
2008	Emergency Government Ordinance no. 162/2008. Initiation of the decentralization process in hospital care (not fully implemented de facto)
2008	Pilot phase of hospital decentralization in Bucharest and Oradea
2010	Emergency Government Ordinance no. 48/2010 adopted under financial stringency and strict agreements with the IMF. Amended previous legislation and stipulated the decentralization of most local and county hospitals which are now owned locally. More emphasis placed on the role of professional hospital management
2010	National Strategy for the Rationalization of Hospitals designed by the Ministry of Health on the basis of a number of World Bank reports. Clearly emphasizes the remodeling of healthcare demand and placed a greater role on increasing the type and extent of services treated in primary care to reduce hospital care and foster efficiency of the healthcare system as a whole

(continued)

Table 6.1 (continued)

Year	Reform or policy initiative
2012	New healthcare legislation under consultation (first half of 2012). Major changes are envisaged, such as amendments of the legal form of hospitals and the extent of hospital autonomy. Primary care is seen as a major means to reduce system-level healthcare costs (not yet adopted by law)
2014	National Health Strategy 2014–2020, Health for Prosperity, a comprehensive strategy aiming to cover and prioritize different types and levels of care in an integrated manner in line with the Europe 2020 strategy and EU structural funds for 2014–2020

Source: Adapted from Vlădescu, Scîntee, and Olsavszky (2008, p. 138) (for changes up to 2007) and Dan and Savi (2012, p. 24) for developments since 2008 complemented by the author with changes after 2012

2010). We now turn to the two prominent areas of reform that pertain to public hospitals specifically: reducing hospital capacity and decentralization of hospitals.

PUBLIC HOSPITAL "RATIONALIZATION"

Reducing capacity in public hospitals is a fairly new phenomenon in the healthcare system in Romania. The idea itself is not novel, but it has only in recent years started to be put into practice. Up until 2011, when it dropped significantly, the number of public hospitals remained almost the same as in 1990 (Table 6.2). This reflects changes in the system that occurred in 2010–2011 including hospital decentralization reform, a commitment to reduce what was considered excessive hospital capacity, and an emphasis on primary, outpatient and day care. Treatment in private hospitals developed timidly and was virtually non-existent until the early 2000s. Nevertheless, in recent years, the number of private hospitals has grown considerably from 30 in 2008 to 109 in 2012 and further to 161 in 2014 (Table 6.2). This growth can be contrasted with the decrease in the total number of public hospitals.

A number of international consultancy studies had been carried out and reports written before the outbreak of the 2008 financial crisis. They recommended major restructuring and systematic planning of hospital facilities and hospital care more generally (Government Decision 1088/2004; Presidential Commission, 2008; World Bank, 2003). This process came to be known both in law and policy documents as

Table 6.2   Number of hospitals in Romania, 1990–2014

Hospitals Year	Total number	Public	Private
1990	423	423	0
1991	427	427	0
1992	430	430	0
1993	433	433	0
1994	415	415	0
1995	412	412	0
1996	413	413	0
1997	418	416	2
1998	416	414	2
1999	428	425	3
2000	442	439	3
2001	446	442	4
2002	447	442	5
2003	427	422	5
2004	425	416	9
2005	433	422	11
2006	436	419	17
2007	447	425	22
2008	458	428	30
2009	474	431	43
2010	503	428	75
2011	464	367	97
2012	473	364	109
2013	499	365	134
2014	527	366	161

Source: National Statistical Institute of Romania (2014a), Tempo online time series, Health Statistics

"hospital rationalization." In 2009–2010, the National Strategy for Hospital Rationalization was developed—a fairly comprehensive document proposing major change to the public hospital system. The government approved the strategy in March 2011 (Government Decision 303/2011). In the context of the financial crisis that endangered the financial stability of the country, the government in office at that time criticized previous governments for excessive public spending and failure to adopt needed reform. In 2009 as part of the financial package agreed with the EU, IMF and the World Bank, the Romanian government received financial support from the World Bank in the form of policy development loans. The agreement included sector-specific provisions, and hospital restructuring and "rationalization" were part of the agreement and deemed a priority. De facto reform in this area constituted a conditionality in the loan agreement and a basis for assessing the possibility of future assistance.

The National Strategy for Hospital Rationalization (the Strategy), a 66-page document, was developed on the basis of previous studies with a significant contribution from international consultants working for the World Bank. The Strategy included a list of general and specific goals and an action plan. The goals were divided into two main categories: (1) "hospital rationalization" and (2) "complementary strategic priorities." Together, they consisted of five general and nine specific objectives, as shown below (Ministry of Health, 2010, pp. 42–43):

I. Hospital rationalization

1. General objective

Creation of a well-performing hospital sector by means of hospital reorganization, decentralization and informatization

Specific objectives:

1.1. Hospital reorganization and improvement in hospital efficiency

1.2 Hospital management decentralization

1.3 Adoption of a clear hospital classification system, the development of a general national hospital plan and accreditation system on the basis of the new classification system

1.4. Hospital system informatization

2. General objective:

Ensuring sustainable and efficient financial resources through remodeling hospital financing

Specific objective:

2.1. Change in the health insurance system for hospital financing

II. Complementary strategic priorities

3. General objective

Remodeling demand for healthcare services

Specific objectives:

3.1. Rationalizing demand for hospital services

3.2. Developing and qualitatively improving primary and outpatient healthcare

4. General objective:

Improving the organizational and functional efficiency of the social health insurance system

Specific objective:

4.1. Attracting private funding within the insurance system

5. General objective: Development and implementation of a coherent human resource strategy

Specific objective:

5.1. Introduction of modern human resource planning and management practicesIn addition, the Strategy included a list of specific targets and indicators. For the purposes of this study, the most relevant are the following (Ministry of Health, 2010, pp. 62–65):

- 7 % reduction in hospital beds
- Hospital personnel costs must not exceed 70 % of each hospital's budget
- 15 % reduction in the number of public hospitals
- 85 % of public hospitals must be decentralized (i.e. hospital ownership transferred to local authorities)
- Creation of a legislative framework to enable an increase in de facto hospital management autonomy
- Creation of a legislative framework establishing the criteria for hospital classification based on competence
- 8 % reduction in the number of hospitalizations in the context of developing a new national hospital plan and eight regional hospital plans.

The main institutions responsible for implementation were the Ministry of Health and the National Health Insurance House, and operational activities were to be finalized by the end of 2012 (Ministry of Health, 2010, Annex 2). The quality of care was not a central focus of these measures—it was somehow assumed that the changes will lead to improvements in quality. Quality was considered an important outcome, but no specific plan was put in place to assess the effects of the proposed changes on quality. This in our view is a main criticism of the Strategy, which overall gives the impression of being reasonable and ambitious enough to tackle some of the root causes of deep-seated inefficiencies that seem to have long been ignored. The rationale for the reform needs to be placed and understood in the context of the financial crisis, during which the Romanian government had to reduce public spending.

The critical financial situation of public finances seemed to offer a favorable environment to push reform forward. The key phrase was reducing what was thought to be in excess—cutting down the fat without hurting the muscle. This approach reflects the state of the hospital sector, which first needed systematic planning, organization and management—some of the preconditions to enhance quality—before it can deliver improvements in outcomes. Setting up the system on a more financially sustainable basis first seemed a more reasonable expectation. The action plan put forward in the Strategy comes across as being a result of considerable policy analysis and evidence derived from both an evaluation of the current situation on the ground and international good practice. There is frequent reference to evaluations on the ground and consultations conducted in 2009 and 2010 by the Ministry of Health before the actual design and implementation of the measures. The document is also presented in an optimistic tone as incorporating needed change that would lead to improvements in efficiency and overall performance. The various measures proposed are said to converge toward this overarching goal. Hospital decentralization and increasing hospital management autonomy were two important reform strategies—seen not as ends in themselves but important prerequisites in line with the situation on the ground and international good practice. There is, nevertheless, little analysis presented in the document of other potential options for reform. Similarly, little space in the Strategy is devoted to implementation, monitoring and evaluation (half a page and a one-page action plan with a listing of responsible actors and deadline, see Annex 2 of the Strategy). This is the case despite the observation that policy implementation and evaluation capacity are two of the hurting spots of the Romanian public sector (e.g. World Bank, 2010).

All these observations indicate that the Romanian hospital system in recent years has been going through a major process of structural reform that is still current today. It is to be expected that changes in hospital capacity and restructuring will continue in future years before the system reaches a certain degree of stability. The current hospital system structure is inherited from communist times and, despite the 2010–2011 reform, many small, local hospitals are still expected to be restructured and turned into long-term care facilities. Mergers and integration of dispersed hospital buildings in medium and large cities, which have occurred and occur elsewhere in Europe, are equally likely to continue to be needed to improve efficiency, effectiveness and the overall financial sustainability and performance of hospital care. This need to improve quality, performance and financial sustainability needs to be reconciled with the need for improved access. Though the hospital system appears oversized in absolute terms, when accounting for population density the situation is in fact different. The number of hospitals in Romania per 100,000 inhabitants is slightly low compared to average European levels. In recent years, in a context of reductions in hospital capacity across Europe, the difference has diminished. At the same time, Romania's population has been constantly declining since 1990. The number of registered residents in 2013 numbered 20.02 million compared to 21.83 in 2002, while the official number of emigrants during the same period increased from 1.06 million to 2.34 million (National Statistical Institute of Romania, 2014b). In addition to growing emigration (predominantly of young people), the effect of decreased fertility is slowly contributing to an aging of the population which, though a wider European concern, is increasingly worrisome in Romania (World Bank, 2011, p. 5). In terms of the number of hospital beds in acute, short-stay hospitals, the numbers in Romania are among the highest in the EU (Fig. 6.1). There has been a clear decreasing trend across Europe, including Romania, with a sharp decrease in 2010–2011 (411 acute care beds per 100,000 inhabitants in 2011 compared to 538 in 2000 and 423 in 2013). The values of this indicator are comparable to other EU12 states but significantly higher than both the EU15 average and Estonia.

DECENTRALIZATION AND AUTONOMY OF HOSPITAL MANAGEMENT

Decentralization Reform

Decentralizing public hospitals has been a process that manifested itself as one component of the public administration reform and transition period more generally. The approach taken included a number of steps to create the legal framework that would later enable de facto decentralization to occur. In 2002, three government decisions (866/2002, 867/2002 and 70/2002) sought to transfer the administration of certain county and local public hospital facilities from the Ministry of Health to county and local councils. The nature of this transfer was largely administrative. Government Ordinance 70/2002 included provisions concerning the financial decentralization of public health facilities and attempted to clarify

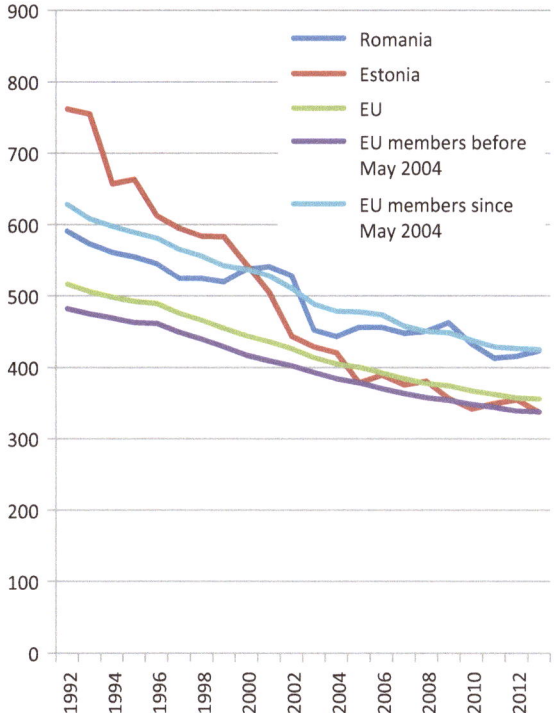

Fig. 6.1 Number of acute hospital beds per 100,000 inhabitants in Romania, 1992–2013
Author's own compilation *Source*: World Health Organization, European Health for All database, updated December 2015

the financial roles between the main players in the system: the Ministry of Health, county public health authorities (representatives of the central government in each county) and county and local councils. These decisions aimed at creating the premise for both administrative and financial decentralization to occur in a context of scarce resources and centralized decision making. Local authorities were expected to contribute financially to the much-needed renovation, consolidation and maintenance of hospital buildings and property. Six years later, in 2008, after a number of amendments to the 2002 legislation, the process continued with the adoption of a government emergency ordinance (OUG 162/2008). One year later, another government decision (HG 562/2009) embraced the concept of healthcare decentralization *strategy*. Three specific goals were envisaged, some of which were not new, but needed reiteration and implementation support (Ministry of Health, 2010, p. 23):

- The creation of the operational framework for decentralization to occur in practice
- Transfer of the range of competences concerning the administration of public hospitals and the management of healthcare facilities to county and local public authorities
- A redefinition of the role of the Ministry of Health concerning the development, implementation and monitoring of public health policy and legislation needed to ensure effective operation of the healthcare system.

Though they included provisions for managerial and financial decentralization, the initiatives up to that point had largely been administrative in effect. Financial decentralization was still minimal, and modern management principles in hospitals were still in their infancy. Stimulated by the financial crisis, international pressure and foreign expertise, 2010 proved to be a crucial year in the process for greater decentralization. For the first time, policy makers took concrete steps to decentralize hospital management. The Ministry of Health first conducted two pilot projects and chose the capital city Bucharest and the city of Oradea as experimentation sites. The projects consisted of transferring the management of 18 out of the total of 42 public hospitals in Bucharest and four hospitals in Oradea to the two municipalities. An evaluation of the pilot projects concluded that the two municipalities possessed the administrative capacity needed to manage the healthcare facilities (Ministry of Health, 2010, p. 24). Policy makers in the Ministry of Health built on this experience and in June 2010 issued a government emergency ordinance (OUG 48/2010) which created the legal basis for the decentralization of 370 local and county hospitals—out of the total of 435 public hospitals in Romania at that time. The list of hospitals to which management was transferred was included in a government decision (HG 529/2010), and at the same time, a directive of the Ministry of Health (OMS 910/2010) approved the template of the document for the transfer of ownership. As a result of this act, the Ministry of Health, represented by the county public health authorities, was no longer the owner of most public hospitals. A selective number of regional hospitals providing tertiary care, single-specialty institutes and health centers remained under the direct responsibility of the Ministry of Health. The same is the case for clinical emergency hospitals and emergency units. In this way, the Ministry of Health hoped to retain the responsibility for providing integrated care in case of emergencies as well as conducting national research and ensuring the implementation of national public health programs in various specialties. A number of complementary changes were envisaged that sought to augment the role of local authorities in administering, managing and funding the hospitals:

- Local authorities were encouraged to create healthcare departments within their administrations that would be responsible for governing hospitals depending on the size of the hospital network;
- Local administrations were given the responsibility to hire hospital managers who would sign a contract with and be accountable to the local authorities rather than the Ministry of Health;
- A number of management decisions need to be approved by the mayor, in case of local hospitals, or by the president of the county council, in the case of hospitals owned by counties. The Ministry of Health still needs to give its notice, but this role is thought to be less prominent than before. This is also reflected in the structure of the administrative committee which is now composed in such a way to enable more decentralized decision making than before. Out of the five members of the committee, two members are appointed by the county or local council and one by the mayor or county council;
- Hospital care will continue to be funded through the national health insurance fund or through the state budget for investment, as before the reform. However, the 2010 reform encouraged local authorities to complement these sources and assume a more prominent financial role than in the past.

The substantiation note to the reform clearly states that making local administrations more responsible by assuming a greater financial role was one of the main reasons underlying the reform (Substantiation note to Government Emergency Ordinance 48/2010). Another expectation was that efficiency in allocating and using resources would increase as a result of financial and managerial decentralization. If local authorities allocate a greater budget in funding hospitals, then, it was believed, that money will be used more efficiently and effectively. Effectiveness and quality were indirectly expected to improve through the following mechanism. If local administrations support to a greater degree the maintenance and functioning of facilities, then hospitals could use more money to improve service quality, rather than fund basic infrastructure. Similarly, transparency and accountability were expected to improve following a typical argument in support of decentralization which claims that local needs are best understood and met when decisions are made locally.

Unlike previous efforts to increase decentralization, the 2010 reform made it through to implementation. It is debatable whether the reform led to a change of substance or was mere window dressing in reaction to fiscal pressure and international trends. Some interviewees consider that the reform does not address the problems in the hospital system. They argue that it makes little difference who the owner of the hospitals is— whether central institutions or local administrations. Decentralization is like a "china item on a shelf," one interviewee claimed as long as local administrations do not possess the administrative capacity and financial resources to support the development of hospitals (Interviewee 24). This is not one person's opinion only. Other respondents have claimed that decentralization is a step forward, but there is great variation in administrative capacity and financial resources from one place to another. This would affect the good intention of the reform. It is manageable for a large municipality to support the hospitals in their jurisdiction as they can mobilize staff and resources more easily than a small municipality in a poor region that is already experiencing financial problems. The reform did not draw a distinction between high and low capacity municipalities—all local hospitals were proposed for decentralization regardless of the financial situation of local administrations or the financial situation of the hospitals within those jurisdictions. Furthermore, the pilot projects included two large and relatively well-resourced municipalities, Bucharest and Oradea, but they are clearly not representative of the entire country. Some hospitals had accumulated debt, and although the Ministry of Health promised to pay the debt, local authorities feared they would have to take the financial burden on their already crippled shoulders. Some local administrations rejected the proposal initially which exacerbated the already tense relationship with the center—and the political parties in power. Some local authorities in opposition and under fiscal pressure boycotted the reform, which was seen as unreasonable and unsustainable.

The public hospital decentralization reform is now a few years old, and some of its effects and long-term impacts are still in the making. However, on a short- and medium-term basis, we can already assess what changed, if anything, since the reform. Notwithstanding local resistance from some hospitals and local authorities undergoing financial stress, overall the reform passed the implementation test in 2010, the year when the legislation was adopted. In the case of most hospitals, "take over protocols" were signed in 2010 which heralded the legal transfer of ownership to the local authorities. There is evidence that the reform produced changes concerning local financial responsibility and the relationship between decentralized hospitals, local authorities and the Ministry of Health. It is important to note that it was not the 2010 reform that reshaped all these relationships, but the 2010 reform represented the climax of a longer process toward greater decentralization.

Financially speaking, there is evidence that the reform further strengthened the involvement of local authorities in hospital financing within their jurisdiction. By taking over the assets of decentralized hospitals, local authorities were stimulated to invest in the infrastructure and administration of hospitals. The problem is that this has not been uniform across all local authorities. Lack of financial and administrative capacity burdened some local authorities, particularly those in poor and small localities. Rather than thanking the Ministry of Health for the "gift," they felt they had to take over what was considered financially insecure and politically delicate. Administering hospitals and healthcare services was also a completely new task for these administrations, different from other less specialized and possibly less problematic services. This was a policy mistake that seemed to ignore the local context, but at the same time, the decision to de facto decentralization had already been postponed a number of times before the 2010 reform. There was also little hope that the financial situation of both local authorities and public hospitals would change significantly in the coming years. In this sense, the decision had to be made, though not all prerequisites were in good order. The Ministry of Health going through its own financial challenges reinforced by the financial crisis, took major steps to relieve itself of part of the financial burden. Though far from uniform, well-resourced local authorities did become more interested in hospital governance following the reform. They started to assume the new role more confidently and develop hospital governance skills. The material and financial state of most of the hospitals interviewed improved as a result:

"Local authorities, having income sources through local taxes, can support these hospitals and medical centers. Without the money from the local

> authorities we would have only had money for salaries until October. We've seen that since the transfer to the local authorities we have been much better financed and we were able to receive funds for investment in modern medical equipment [...] The Ministry still has an important direct role in managing the national public health programs but through the reform the Ministry is relieved of some tasks and of course the system is heavy, we would like it all to start working all of a sudden, but it has started to work."
> (Interviewee 16)

This is an example in a large municipality with a long tradition of medical care and education where local decision makers were both capable and willing to support the development of local hospitals. It is not the only fortunate case, and this effect is not specific to large and generally well-resourced municipalities only. Some local authorities were in a position to build units within their organizations specifically responsible for the administration of hospitals and the coordination of healthcare services within their jurisdiction. In this context, hospital managers assessed decentralization positively but with some reservations. The manner in which decentralization is perceived heavily depends on whether a specific hospital received funds from the local authorities as well as more generally how they view the relationship with local authorities. This relationship is influenced in turn by the manager's leadership and lobbying skills. Since both hospital managers and local decision makers can change frequently, identifying windows of opportunity is a highly valuable skill. In addition to finance, some hospital managers have identified other benefits of decentralization. These include a reduction in politicization and central control and the perception that local authorities possess a better grasp of the situation of the hospitals than the Ministry of Health. These benefits, nonetheless, are not universally shared. Whether decentralization is perceived as beneficial depends on local contextual factors that are hard to pin down and control over time. Some hospital interviewees have emphatically argued that decentralization increased red tape. Rather than reduce bureaucracy, the reform added an extra layer of local red tape on top of the central red tape which has continued to persist, despite the decentralization process:

> "Our perception in the hospital is that bureaucracy increased as a result of decentralization. It did not decrease... Before the reform, things were clear and there were certain routines that worked. On the other hand, for almost any change, for example change in structure or personnel, except

just a few responsibilities that the local council is now responsible for, we need to also ask for the Ministry of Health's approval. So things have not become simpler; they have become a little bit more complicated." (Interviewee 18)

Again this is an opinion that is not universally shared by all interviewees (although our list of interviewees cannot be considered representative of the entire country). A complex reform such as decentralization, involving many actors with different interests across different levels, is likely to be assessed differently from one institution to another. Those who have perceived an increase in red tape and no change in central control are likely to question whether decentralization has occurred in reality:

"In our case a potential recentralization would be easier to implement since the decentralization has not really been real. It's likely that in three, four or five years' time the system will recentralize." (Interviewee 18)

Despite this pessimistic view, we have seen however that financial decentralization did occur to some extent and in some cases. We have also found evidence of local authorities actively assuming their new role and investing in developing a coordinated strategy for governing hospital care locally. As any other major change, there are actors who lose and actors who win and perception of whether reform works or not depends on which side one finds himself at a particular point in time.

Autonomy of Hospital Management

There has not been so far a distinct piece of legislation specific to hospital autonomy alone. The same is true for the 2010 decentralization legislation and complementary policy documents, including the Strategy. However, the Strategy had much to say about managerial autonomy and what needed to be changed. Hospital management autonomy was part of the same "package" as decentralization, both of which were seen as key means to improve the state of hospital care organization, management and provision across the country. Before the 2010 reform, the Ministry of Health and its decentralized authorities were responsible for a wide range of administrative decisions in addition to a policy, control and governance role. These included the responsibility to issue proposals and approvals to found or close a public hospital, the internal structure and organization of a hospital, the number of hospital beds or the name and address of a hospital. Hospital directors, as they were typically called at that time (no managers yet), could consult with local councils in their jurisdiction, but the final approval lay with the Ministry of Health through the local public health authorities. The main hospital governance body was the consultative committee, comprised of several members who according to the law had to be representatives of the Ministry of Health, local authorities, academic institutions (in the case of university hospitals), the business community and labor union. The autonomy of this committee, however, was assessed as limited in practice and could in reality only issue recommendations rather than make final decisions (Ministry of Health, 2010, p. 23). On paper it seems that a hospital manager had some degree of autonomy but had to operate in a highly regulated environment and a financial context in which most financial resources, typically more than 70 %, were used to pay salaries following a centralized standard remuneration system. It could make various recommendations, which later could be implemented, but only after being approved from above. The manager was responsible for appointing department heads after a competitive examination approved by the Ministry of Health with the exception of clinical university hospitals in which the post of department head had to be occupied by staff with the highest medical degree, following the recommendation of the university senate. These decisions had to be approved by the hospital manager and the Ministry of Health. This system can have its merits, but it can also lead to appointments based on informal networks rather than competence and fit for the job. Hospital managers signed a three-year standard contract and were evaluated yearly based on a list of standard performance indicators which were included as an annex to the contract.

Policy makers promoting the Strategy seemed to agree at that time that what was needed was a significant increase in the actual decision-making autonomy of hospital management. Management needed to be empowered, to have the legal and practical authority to decide on a wider range of issues over which previously had only little control in reality. This, it was believed, would unleash management expertise and improve service organization and delivery. As clearly underlined in the Strategy, policy makers hoping to increase hospital autonomy relied on the framework developed by Preker and Harding (2003) to assess the status quo of the hospital sector. This model aiming at corporatized hospital management was seen as the direction to go, and success seems to have been evaluated based on the extent to which hospitals in Romania fitted this framework. It was concluded that hospitals in Romania did not yet follow the principles of corporatized hospital management, and the recommendation was to "increase hospital autonomy and introduce the corporatized management model along with systematic hospital planning" (Ministry of Health, 2010, p. 29).

A 2009 technical report supporting the Strategy concluded that public hospitals were part of a "highly centralized, bureaucratic, and rigid governance system where almost all management and governance decisions have to be approved centrally by the Ministry of Health. Such an environment is not conducive to efficient and appropriate governance and it does not empower management to react to the rapidly changing market conditions. Another concern is that despite the existence of criteria that managers have to meet to be hired and of performance measurement systems, transparency in the hiring of managers leaves much to be desired […] and changes in hospital management often occur soon after elections and shifts in alliances in the local and/or national political balance. In other words, there are strong indications that politics plays a role in the choice of hospital managers." (Pikani & Sava, 2009, p. 6)

Although most public hospitals have been the object of decentralization, the reform has not led to an increase in the autonomy of hospital managers. On the contrary, it can be argued that the decision-making power of hospital managers decreased in some areas, most notably public procurement or remained unchanged in other respects. Despite the plea for greater hospital management autonomy, as articulated in the Strategy, there is no clear evidence of an increase in autonomy. Following the Strategy, reform ideas aiming at greater autonomy continued to be proposed in 2012 as part of a larger proposal for a new healthcare law which was recommended for public debate at that time and soon thereafter. These ideas have faded away in the meantime, and changes in the leadership of the Ministry of Health brought a shift of ideas. Some policy makers preferred centralization to management autonomy. The decentralization legislation, nonetheless, did include some provisions to increase hospital management autonomy. For example, the consultative committee was replaced by an administrative committee which is said to have real governance responsibilities in approving the hospital budget and other financial matters, the hospital strategy, the yearly procurement plan as well as organizing the competition for appointing the manager, evaluating the manager's performance and revoking the manager from office in case of incompatibility, serious culpability or underperformance. The legal basis, it is stated in the Strategy, allows more flexibility than before concerning structural and human resource changes in hospitals, as well as in the internal reallocation of hospital budgets and a series of other organizational and administrative aspects (Ministry of Health, 2010, pp. 46–47). Nevertheless, these changes have either not been implemented, for example concerning procurement, or have had merely formal connotations with no real impact on hospital autonomy. Interviewees representing both centralized and decentralized hospitals agree that decision making is limited, and the system has either remained the same or become more bureaucratized and controlled following the 2010 decentralization reform. If central and local decision makers want hospitals to enjoy more autonomy and, as a result, want them to actively use modern management tools, then there needs to be an actual change in autonomy. So far, there have been ideas, proposals and promises, but little change in reality:

"The concept of self-governing hospitals does not exist in our case in my view. [...] For instance, in case of a vacancy there is competition between applicants organized by the Ministry of Health or by the local authorities with the Ministry of Health's approval. [...] The change of the organizational form and hospital autonomy have not occurred yet either, though these have been discussed in recent years. The reason is that this would be a major change with all kinds of implications, including of a political nature... I believe this is a trend towards which we are aspiring... I think it would be good to increase hospital autonomy, to change this aspect of a budgetary institution as it is the case today." (Interviewee 17)

"The relationship between the Ministry of Health and the hospitals is one of subordination; it is a hierarchical relationship... given the size and importance of our hospital, the Ministry of Health is interested in it and acknowledges its role in our region and so it supports the hospital to the extent possible, for example in case of renovations and equipment. This is a positive thing. However, in terms of issues, the decision is very centralized, bureaucratic and inflexible which makes things work more difficult." (Interviewee 17)

What is particularly interesting is that this view is not shared only by the hospitals which remained under the direct coordination of the Ministry of Health, as in the case above, but also by decentralized hospitals. This shows that decentralization and hospital management autonomy do not necessarily change in the same direction. Changing the ownership of hospitals does not necessarily involve an increase in the autonomy of hospital management. In fact, as argued in this chapter, in the case of Romania, decentralization has meant that hospitals in reality have two owners instead of one as it used to be before. For example, this member of an executive board of a decentralized hospital explained the situation in this way:

"In terms of hospital autonomy, the situation has not changed as a result of decentralization reform. We have still remained a budgetary institution, i.e. institution governed by the state budget law and in this sense the Ministry of Finance is our master. When it comes to money and administration, the Ministry of Health only offers methodological support. However, as mentioned earlier, for any change concerning personnel, practically anything... setting up a new unit in the hospital, all these decisions go all the way up to the Ministry of Health. [...] Approvals from the Ministry are not merely consultative; they are mandatory and if the answer is no, then it's a no, and that change cannot be applied... It is not merely formal either; it involves an analysis of the request." (Interviewee 18)

The same idea—increase in red tape and having two owners instead of one—is also usefully echoed by this hospital manager:

"The decentralization strategy was well intended. The goal was to get local authorities involved in hospitals in order to address certain aspects and issues locally rather than centrally. However, this reform also had to include a decentralization of decision making which has not been the case. It only happened to some extent. For instance, if I, as a hospital under the Ministry, want to hire somebody or if I want to develop or stop the activity of a hospital unit, I need to ask for the Ministry's approval. Decentralized hospitals, on the other hand, need to make an additional step; they also need to ask for the approval of the local authority but also the approval of the Ministry of Health. As a result, my decision making instruments today are the same as the hospitals under the local authorities. In fact there is lack of flexibility because the decision is still made centrally ultimately." (Interviewee 17)

Hospital autonomy is limited not due to hospital policy, but also as a matter of limited resources. If hospitals, for example, had been granted more autonomy by law, they would not necessarily be able to make use of it without adequate resources. In this sense, autonomy becomes a double-edged sword which promises much but can be easily misused and abused in practice. This has been a main theme throughout the course of the

research, and a number of interviewees have emphasized the possible problems of increasing hospital autonomy in the Romanian context:

> "Concerning hospital autonomy we see the following factors as important:
> insufficient human resources, a freezing of vacancies and insufficient finan-
> cial resources. Due to low salaries, doctors are working abroad and there is
> also a crisis of essential medication (cytostatic, anti-HIV, diabetes and oth-
> ers) and as a result in some cases patients need to procure their own medica-
> tion during hospitalization. So the autonomy that exists, though limited, is
> also limited by insufficient resources." (Interviewee 19)

> "Decentralization is an important principle of the reform, but if it is not
> adapted to the situation on the ground, and is not nuanced, it can nega-
> tively affect coordination. Concerning hospital management autonomy, the
> situation is the same: it can have negative effects due to managers' different
> specialized capacity and training. There are many examples today of manag-
> ers who were dismissed due to poor management as a result of investigations
> which discovered unlawful behavior concerning public procurement, which
> is a frequent charge in Romania." (Interviewee 19)

Mechanisms and Instruments of Coordination

The main national players are the Ministry of Health and the National
Health Insurance House. Other important national actors include the
College of Physicians—the association of Romanian physicians—and the
National Commission for Hospital Accreditation, a quasi-independent
agency operating under the supervision of the prime minister (rather than
the health minister). The task of the commission is to manage hospital
accreditation. The commission is a central government agency governed
by a board whose members represent both the political and professional institutions: the administration of the President of Romania, the
Central Government, the Romanian Academy, the College of Physicians
and the Association of Nurses and Midwives. The members of the commission are appointed for a four-year term under the recommendation
of the institution they represent and need to be approved by the prime
minister (National Commission for Hospital Accreditation, 2014a). The
commission establishes the norms and the framework for hospital accreditation which is carried out by approved evaluators. The object of hospital
accreditation, according to these norms, refers to both form (e.g. compliance with existing regulation) and substance (evaluation of performance)

(National Commission for Hospital Accreditation, 2014b). The Ministry of Health is the main central policy institution and is entrusted by law with a wide range of responsibilities. Before the decentralization reform, among others, these included the role to:

- Design, coordinate and control the implementation of health policy, programs and strategies nationally, regionally and locally in accordance with the central government's governance program;
- Evaluate and monitor the health of the population;
- Take measures to improve public health and inform the central government concerning changes and trends in healthcare;
- Regulate the organization and operation of the healthcare system;
- Monitor, control and evaluate the activity of hospitals and take measures to improve the quality of healthcare;
- Ensure, in collaboration with central and local public authorities, the necessary human, material and financial resources in order for the system to function properly.

The Ministry of Health carries out its central role in the system through 42 public health authorities which represent the Ministry of Health in each county and the city of Bucharest. These health authorities have the responsibility to make sure that the above tasks are put in practice locally. Through them, the Ministry of Health has sought to ensure coherence across the country and the implementation of national policy locally. Following the decentralization reform, local public administrations were expected to exercise a greater role in coordinating the newly decentralized public hospitals within their jurisdiction. The 42 health authorities no longer owned the newly decentralized hospitals, but they continued to own and coordinate the hospitals that did not undergo decentralization. It is, however, a question of empirical research if this formal change has thus far produced significant change concerning the role of the health authorities.

Two of the goals included in the Strategy consisted of first, the adoption of a simple hospital classification system for all hospitals based on competence and, second, the elaboration of hospital plans on the basis of this classification. It was intended that hospital planning would cover three layers: national, regional and local. To this effect, the Ministry of Health issued a ministerial directive which included the methodology and mandatory minimal criteria for classifying hospitals into five categories based on competence (OMS 323/2011). According to this directive, hospitals were classified into one category ranging from V to I. Category V hospitals offer basic chronic, palliative and single-specialty care; category IV hospitals have the capacity to provide basic services to simple cases in a limited catchment area (small town hospitals), whereas hospitals included in the third category can serve patients in a specific county for cases of medium complexity (county hospitals). The two highest categories, II (high competence) and I (very high competence), differ based on competence and catchment area. Hospitals included in the second category typically provide services within a county and neighboring counties, whereas category I hospitals are regional hospitals and are expected to cover the need for high-level healthcare in a wider geographical area.

The classification was designed to be a first important step in improving the systemic coordination of hospital care with expected improvements in efficiency and transparency. The new system, it was hoped, would stimulate the use of performance budgeting while reducing costs due to treatment at a different level of care than adequate (Ministry of Health, 2010, p. 48). By reducing duplication between hospitals, it was also expected that efficiency would improve. The different categories of competence would also help with investment decisions in equipment and infrastructure as well as service contracts with the National Health Insurance House. The classification system has been the object of considerable amendment since it was first proposed. This has been due to different interpretations of the classification criteria, with some hospitals claiming the right to be included in a higher category than the one to which they were originally assigned. These hospitals have lobbied their way up to a greater status.

Along with the new classification system, policy makers initiated the process of hospital planning. The national plan would ensure the functional coherence of the system as a whole following decentralization. Three principles formed the backbone of the new project for the development of a hospital master plan, the first of its kind in Romania:

- Equitable access to specialized acute care within one hour under normal weather conditions;
- Optimal distribution of diagnostic and treatment equipment;
- Optimal size and structure of the area, and acute hospitals need to be situated in the natural center of this area.

It was also expected that regional and local plans would be developed starting from the master plan, and these would form the basis for hospital restructuring, closing or the construction of new facilities, if need be. Importantly, the Strategy only discussed in very general terms how hospitals would interact and coordinate their activity horizontally and vertically with other levels and types of care. Reform has reached the stage of proposing a new structure—reshaping the system—while the rules for operating within the structure have yet to be thought through and adopted. These instruments of coordination are fairly new—regulation, in fact, is the primary coordination mechanism at the disposal of the Ministry of Health. This takes the form of comprehensive healthcare law, that is, Law 95/2006, and a variety of specific legal acts such as emergency ordinances, government decisions and ministerial orders. These legal instruments target a particular matter, such as the methodological norms for the centralization of public procurement of hospital equipment, the approval of the framework contract for hospital managers (Ministerial Order 1384/2010), the classification of hospitals (Ministerial Order 323/2011) or the monitoring of hospital costs (Ministerial Order 858/2012). These are legally binding, and noncompliance is sanctioned. Authorized institutions and agents are entitled by law to control (a word used in the legislation) and investigate the activity of hospitals, including costs and quality, and general compliance with the law. Following decentralization, local authorities can exercise control in the decentralized hospitals in their jurisdiction, but the Ministry of Health through the local public health authorities in each county can also control the activity of decentralized hospitals. In the case of the hospitals that have remained under the ownership of the Ministry of Health, the mechanisms and instruments of coordination did not change. The standard hospital management contract, approved through ministerial order, includes a list of performance indicators on which hospital management needs to report. These include four types of indicators pertaining to human resource management (six indicators), service utilization (ten indicators), finance and economics (six indicators), and quality (six indicators) (Ministerial Order 1384/2010). To exemplify, the quality indicators hospital management is held accountable for comprise the following: the mortality rate per hospital overall and per hospital unit, nosocomial infection rate per hospital and hospital unit, readmission rate within 30 days after discharge, concordance index between the diagnosis upon admission and discharge, the percent of patients transferred to other hospitals out of the total number of admitted patients and the number of recorded complaints. These are fairly standard hospital indicators nowadays and much depends on how accurate the collected data is.

CASES AND PROBLEMS OF COORDINATION

Coordination of Financial Resources: A Problem of Contradiction

The healthcare system in Romania is based on social insurance and characterized by purchaser-provider split. Within the social insurance system, the National Health Insurance House is the principal actor. The insurance house is currently organized as a quasi-independent public body, the main function of which is to purchase and pay services from different providers in the healthcare system, be they primary care practices, hospitals or other providers. In addition to the national insurance house, there are 42 local insurance houses (one in each county), including one in Bucharest serving the area surrounding the capital. The local insurance houses are public institutions with their own juridical status and budget. They operate locally on behalf of the national insurance house and are responsible for local implementation of the policy and strategy of the national organization. They have their own statute but function within a general framework approved by the mother organization. The share of statutory insurance in the total health expenditure has constantly grown since 1998. While in 1990 the system was funded 100 % through general tax, in 1998 general tax represented 31.8 %, local tax 0.6 % and the biggest share was statutory insurance with 64.6 %. This share of the statutory insurance grew constantly and reached 80.7 % in 2001 and 82.7 % in 2004 reflecting the new realities of healthcare finance in Romania based on social insurance. The share of noninsurance revenue (i.e. general central tax) fell as a result of the change of the system with the adoption of the social health insurance system. The national insurance house distributes funds to local insurance houses according to a formula that accounts for the number of insured persons and the mix of population risks in each county. In a context of scarce financial resources and the financial crisis, there has been (and continues to be) ongoing interest in finding additional sources of revenue, including co-payments and local tax. The hospital decentralization reform aimed at creating the premise to increase local financial responsibility as a means to create additional funding sources in healthcare. The collection of funds is sensitive to the state of the economy and employment rates, which have fluctuated considerably. Romania's GDP has grown significantly in the past 15 years, starting in 2000. In the first decade after 1989, the industrial output dropped significantly following measures to restructure the former communist economy centered on heavy industry (Fig. 6.2). In the years preceding the outbreak of the financial crisis in 2008, GDP per capita had increased more than five times. Similar overall economic trends can be observed across the European Union with the important qualification that there are significant differences in absolute terms between the different regions of Europe. Romania's GDP per capita, though it has grown significantly, is still among the lowest in Central and Eastern Europe, and considerably smaller than in Western Europe (Fig. 6.2). Whereas Estonia's per capita income fares better than the average in the EU12, Romania's GDP per person is situated below the EU12 average despite a positive long-term trend.

The percent allocated to health from both public and private sources is comparable to that of other countries in Central and Eastern Europe, and fluctuated slightly around 4 %. In 2000, for instance, the share of GDP from public sources was 3.5 %, but since then the trend has been slightly ascending reaching 4.8 % in 2010 and 4.3 % in 2013 (Fig. 6.3). Nevertheless, the share is still among the lowest in CEE, and significantly smaller than the EU average, which exceeds 7 %. Interestingly, Romania's share of health expenditure as percent of GDP has been close to Estonia's share, and in recent years starting in 2010, they have both fluctuated around 4.5 % of GDP (Fig. 6.3)

There are two severe problems concerning the coordination of financial resources: the total funding of the system and the funding mechanism. As the previous graphs clearly show, the financial resources allocated to health are relatively low compared to the EU average. Healthcare in Romania, relative to other countries in the EU—both EU15 and EU13—has been severely underfunded and has remained so 25 years after the collapse of communism. This is a clear theme that has emerged from both the primary and secondary data collected. In a poorly resourced context, there is a contradiction between the actual costs of services and the reimbursed amount. Hospitals receive less money than the actual costs, which has led to accumulated debt (hospital arrears). Some hospitals also treat more patients than they receive reimbursement for, which has the same effect of accumulating debt and endangering the functioning of the hospital and possibly the quality of healthcare. For example, one member of the executive board of a large hospital shows how large the difference is between the number of treated patients versus the number for which the hospital was paid:

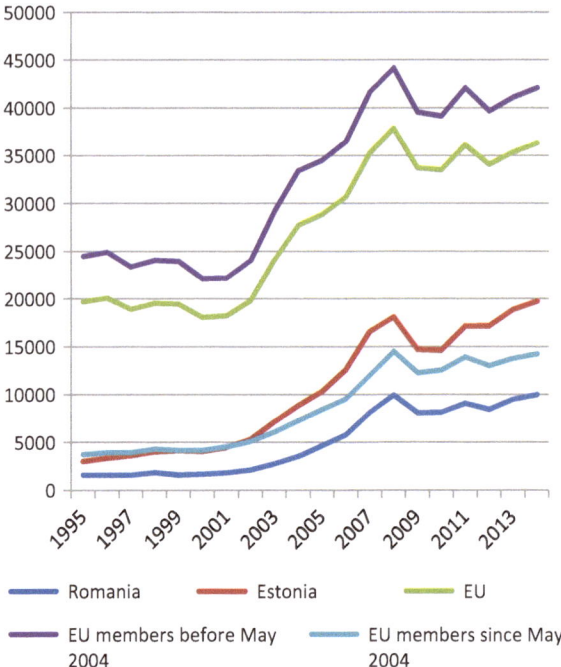

Fig. 6.2 Gross Domestic Product per capita in Romania in USD, 1995–2014 Author's own compilation *Source*: World Health Organization, European Health for All database, updated December 2015

> "We were reimbursed for 39,000 patients though in reality we treated 42,000. This led to arrears which subsequently had to be financed from the state budget. There is not enough money for all this volume; we are talking here in the case of an emergency hospital and emergency services are free." (Interviewee 27)

The financial arrangements are not realistic and the same is the case with the structure of healthcare provision which still is disproportionately geared toward inpatient care. Although measures have been taken in recent years to foster a greater role for primary, ambulatory and day care, the extent of the use of inpatient care is overwhelming and financially suffocates the healthcare system. In this context, hospitals exercise their creativity and find ways to cope with the situation through corrupt means, such as altering the diagnostic or fabricating cost-related data:

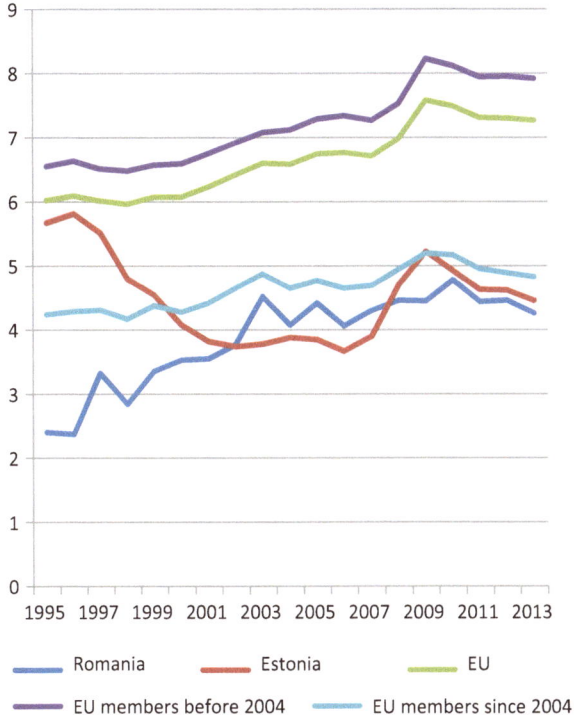

Fig. 6.3 Public sector expenditure on health as percent of Gross Domestic Product in Romania, 1995–2013
Author's own compilation. *Source*: World Health Organization, European Health for All database, updated December 2015

"There is a tendency to alter the diagnosis to receive more money from the insurance house which funds hospitals based on a historic budget plus negotiations between the hospitals and the insurance house... it's also possible through personal contacts to share the remaining pie after the budgets have been divided. What is left can be given preferentially on the basis of informal grounds." (Interviewee 25)

Not only is the pie small, but the way in which the pie is shared is also considered to be severely flawed. The DRG mechanism, though it has gone through change since it was first adopted, is assessed to be unrealistic and lacking in transparency. It produces severe dysfunctions in the financing of hospitals and perpetuates a culture of "fooling ourselves," as one inter-viewee vividly characterized it:

> "In addition to issues with the lack of personnel and underfinancing, we experience two other contextual problems that affect our activity. First, the DRG system which has not been adapted to Romania and it was taken first from the American DRG and then the Australian one. The DRG costs are unsuitable for Romania and they do not reflect the real costs and as a result the Romanian creativity leads us to hide certain things to look better and be funded better. Practically we are deceiving ourselves, but if everybody does this then you also have to do it because otherwise you end up with a sum of money with which you can barely pay the salaries." (Interviewee 18)

Another interviewee sheds further light on why the DRG is flawed:

> "The current financial mechanism used to finance hospitals, based on the DRG system, produces major dysfunctions in how hospitals operate. This is because it was poorly implemented from the beginning. At first it was based on the American system, then it was replaced with an Australian one and when it adopted the Romanian values, what happened in fact was that we put some-thing Romanian on something that did not fit our country... In Romania the money included in the DRG also included other costs, not just the treatment costs, such as utilities, renovations and so forth so all hospital costs were in fact included in this DRG which was not the same as the American DRG and so it could not work. The Australian DRG tried to regulate things a little bit and to look at things from a different perspective but eventually the same thing happened as before. Currently the money allocated to health is not sufficient to cover what is needed in reality and the allocation mechanism between dif-ferent types of medical assistance could also be improved." (Interviewee 17)

Adopting a finance mechanism uncritically proved to be highly prob-lematic. The DRG system is, however, widely used across the world, which leads us to question if it is the mechanism itself to be blamed. The issue at stake is that the DRG prices are not concordant with the reality in Romania. There is no easy answer to the question why Romanian author-ities did not insert realistic prices into the DRG system. Compared to the first versions of the system, the compatibility between DRG and real prices has improved, but there are still significant gaps, as shown in this chapter. This is at least partly due to the limited financial resources of the healthcare system and also limited administrative capacity to manage the system properly, though the latter has improved as experience and expertise have accumulated. We question the wisdom of the decision to use a DRG system that was not suitable for the reality on the ground—following an international fashion and applying it to a context that was not yet ready for such change.

Centralizing Public Procurement

Public procurement of medical equipment is a special case that has been the object of much debate and change in the context of decentralization reform and discussions about hospital autonomy. Since the trend in hospital policy in Romania has been toward greater decentralization and timidly toward an increase in hospital autonomy, one can expect the same change in the important area of public procurement. However, this has not been the case. Procurement of medical and sanitary equipment was the responsibility of hospital administrations, but in 2012, a government emergency ordinance (OUG 71/2012) designated the Ministry of Health as the only centralized public procurement unit. A subsequent ministerial order established the methodological norms for the organization of centralized procurement. The ministerial order, among other provisions, includes the list of products that form the object of centralized procurement. The list comprises medication, medical, sanitary and safety equipment as well as auxiliary services such as automobile fuel and lubricants. The order clearly establishes the Ministry of Health as the authority in the matter, but leaves some room for hospital management who can make recommendations on what products the list should include. It is important to note that the emergency ordinance and ministerial order are universal in scope—they apply to both centralized hospitals under the direct coordination of the Ministry of Health as well as to the decentralized hospitals under the direct coordination of local authorities. There is one exception here: central policy makers decided that medical equipment financed from local sources granted by local authorities, donations and funds from other projects does not form the object of centralized procurement. The procurement procedure includes a number of provisions concerning the role of each institution, as specified in the government ordinance:

- The Ministry of Health first signs framework contracts on behalf of the centralized and decentralized public hospitals;
- On the basis of the framework contracts, public hospitals sign subsequent contracts with the providers of medical equipment and the contracts need to be approved by the Ministry of Health.

The entire procedure includes a number of steps, as described in the ministerial order. The Ministry of Health is the principal actor and is tasked, among others, with:

1. Developing the list of medication, sanitary materials, medical equipment, safety equipment, services, automobile fuel and lubricants

In response to this first step, within 15 days since the publication of the list, public hospitals must report the following data to the public procurement unit in the Ministry of Health:

- The minimum and maximum quantities and volumes of materials and services needed for a year;
- Technical specifications of products and services that were used in the past before the request for data;
- Prices per unit for the products and services used in the past;
- Any other data requested by the centralized public procurement unit.

2. Developing the documentation for attribution

A commission is established for the purpose of developing the documentation that will form the basis for the procurement decision. Three of the members are experts in the field and representatives of three different public hospitals or public institutions (e.g. chief doctors) while two are representatives of the Ministry of Health. It is important to point out that ultimately it is the Ministry of Health that decides on all five members of the commission. All members need to be appointed by the Ministry of Health.

3. Asking for a second expert opinion

To validate the technical specifications of materials that form the object of public procurement, the Ministry of Health proposes and selects two additional independent experts. The substantiation note to the government decision explains the need for centralized procurement on efficiency grounds. It argues that there are major price differences, in some cases as high as ten times, from one public hospital to another for the same products and services. By centralizing procurement, the Ministry of Health hoped to achieve economies of scale, reduce price variation from one medical institution to another, standardize the quality of purchased materials and improve the continuity in the acquisition of products and services. The substantiation note argues that this change is part of a trend occurring in many other European countries seeking to do more with less. The case of centralizing public procurement is a case in point and ultimately shows the fragility of policy ideas in a changing context. The argument for the centralization of public procurement, interestingly enough is framed in a context of financial hospital autonomy, but there is no discussion of how centralizing procurement might affect the autonomy of hospitals. Considering that improving the autonomy of hospitals has received much interest from some health policy makers in recent years, the decision to centralize procurement is a move against the tide triggered by economic considerations and an interest in keeping things under control. There is evidence originating from the Ministry of Health itself that centralized public procurement led to savings in 2013, the first year since procurement was centralized, and is expected to improve continuity and standardization of the quality of materials purchased. It is too early to evaluate whether the latter two benefits have occurred in reality. Concerning savings, the Ministry of Health leaves no room for interpretation. In some cases, savings have reached 33.6 % as, for example, in the specific case of the purchase of 1.4 million doses of hexavalent vaccine (Ministry of Health, 2013). In other cases, such as the purchase of tuberculosis medication, the Ministry claims to have obtained savings up to 28 %. A third product included in the savings list includes the purchase of automobile fuel, for which a 6 % discount was obtained compared to the regular price at the gas station. Despite these optimistic figures, the question remains whether centralized procurement is beneficial in the medium and long term. Assuming that hospital autonomy is the way to move forward, which seems to be the case judging by the recent policy ideas, procurement is, however, one example of a state of affairs that is still favorable to central control. It is a signal that in fact central control is necessary, despite the ongoing talk about hospital autonomy. As attractive as savings and standardization may be, centralization of procurement sends out different and conflicting messages that, in our view, are difficult to reconcile:

> "Though the idea is well motivated and we understand the reasons, it affects us and contradicts the principles of decentralization which were so actively promoted in recent years." (Interviewee 27)

EXPLAINING COORDINATION

As in the previous chapter, in this section, we return to the theoretical propositions introduced in Chap. 3. We seek to explain the empirical findings in light of the propositions derived from principal-agent theory and sociological institutionalism. We begin the theoretical discussion with the propositions derived from principal-agent theory and then continue with the role of the hospital system culture.

Positive and Negative Incentives

Proposition 1: Positive incentives designed by central institutions with a coordinating role enable hospital system coordination

Proposition 2: Negative incentives (or penalties and sanctions) designed by central institutions with a coordinating role enable hospital system coordination

The principal-agent theory posits that the use of positive incentives such as financial stimuli employed by coordinating institutions facilitates the coordination of hospitals. This is expected to improve coordination and the alignment of goals between the principals and the agents. Coordination problems are expected to be ameliorated if not resolved. It is also assumed that hospitals—the agents—favorably respond to these incentives, if they are strong enough, and choose to be coordinated according to the principal's intention. These incentives are expected to resolve potential conflicting interests and differing goals between the two sides. The agents are public hospitals while the principals are the insurance house, the Ministry of Health and, importantly, local authorities that can and have provided positive incentives to decentralized public hospitals in their jurisdiction. Positive incentives principally take the form of financial contributions which in a low-resourced context can be expected to make a significant difference. If we consider the incentives developed by Romanian national healthcare institutions in the context of the decentralization reform, we can conclude that these have been negative rather than positive. The main message has been to reduce "the excess fat" and increase the control of what was considered to be poorly managed. Furthermore, the financial restrictions that accompanied the financial crisis led to a 25 % reduction in the salary of the medical personnel operating in the public sector. This measure was accompanied by a "freezing" of new employment contracts in the public hospital system, despite the observation that there were already shortages. In some specialties, this has exacerbated the existing problems and posed further strain on the already ailing system. The problem has become so acute that it convinced some that the shortage of medical personnel has become the main problem of the system in recent years. This market effect is similar to the one found in the case of Estonia:

"What we are most affected by at the moment is the personnel structure and lack of personnel since, as you know, hiring is blocked nationally and we have still had a deficit of a number of posts. Practically this affects us to the extent that we don't have enough specialists to use some of the super-modern equipment and laboratories, worth hundreds of thousands of euro we had invested in previously. We had spent the money, 1 million euro, for instance in an angiography laboratory, but we cannot use it, I mean we use it but not at full capacity because we don't have enough specialists. [...] I don't think that this problem is specific to our hospital only; I think it's more general and in fact all state hospitals are experiencing this challenge. At this moment, I mean some state hospitals are also experiencing financial problems but all hospitals lack personnel. The latter has perhaps become a greater issue than the problem with underfinanced healthcare. Money perhaps you can find here and there but you cannot make specialists that fast and in the case of Romania people only leave, almost nobody comes in from abroad." (Interviewee 18)

"Medical personnel can move freely and although some private medicine faculties were created, the outflow is greater than what we produce. Furthermore, it's difficult to plan for the future how many specialists you need in a specialty since, let's say, radiologists or anesthesiologists leave the country, which is what is happening in reality. This is a relatively new phenomenon and is acute. So far we have always complained about the lack of money and said to ourselves that if we had more money we could do anything, but now we see that having money is not enough, and you realize that you face other problems." (Interviewee 18)

Reducing already low salaries by 25 % and the opening up of the borders especially since 2007, when Romania joined the EU, constituted strong incentives which the medical personnel reacted. The issue, as the above quotations show, has become pervasive and systemic. We can argue that these negative incentives were not initiated by central coordinating institutions, but were rather a necessary response in a difficult time. On the positive side, central institutions have attempted to develop policies to regulate the ailing system, but these, though promising, have not yet produced significant results. The culture of the hospital system, characterized by low mutual trust between stakeholders and low compliance with ethical standards, has resisted the central positive incentives. They may make sense to national policy makers, but they make little sense further down into the trenches of day-by-day hospital management.

Locally, following decentralization, we have seen that local authorities were given the responsibility to contribute financially to the operation and development of local hospitals. This is a type of positive financial incentives developed by the local principals with the aim to ensure the ongoing operation and growth of local hospital facilities and hospital care. This is a new development in Romania, and there is evidence that some local authorities possessing the financial and administrative capacity, as well as the political will, have positively assumed this responsibility and made a significant contribution to hospital budgets. However, only some of the local authorities have had the administrative and financial capacity to actively assume these new responsibilities—our data do not allow an exact estimate of what proportion.

At the same time, some local authorities have actively assumed their coordinating role and made decisions to reorganize the local hospital network. This meant in practice that not all individual hospitals benefited from decentralization—some were closed or reorganized while others were further supported. Finally, it is useful to question the purpose of these incentives—both positive and negative. For our purposes, we assumed that the incentives are used with the aim of improving coordination and tackling coordination problems. The negative incentives cannot be said to be means to improve coordination—they were something that had to be done, but that nobody seemed to want to do. The financial contributions made by local authorities, however, can be said to have aimed at improving coordination, but this was not necessarily the main or the only purpose. In a poorly resourced environment, other more urgent matters came first such as renovating existing buildings, replacing old equipment, paying arrears, buying medication and so forth. Coordination may have had to do with these purposes, but the incentives were not primarily targeted at improving coordination. The need for coordination exists, particularly avoiding duplication resulting from a multi-site hospital infrastructure—a legacy of the oversized communist hospital sector. Nonetheless, this goal is perceived to be less urgent and receives less attention than the crisis of medical personnel, medication and sanitary equipment. These affect the very ability of hospitals to deliver treatment while duplication and coordination, though important, can wait. This hospital manager of one of the largest hospitals in the country explains how the multi-site—more than 30 different locations—hospital infrastructure leads to duplication:

"Concerning duplication, this is a problem in our hospital; this is due to the building structure of the hospital, we are located in more than 30 different buildings scattered across the city. So inevitably we cannot have one centralized laboratory only, for example, I need to have this possibility in many of the other existing buildings, so redundancies exist. The hospital would function better if it was located in one major building only. These redundancies would no longer be an issue; we would have them centralized in one place. They are more economical; our hospital is not economical, we have to pay a lot of fixed costs for a wide range of services. So this is the situation." (Interviewee 17)

This case is not solitary—many large hospitals still inherit the basic infrastructure built years ago and though there are plans to create integrated regional healthcare centers in each main region across the country, this ambitious goal can only be achieved in the long run. For these reasons, in the case of public hospitals in Romania, we can legitimately question the effectiveness of incentives for coordination purposes. In those cases when incentives specifically target coordination, the situation may be different, but thus far, this has only rarely been the case.

Information Asymmetry and Imperfect Monitoring

We now turn to the proposition concerning information asymmetry and imperfect monitoring.

Proposition 3: Information asymmetry and imperfect monitoring hinder central hospital system coordination

By possessing information that principals do not entirely have access to, agents can eschew the control of principals. The monitoring tools at principal's discretion can be imperfect which in practice means that the principal does not have enough information to control the agent's activity. It is either due to insufficient or inaccurate information or to poor monitoring. Translating this arrangement for the purposes of our research, we are interested in the role that potential information asymmetry and imperfect monitoring play in the coordination of public hospitals in Romania.

Under information asymmetry, public hospitals have information that central and local authorities do not have. Under these circumstances, ineffective coordination is attributed to lack of information about the activity and behavior of public hospitals. Our research suggests that information asymmetry does not adequately explain coordination in the Romanian public hospital system. We have not found empirical evidence in this sense. Our findings suggest that the coordinating institutions do possess the needed information. The problems are known, but this does not necessarily facilitate coordination. One case in point is the financing system in which case there is a major problem of contradiction between the real costs and the amount covered by the insurance fund. In this case, it seems naïve to believe that national institutions do not have information on the actual costs of services. The DRG is on the one hand not new and, on the other hand, there has been much debate about the contradictions in the DRG system. Some interviewees, however, have argued that in reality there is much more confusion about actual costs than it may seem at first. Some have claimed that without accurate information on the costs of healthcare, it is difficult to develop a realistic funding arrangement. The costs that fed into the DRG were produced "in the office," and information on actual costs is perceived to lack in transparency (Interviewee 21). Nonetheless, this statement, which is shared by some hospital interviewees, may come as a surprise at first. The reason for this is that hospitals are required to report, and are controlled for, their financial situations. According to a recent ministerial order, hospitals need to report, for instance, the value of each type of contract with the insurance house (Ministerial Order 858/1194/2012). The reporting tools seem to be in place. The Ministry of Health and local authorities are supposed to evaluate the performance of hospital management on the basis of the performance indicators in the standard management contract. There is some evidence that this occurs in reality and is not a simple formal exercise:

> "The Ministry of Health exercises its duties. If you look at the standard management contract there are performance indicators there... the Ministry goes to check and control these performance indicators. So I cannot say that given its capacity, the Ministry has not done its job." (Interviewee 16)

It is debatable how accurate this reporting is, considering the specific hospital system culture affected by poor management and corruption. Nonetheless, there is no clear indication that coordinating agencies lack the information to perform their coordinating functions. The specific details of costs and quality may not be known entirely, but the main problems are well known and yet little is achieved in practice, which means that there are other more important factors at play.

The second point concerns imperfect monitoring. In essence, principal-agent theory posits the same idea in the case of monitoring as in the case of information asymmetry. It is the asymmetry of information that is central to the theory and not the type of and manner in which monitoring is performed. Ultimately in principal-agent theory, the effectiveness of monitoring is assessed by how much useful information the principals obtain as a result of monitoring. The added element in this case is that lack of information is explained by how effectively the principal monitors the agent's activity. However, how monitoring is conducted may be as important as the purpose for which it is carried out. Monitoring and evaluation are important ingredients of good coordination in any hospital system. This is particularly so considering the relatively complex Romanian healthcare system and accountability lines (World Bank, 2011). On the one hand, decentralized hospitals are supposed to be coordinated locally, but at the same time need to report nationally to the Ministry of Health and the National Health Insurance House for national, systemic coordination to be effective. On the other hand, local administrations are subject to the supervision and regulations of the Ministry of the Interior, rather than those of the Ministry of Health. This may weaken national health coordination and further blur already complex accountability lines. Another area of criticism concerns the actual role, in addition to the manner in which the role is carried out. Changes in healthcare systems internationally, especially in the Western world, have included a reconsideration of the role of central government players. In the case of public hospitals, ministries of health have sought to strengthen their policy and regulatory function while administrative and management tasks have been devolved locally. Hospitals, likewise, have been granted increased managerial autonomy so that ministries of health have taken a step back from management and assumed the role of steward rather than administrator. Performing a wide range of responsibilities comes at the cost of weak policy and planning particularly in a context of limited capacity. The 2010 legislation and substantiation notes have emphasized these limitations and included provisions for change along the lines underlined above (Substantiation note to Government Decision 303/2011, p. 4). Despite this general direction, official documents still emphasize the role of the Ministry of Health as one of control—a word that appears frequently in the documents. For instance, in the section "Expected changes" of the Substantiation note to the decentralization act, we read that "the *control* over the medical activity undertaken in the decentralized public hospitals as well as in private hospitals is exercised by the Ministry of Health" (emphasis added) (Substantiation note to Government Emergency Ordinance 48/2010, p. 3). Rather than framing the role in terms of governance, coordination or stewardship, policy makers still prefer to use a hierarchical terminology. Hospital interviewees also perceive this idea of control as the main coordination mechanism. This culture of control is a key element of the hospital system in Romania. It reflects the interaction between the main stakeholders and is related to the low level of trust between central authorities and public hospitals.

In performing its financial control functions, the Ministry of Health is perceived to use control as a means to punish rather than recommend improvements (Interviewee 27). There is no concrete evidence that this form of top-down coordination has proved effective, but it is difficult to explain whether the type of coordination itself explains this finding. Other types of coordination need to be assessed and compared with control and conclusions need to be drawn about the potential merits of alternative coordination mechanisms. In terms of information asymmetry, we can conclude that it plays a minor part in explaining coordination. We suggest that other alternative explanations, to which we now turn, are better aligned with the collected evidence.

Conflicting Interests and Goals and the Hospital System Culture

A fourth proposition derived from principal-agent theory concerns the presence of conflicting interests and goals between principals and agents.

Proposition 4: Conflicting interests and goals between principals and agents hinder central hospital system coordination

The specific propositions concerning the role of the hospital system culture in explaining central coordination of public hospitals are as follows:

1. The interaction between health policy makers, medical profession, hospital management and patients influences central coordination of public hospitals

2. Mutual trust between health policy makers, medical profession, hospital management and patients is helpful to central coordination of public hospitals
3. Stakeholder compliance with ethical standards affects central public hospital coordination. Usually, high levels of compliance with declared standards will assist in the implementation of official attempts at coordination
4. Hospital system culture is one reason for the differences in coordination across the selected hospital systems.

Principal-agent theory postulates that due to different interests and goals, the principal encounters difficulties in controlling the activity of the agents. Rather than pursue the goals of the principal, the agents are supposed to be interested in their own welfare, which is assumed to be costly to the principal. To address this misalignment of interests and goals, and reduce the cost, the principal can create incentives to bring the agents on the same page as the principal's. In the context of public hospital coordination, the idea of differing interests and goal is very fitting. In a complex world as that of healthcare with different actors and professional groups, we can safely expect that hospitals' interests and goals differ from those of the coordinating agencies, be they the Ministry of Health or local authorities. Coordinating institutions are expected to be interested, for example, in the efficiency and sustainability of the hospital system as a whole, whereas specific hospitals or local authorities might be expected to pursue their local and organizational interests and goals. They may lack the systemic perspective. Our research shows that conflicting interests and goals are a useful lens to explain coordination of public hospitals in Romania. This may be surprising at first if we consider the limited autonomy of hospitals. We would expect that hospitals with limited autonomy might be more easily coordinated than those which enjoy a greater degree of autonomy. Autonomy might pave the way for developing organizational interests and goals which would be more difficult to do in a closely coordinated arrangement. This, however, is not the case. It is especially because of differing interests and goals that the Ministry of Health and local authorities seek to keep hospitals under control. Hospitals react to this control by questioning its logic and usefulness, as expressed by this director of medical care of a decentralized hospital:

"The county council functions differently, in ways that are incompatible with the healthcare system. Any approval takes longer to obtain, and any proposal on our part needs the council's approval (i.e. the politicians' approval), and this involves time and sometimes we get innocent questions that reflect the fact that they do not work in the field. They have certain suspicions concerning how the hospital works, and we need to give them explanations why we want this or that." (Interviewee 18)

"The budgetary restrictions as a result of this crisis which never seems to come to an end, affected the hospital in two ways: both from the center and from the local council. Each came with their own restrictions, if you like. And we have the impression that these don't make sense." (Interviewee 18)

Local authorities believe that asking "innocent questions" is a justified means of coordination in a context of alleged ethical problems. This creates a situation in which owners question the integrity of hospital management, but at the same time hospital management, in turn, question the politics of hospital governance and the capacity of the governing bodies. This turns into a blame game characterized by strong ethical and political connotations. It constitutes a vicious circle which perpetuates the lack of trust between institutions and as a result perpetuates a culture of control, which leads to bureaucracy, duplication and frustration.

The dimensions of the hospital system culture incorporated in our understanding of the term proved highly useful in making sense of why coordination has proved ineffective in Romania. It shows how well-known values, norms and behavior patterns are shared and constitute a culture in their own right which proved highly resistant to change. Concerning the interaction and power struggle between the central health policy makers, local politicians, the medical profession, hospital management and patients, we found that the key players are central policy makers, the elite medical profession and pockets of local political influence. This role of local politics has intensified following the decentralization reform. We have not found evidence suggesting that hospital management, as a distinct profession, or patients constitute important stakeholders in hospital coordination in Romania. This is not surprising considering that the autonomy of hospital management (or directors, as they are still more commonly referred to) has been and remained limited. The medical profession, particularly the elite medical profession, is much stronger in Romania than hospital management. Moreover, a culture of limited civic engagement, despite progress, has meant that in reality patients do not yet have sufficient power to significantly influence organizational reform. Furthermore, both the low level of trust between these stakeholders and limited compliance with ethical standards and existing regulation are important cultural factors that help explain coordination problems in the Romanian public hospital system. In what follows, we further describe the specific mechanisms through which these cultural factors affect central coordination.

The ideas of decentralization and hospital management autonomy promoted by central policy makers in recent years are desirable and a step in the right direction. These changes, if well adapted to and implemented in the context of Romania, are aligned with international trends and can prove beneficial. In the case of decentralization, the opposition to reform had a practical rather than ideological connotation—decentralization in the Romanian context is perceived as a good idea, but practical limitations hinder it. Hospital autonomy is associated by some with privatization and is a more contested type of change both ideologically and practically. Efforts to reform the system more profoundly than a simple change of ownership have been faced with professional resistance which is led and controlled by old-school chief doctors and heads of specialties who dominate decision making in hospitals.

Some interviewees, for instance, have described them as displaying a "caste behavior"—a sort of elite epistemic community—that is averse to new and is interested in preserving the status quo to their advantage. They are averse to new organizational arrangements that shake up their position but may, nevertheless, support change that would reinforce it, such as investments in new medical technologies. Others have preferred to use the phrase "feudal system" characterized by hierarchy that tends to rule over peers that have not arrived at the top. Elitist thinking and acting is representative of these heads of unit who are "running the show" of health policy making in the country nationally and locally:

> "The Ministry of Health is involved and it tries and has found solutions, see for example the decentralization reform, so I cannot say that the Ministry is not active. But it works slowly and is faced with decision makers in hospitals. These are people who want to maintain the status quo, to keep oversized hospitals and an oversized system. Some chief doctors (the heads of different specializations) don't want to lose existing posts, they say they need to have a certain number of beds, etc. This is where the Ministry hits the wall. It's not that the strategy of the Ministry is not right." (Interviewee 16)

The above quotation sheds light on how the elite medical profession resists ideas that are otherwise considered necessary. Thinning down the system more deeply than has been the case so far, to improve quality and efficiency, has met professional resistance from the top of the medical hierarchy. Hospital managers, some of whom are doctors themselves, but not "top" doctors, are lost as in a labyrinth that seems too complex to manage. This interviewee possessing an economic background helpfully explains the dynamics between hospital managers and the elite medical profession. If doctors must be the heads of specialties and if a head of specialty needs to perform management tasks, then what we can conclude is that doctors need to develop management skills in addition to their medical profession. The role of head of specialty involves management tasks. However, it is questionable whether in reality chief doctors are competent and interested in management. They may want to control the management decisions but not perform the management tasks:

> "Let's not forget that it is doctors who are the heads of specialties, so when you talk to them about management you need to transpose them into a different dimension, an economic dimension and not all of them understand this dimension... Cost management training for these chief of units would be very beneficial. They need to know what is efficient and what is needed and what they need to do as a consequence [...] It's important that managers have a medical director in the management team... the manager needs to be involved in the medical world too and needs to understand it and there needs to be harmony [...] Doctors care about their status, but working together with managers would be beneficial. Doctors, however, often act as a separate caste, with their own professional pride and it's hard to make them think differently. I have met good professionals in my 40-year experience in the system but they were bad managers. [...] Each chief doctor and head of specialty has inevitably some management tasks to perform... Some heads of unit don't want to get involved in management tasks, they want to work only in their profession but if they are head of units they inevitably need management skills." (Interviewee 16)

Concerning compliance with ethical standards, we have shown in this chapter the acuteness and scale of this problem, and the implications that stem from it. We have shown specifically how this unethical behavior takes different forms, such as the acceptance of informal payments, misreporting of data and information and illegal procurement procedures. The extent of the problem was usefully summarized by one of the interviewees who described the pervasiveness of misreporting financial information based on the ailing DRG system:

> "The DRG costs are unsuitable for Romania and they do not reflect the real costs and as a result the Romanian creativity leads us to hide certain things to look better and be funded better. Practically we are deceiving ourselves, but if everybody does this then you also have to do it because otherwise you end up with a sum of money with which you can barely pay the salaries." (Interviewee 18)

"If everybody does it then you also have to do it" may sound like a good excuse, but we can question if financial survival based on deceit is likely to lead anywhere in the medium and long term. Not only is this deceiving, but it also perpetuates a culture in which it is acceptable to do what is illegal. Managers are not excluded from this picture—the Romanian hospital system culture is inclusive enough to affect various actors and professions. These behaviors eschew coordination and question the effectiveness of reform. Granting autonomy to hospitals is especially problematic in this context, and it opens more opportunities for abuse. This abuse would then trigger political and administrative control which in turn would lead to possibly less autonomy than before the reform, as it was the case with the centralization of procurement:

> "Managers have autonomy, but managers must be capable. I doubt whether managers in our country have the needed administrative capacity to use their autonomy properly and effectively. There are a number of reasons why. First, often time doctors are called to act as managers; there is a requirement that managers need to have a management education but that education could be anything (like a short course or something). A good manager needs to be practical, to have a vision, to be experienced, responsible and an ethical person. He needs to be ethical because there are many temptations as manager concerning granting contracts, etc. Why do you think that the Ministry of Health wants to centralize procurement?" (Interviewee 16)

> "The autonomy is a double-edged sword. Too much autonomy can be harmful… it can lead to abuse. The managers as well as the society need to be socialized in this respect. It's hard to change from one extreme (no autonomy) to the other extreme (great level of autonomy) very fast. We have, anyway, inherited some strange habits and it's very hard to get

rid of these as individuals as well as society. That's why I am saying that the hospital autonomy is desirable but it needs to be granted gradually. I don't think a quick increase in autonomy would be beneficial. That radical change involving a quasi-total autonomy would be risky because of the culture especially if the system continued to be under-funded." (Interviewee 18)

In this context, it comes as no surprise that the reform to increase hospital autonomy, though actively promoted, has not yet been adopted. Decentralization, by contrast, was seen as an operation to improve responsibility and accountability locally. Local authorities by owning and financially supporting the hospitals would be in a good position to hold hospitals to account. It is early to conclude whether this has been achieved. For this to happen, one needs capable and ethical coordinating agencies, to start with, and a more profound change of culture which is unlikely to occur in the short to medium run. There is, however, hope for the future. Under growing internal and international pressure as part of the European Commission's Co-operation and Verification Mechanism, the judicial system in Romania has made significant progress in the fight against high-level corruption (European Commission, 2015). The challenge, however, is to sustain this positive trend and translate it to the nitty-gritty of daily interactions in society and the healthcare system specifically.

BIBLIOGRAPHY

Boia, L. (2012). *România: Țara de frontieră a Europei*. Bucharest: Humanitas (Romania: Borderland of Europe).

Boia, L. (2013). *De ce este România altfel? (Why is Romania different?)* (2nd Rev. ed.). Bucharest: Humanitas.

Dan, S. (2015, February). The new public management is not that bad after all: Evidence from Estonia, Hungary and Romania. *Transylvanian Review of Administrative Sciences, 11*(44), 57–73.

Dan, S., & Savi, R. (2012). *Payment systems and incentives in primary care in transition healthcare systems: Implications of recent reforms in Estonia and Romania*. Paper presented at the 4th ECPR conference, Bremen, 4–6 July.

Dan, S., & Savi, R. (2013). Payment systems and incentives in primary care: Implications of recent reforms in Estonia and Romania. *International Journal of Health Planning and Management, 30*(3), 204–218.

European Commission. (2015, January 28). *Report from the commission to the European parliament and the council on progress in Romania under the cooperation and verification mechanism.* Brussels: European Commission.

Government Decision 1088/2004 (HG 1088/2004) concerning the approval of the national strategy for healthcare services and action plan for healthcare reform, Bucharest: Government of Romania.

Ministerial Order 1384/2010 concerning the approval of the management framework contract and the list of performance indicators for the public hospital managers.

Ministry of Health. (2010). *National strategy for hospital rationalization.* Bucharest: Ministry of Health.

Ministry of Health. (2013, December 27). *Communicat de presă, Discursul ministrului sănătății cu privire la Strategia Națională de Sănătate și achizițiile publice centralizate (the discourse of the Minister of Health concerning the National Health Strategy and centralized public procurement).* [Press release]. Bucharest: Ministry of Health.

Molnar, M. (2000). Poverty measurement and income support in Romania. In S. Hutton & G. Redmond (Eds.), *Poverty in transition economies.* London: Routledge.

National Commission for Hospital Accreditation. (2014a). About the National Commission for hospital accreditation. Bucharest: National Commission for Hospital Accreditation. Available online. Accessed November 04, 2014.

National Commission for Hospital Accreditation. (2014b). Order Nr. 51 of 05.02.2014 concerning the approval of the norms concerning the activity of the evaluation commission for the purpose of hospital accreditation. Bucharest: National Commission for Hospital Accreditation.

National Statistical Institute. (2014a). *Tempo online time series, Health statistics.* Bucharest: National Statistical Institute. Accessed April 30, 2014.

National Statistical Institute. (2014b). *Key indicators, resident population, 2002–2013.* Bucharest: National Statistical Institute. Accessed May 03, 2014.

Pikani, J., & Sava, D. I. (2009, August). *Technical assistance to support the updating of the hospital strategy.* Report prepared for the Government of Romania with support from the World Bank, Bucharest.

Preker, A. S., & Harding, A. (Eds.) (2003). *Innovations in health service delivery: The corporatization of public hospitals.* Washington, DC: World Bank.

Presidential Commission. (2008). *Un sistem sanitar centrat pe nevoile cetățeanului (A healthcare system centered on citizen needs).* Report of the Presidential Commission for the analysis and development of public health policy in Romania. Bucharest: Presidency of Romania.

Vlădescu, C., Scîntee, G., & Olsavszky, V. (2008). *Health systems in transition, Romania health system review.* Copenhagen: European Observatory on Health Systems and Policies.

World Bank. (2003). *National strategy for the rationalization of hospital services.* [Report coordinated by Ray Blight]. Washington, DC: World Bank

World Bank. (2010, October 15). *Romania—functional review: Center of government.* [Final report]. Washington, DC: World Bank

World Bank. (2011). *Romania—functional review: Health sector.* Washington, DC: World Bank.

CHAPTER 7

Coordination of Public Hospitals in Norway

As the previous two cases, this third empirical case study begins with description, continues with evaluation and ends with explanation. We first describe changes in public hospital policy and hospital trends and then move on to describe the specifics of hospital reforms as they pertain to the decentralization and autonomy of public hospitals. Following this first part, we evaluate the relationship between public hospital reforms and coordination problems drawing on the primary and secondary data sources. Finally, using the theoretical framework introduced earlier, we seek to explain the effectiveness, or lack thereof, of central coordination.

Overview of Healthcare Policies (1984–2014)

Some authors have identified a number of major reform emphases in the past decades in the Norwegian healthcare system (Johnsen, 2006; Ringard, Sagan, Sperre Saunes, & Lindahl, 2013). In the 1970s, equity and geographical access were two of the main goals. In the 1980s, policy makers emphasized cost containment and decentralization; whereas, in the 1990s, achieving efficiency received special attention. In the past 15 years, while all these goals remained important, much emphasis was placed on cost control, structural changes and patient empowerment. In recent years, we have witnessed a growing interest in improving healthcare

© The Author(s) 2017   179
S. Dan, *The Coordination of European Public Hospital Systems*,
DOI 10.1007/978-3-319-43428-5_7

coordination, quality of care and patient safety (Johnsen, 2006, p. 124; Ringard et al., 2013, p. 119). This focus seems unsurprising if we take into account a recent study which found that Norway is lagging behind other OECD countries in a number of areas, particularly concerning quality of care (Davis, Stremikis, Squires, & Schoen, 2014). Table 7.1 below includes a list of the main health policy initiatives in the last three decades.

Of all the different policy initiatives outlined in Table 7.1, the 2002 reform stands out as the main management reform in the hospital sector. The more recent coordination reform is of particular interest to researchers interested in coordination in healthcare, but for the purposes of this study it is only of secondary interest. This is because it primarily concerns coordination between primary care and specialist care rather than coordination between hospitals. It also deals with coordination more locally rather than centrally or regionally. However, the reform does include certain provisions for improving inter-hospital coordination, but these were not the main part of the reform (Ministry of Health and Care Services, 2009; Ringard et al., 2013, p. 128). More recently, a conservative government came to office and announced a number of changes and, among others, launched the initiative to develop a new healthcare and hospital plan. The new conservative health and social care minister pledged to emphasize central steering of quality of care and patient safety as well as optimization of the hospital structure to reduce waiting times and improve access to elective care. The total number of hospitals in Norway, as in other countries, has followed a slightly decreasing trend in the recent decade data on change in the number of acute hospital beds per 100,000 inhabitants show a decreasing trend across Europe over the last decade. A significant drop can be observed especially during 2005–2013 so that in 2013 acute hospital beds per 100,000 population decreased to 229 from 303 in 2005. We see that the number of acute hospital beds in Norway per 100,000 inhabitants is lower than the average number in both the EU and across Europe more generally (Fig. 7.1).

THE 2002 HOSPITAL REFORM

The most significant organizational reform in hospitals was the 2001 healthcare law, which entered into force on January 1, 2002 (hereafter the 2002 hospital reform). The reform included a number of changes that reshaped the hospital system. Proposition 66 (2000–2001) to the Parliament, developed by the then Ministry of Health and Care Services, provides a

Table 7.1 Healthcare policy initiatives in Norway, 1984–2014

Year	Policy initiative	Purpose
1984	Municipalities healthcare reform	Improve coordination locally between healthcare and social care
1992	Mental and Developmental Care Reform (HVPU)	Downsize institutions for people with developmental disabilities
1997	Activity-based financing	Give economic incentives to increase patient flow
1998	Action plan for elderly care	Strengthen local services for the elderly
1999	Escalation plan for mental health	Strengthen and transform mental care both locally and regionally
2001	New healthcare legislation	Strengthen patient rights
2001	Medical overseas project	Decrease waiting times for hospital care by referring patients to treatment abroad
2001	Regular General Practitioners' scheme	Improve quality of medical care locally and patient-doctor relationship
2001	Liberalization of pharmaceutical market	Increase availability of pharmacies and medication
2001	Individual plan	Tool to improve coordination of long-term care
2002	Central government reorganization	Increase efficiency and coordination of central government bodies
2002	The hospital reform	Improve specialist care through reorganization and change of ownership
2003	Broad Policy for Public Health white paper	Improve and strengthen public health
2004	Substance abuse treatment reform	Strengthen treatment and access to specialist care for substance abuse patients
2006	Changes in sick leave regulation and improving capacity in specialist care	Reduce absence from work by expanding capacity within specialist care
2007	Restructuring of the Regional Health Authorities (RHAs)	Implement a new organizational structure by merging the south and the east RHAs
2008	New resource allocation formula for RHAs financing	Provide a more equitable resource allocation formula for specialist care
2011	National Health Registry Project	Modernize and coordinate the national clinical registries and the mandatory national health registries
2012	Coordination reform	Improve coordination of care between municipalities and hospitals and put more emphasis on public health
2013	Quality and Patient Safety white paper	Provide a comprehensive approach to quality and patient safety issues
2013	Non-communicable disease strategy (2013–2017)	Improve non-communicable disease care and reduce premature deaths by 25 % by 2025

(continued)

Table 7.1   (continued)

Year	Policy initiative	Purpose
2013	Plans to develop a new Health and Hospital Plan	Improve patient centeredness, improve central capacity for steering quality of care, possible reorganization of the hospital model and the RHAs
2014	Launch of the new Patient Safety Program	Promote evidence-based patient safety initiatives particularly community-based healthcare and patient involvement
2014	End of municipal co-financing of hospital care starting with January 1, 2015	Reduce municipal financial risk

Author's own compilation

Source: Adapted from Johnsen (2006, p. 125) for reforms from 1984 to 2004; adapted from Ringard et al. (2013, p. 120) for changes from 2006 to 2013; European Observatory on Health Systems and Policies (2014) and Ministry of Health and Care Services (2014) for developments for 2013 and 2014

detailed account of the reform. For the purposes of this research, the two most relevant changes concern the ownership of public hospitals and the creation of hospital enterprises (also known as hospital trusts). On the one hand, the central government, through a newly established Department of Hospital Ownership in the Ministry of Health and Care Services, took over the ownership of public hospitals from the 19 counties which owned the public hospitals since the 1970 Hospital Act. This involved a transfer of ownership responsibility for specialist care from the county to the central government. This responsibility was added to the existing financing responsibility of the state. On the other hand, the reform led to the creation of hospital enterprises with their own legal status and governance structure and a considerable degree of operational autonomy. In between the state and hospital trusts, the reform created an administrative layer that consisted of five regional health authorities (RHAs): RHA North, RHA West, RHA Center, RHA South and RHA East. The five RHAs became four following a merger of RHA South and RHA East in 2007. Thus, the new structure comprises three tiers: the political (the central government), the administrative (the RHAs) and the operational (the hospital trusts). The overall structure is depicted in Fig. 7.2.

The relationship between these different layers is hierarchical in the sense that the Ministry owns the RHAs which in turn own the hospital enterprises. Hospital enterprises consist of one or more different hospitals which are all

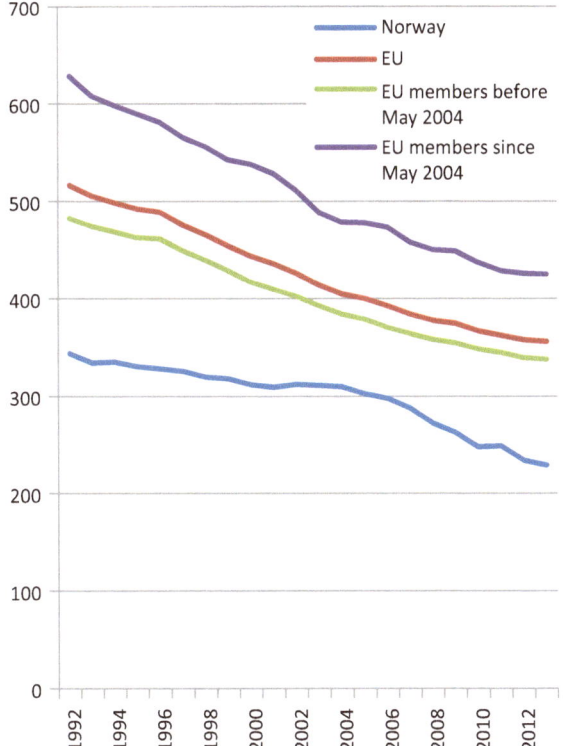

Fig. 7.1   Number of acute hospital beds per 100,000 inhabitants in Norway, 1992–2013
Author's own compilation. *Source*: World Health Organization, European Health for All database, updated December 2015

part of the same enterprise or trust. It is the enterprise that reports to the RHA in their region. Similarly, it is the RHAs which govern the hospital enterprises and these report directly to the RHAs rather than the Ministry. The model thus combines central and regional ownership and governance with decentralized management. Following the reform, the hospitals were no longer part of the administration of the 19 counties, but distinct legal entities.

The ministerial Proposition 66 to the Parliament explains in great detail the rationale and goals of the reform. First, it was believed that good hospital care involved good organization and management, and that these would be strengthened if hospitals received more authority and respon-

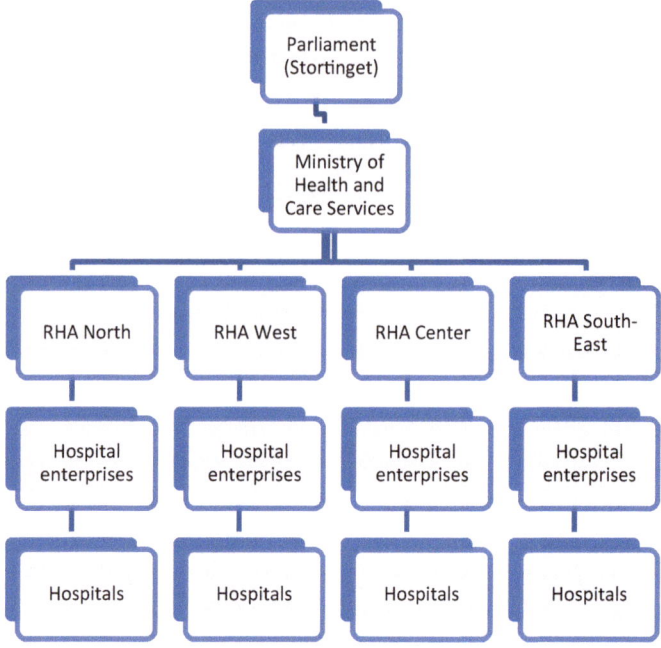

Fig. 7.2 The structure of the public hospital system in Norway, 2014

sibility. It was expected that greater hospital autonomy would lead to a more efficient use of resources, be they capital, labor, money or knowledge. Second, central ownership coupled with regionalized administration and decentralized management was thought to improve national coordination and strengthen the policy and steering role of the Ministry of Health and Care Services. The Ministry would therefore be able to act aggregately and address issues arising from a perceived fragmented system based on county ownership. Policy makers argued that the new model would best address the identified weaknesses of the hospital system at that time, which according to Proposition 66 included (see also Lægreid, Opedal, & Stigen, 2005; Magnussen, Hagen, & Kaarboe, 2007):

- Long waiting times and concerns about "corridor patients";
- Insufficient coordination;
- Large regional and county inequalities in the use of resources and management skills between the different administrations.

These weaknesses were believed to jeopardize the realization of one of the chief policy goals of the welfare state—offering high quality health-care to the entire population across the country regardless of the place of residence when it is needed and where it is needed. Preceding the reform, two reports, developed by the Hellandsvik committee and Sørensen committee, analyzed the managerial challenges in public hospitals and recommended a high degree of independence and flexibility for hospital management and improvement in political control. These changes were believed to be necessary considering the characteristics and complexity of hospitals. The roles of the different administrative layers and players were considered unclear, and it was hoped that centralizing ownership would improve clarity. Proposition 66 acknowledges the international context of healthcare reform and summarizes developments in other Western European countries since the 1980s. The document mentions that "the health reforms in each country must be understood on the basis of a number of political, ideological, historical, cultural and economic factors. Therefore it is not necessarily easy to use experience from other countries in designing health reform in Norway." The reform proposal then moved on to categorize four main areas of reform in Europe stating that some of these developments have also occurred in Norway. They include:

(a) A reassessment of the role of the state and the market in healthcare;
(b) A general trend toward decentralization to lower levels of the public sector as well as to private actors;
(c) Greater emphasis on patient choice and patient rights;
(d) Greater focus on public health measures.

There are also opinions stating that the then Prime Minister of Norway and leader of the Labour Party, Jens Stoltenberg, came in contact with ideas shared by other European Labour Party leaders, most notably the British Prime Minister Tony Blair, the German Chancellor Gerhard Schröder and, across the ocean, the US President Bill Clinton. Anthony Giddens' The Third Way: Modernising Social Democracy or "the modernising left," as Giddens himself put it, a close adviser of the British Prime Minister, may in this way have influenced the 2002 Norwegian hospital reform (BBC News, 1999).

A number of policy changes introduced in late 1990s and early 2000s created the context for the 2002 hospital reform (Proposition

66). First, the funding structure changed in 1997 with the introduction of activity-based funding based on the DRG system. This partially replaced the allocation of funds from the state budget to counties, and led to a correlation between treatment activity and income. Second, in 2001, the Patient Rights' Act introduced the principle of patient choice of hospital across the country. Patients could choose any hospital in the country, but it was the county of residence that had to assume the financial responsibility. These have introduced greater financial risk than was the case before and some counties and hospitals fared better than others. A tipping point that triggered the reform was the year 1999 when hospitals recorded a higher growth in activity than planned and a decrease in the revenue, which made it difficult to finance the growth in activity. The state proposed a 1.25 billion NOK supplementary appropriation to the hospital sector and the Parliament adopted a further increase of 0.5 billion NOK. The counties interpreted these additional allocations as a soft budget constraint and this led to a blame game over the county deficits (Magnussen et al., 2007, p. 2132). However, the state decided that allocating supplementary funds could not continue in the following years and proposed that the financial situation of hospitals be remedied through significant restructuring, cost control and organizational reform. Thus, the need for reform was motivated both on financial and accessibility grounds considering the variation in resource use across counties and regions. There are also unusual access problems in Norway, particularly during wintertime, posed by the mountainous and sparsely populated environment especially in the north, which consists of small and remote settlements. The 2002 hospital reform was inspired by NPM ideas with an emphasis on flexible hospital management and central political steering. These ideas inspired by international NPM reforms were, however, adapted and applied to the Nordic welfare state in a way that was consonant with the national culture. The proposed model represented an important example of a larger shift in public administration and politics, including in the Labour Party (Lægreid et al., 2005, p. 1032).

The reform model combined political centralization and central steering with hospital autonomy hoping that it would reap the benefits of both worlds. Central coordination, however, needed to be exercised "where necessary and appropriate" (Proposition 66). Through creating hospital trusts that would no longer be directly managed by county governments, it was expected that professional management and performance would improve. The organization of hospitals as enterprises was also believed to streamline management, improve access to information, reduce bureaucracy and strengthen adaptability and user orientation. The reform attempted to find a fine balance between different values and political goals in a context of delicate relationships between the roles of the different governing layers and a tradition of delicate geographic politics. Finding this fine balance was emphasized in the policy documents to the extent that it was claimed that the success of the reform would depend on it. It was hoped that the various players would develop a mutual understanding and appreciation of the different parts to be played in the system. Apparently, the model included measures that may, in fact, send opposing signals and may lack internal consistency (e.g. Lægreid et al., 2005). The reform can be primarily viewed as a centralization reform, considering that one main historical feature of healthcare in Norway has been its decentralized structure. Any change from this embedded tradition is likely to be perceived as centralization. With a strong emphasis on hospital management autonomy, however, the reform aimed at improving local decision making. In between the centralization-autonomy debate, the reform also included an element of formalized regionalization through the creation of the RHAs that govern the hospitals and coordinate the provision of hospital care regionally. Though owned by the central government, "the regions" can make a wide range of decisions within the financial and structural framework developed by the central government and the Parliament. Too much central control of the regions would alter the nature of the model. Similarly, too much regional control of the hospital enterprises would come against the principles of the hospital enterprise model. Some authors have called these changes "centralized decentralization" (Lægreid et al., 2005, p. 1036, see also Magnussen, 2013). The creation of the regional administrative layer has been seen by some as unnecessary and possibly conducive to a gap in political accountability (Magnussen, 2013, p. 20). These voices claim that the regional health authorities ought to be removed and replaced by a kind of centralized health administration which would reinforce central coordination and political accountability. The question remains, however, how suitable this solution would be in Norway considering the importance of the regions and local sensitivity toward a growth in the power of the center. Each RHA is governed by a board of trustees appointed by the Minister of Health and Care Services and the boards of RHAs consist of appointed politicians and other representatives of the society. Originally, the board of the RHAs did not include politicians, but this was later changed to include politicians reflecting thus the concerns about lack of political accountability.

MECHANISMS AND INSTRUMENTS OF COORDINATION

Improving central and regional coordination in a context of greater hospital autonomy constituted one of the main goals of the 2002 hospital reform. In proposing the reform, policy makers started from the premise that the quality of specialist healthcare could be improved through better coordination. However, the new plan had to consider the sparsely distributed population in a large country, regional and local politics and concerns about closing down or restructuring hospitals and clinical specialties. Moreover, it was acknowledged that the enterprise model might create or reinforce coordination problems to the extent that hospital behavior became increasingly independent. For this reason, the reform proposed a range of measures aimed at improving coordination centrally, regionally and locally while at the same time protecting hospital autonomy in line with the proposed reform model. To improve coordination, the reform created the RHAs which were tasked with ensuring that hospitals in a specific region collaborate with each other horizontally and vertically, particularly with primary care providers. A region would also seek to foster a common sense of regional identity through standardization of IT systems, reporting procedures, quality assurance systems and the adoption of similar logos and corporate titles. The idea of regional coordination of hospitals was not a product of the reform, but it was formalized once the structure was created and roles were defined. Norway had been divided into five health regions since 1974 with one main university hospital in each region. Up to 1999, when regional hospital collaboration became mandatory, collaboration was voluntary and informal. It was used as a means to identify larger geographical areas in order to obtain economies of scale. Coordinated planning within and between regions was limited but there was an understanding that effective coordination would reduce excess capacity and duplication of services (Magnussen et al., 2007, p. 2131). The differences between counties, with excess capacity in some and large waiting lists in others, were attributed to poor regional coordination and planning. Understanding that hospitals would not voluntarily collaborate to the extent needed, policy makers introduced mandatory cooperation in 1999, a little time before the hospital reform. Regional plans were designed in accordance with national guidelines, which were expected to lead to improved central and regional planning. The 2002 reform sought to further strengthen regional coordination and improve governance effectiveness. Rather than "work" with the central government, hospitals were coordinated by the newly created RHAs—direct regional administration rather than direct central, political coordination. The creation of the three-tier structure raised important questions, however, about the role of each layer and how that role should be exercised. The Ministry through the Department of Hospital Ownership assumed the role of strategic governance and national stewardship while the actual coordination of hospital trusts was delegated to the newly created regions. The central government also appointed the board members in each RHA, established statutes and provided the structural and financial framework within which RHA could operate. In terms of specific governance instruments, the central government provides instructions individually to each region through an annual letter of instruction that accompanies the financial "package." The letter is published immediately after the Parliament's decision on the national budget. A second instrument is an annual circular letter prepared by the Directorate of Health which is also based on the annual budget and is meant to supplement the letter of instruction. This is focused more specifically on performance and quality expectations. In addition, a general meeting takes place yearly between the minister and representatives of the RHAs as well as other meetings, informally, whenever necessary. What the central government can centrally coordinate is supposed to be strategic in nature, such as quality and performance requirements or large capital investment projects. In reality, the distinction between what is strategic and what is not is not always clear, and for political or other reasons, the central government may interfere in what is supposed to be a regional responsibility (Magnussen, 2013).

One level down, the RHAs need to ensure that the population in each region has access to specialist healthcare in accordance with legal and central requirements. They do not provide services directly but own hospital trusts, coordinate the hospital network on a regional basis and channel resources to the different hospital trusts in the region. The coordination instruments are similar to those that govern the relationship between the state and RHAs: annual letter of instruction, general meeting and other more informal meetings throughout the year. It is important to note that RHAs can also purchase services, if need be, from private and non-profit providers, not owned by the region, or from providers in other regions to achieve its mission. It has the mandate to ensure the best possible health-care for the entire population of a region, but it has the freedom to decide on how this can be achieved as long as it complies with the instructions provided by the state. Within the overarching framework, the annual letter of instruction to the regions plays an important coordinating role. This letter includes directives, not only recommendations, but it is a result of much previous discussion and negotiation between the state institutions and the four regions. It does not come as a surprise. The letter is relatively standard across the four regions but it can contain specific instructions depending on the regional context. At first, it tended to be more general and centered on cost control, while in recent years, once the financial situation of hospitals improved, it tended to focus more on medical matters. However, this is work in progress and some interviewees have raised questions about both of these matters. What is interesting in the case of Norway is that hospital managements do not seem to challenge the idea of being coordinated, and they do not see it as an offense to their autonomy. They accept the model. However, some have questioned the object of coordination. There is the perception that even though hospitals for the most part are now financially stable, there is still a strong emphasis on economics at the expense of medical outcomes:

> "The Ministry is able to make its policy more easily in the current structure than when the hospitals were owned by the counties… I find that the regional health authority is useful in some ways though sometimes they try to get involved too much in how to do it instead of measuring the outcomes." (Interviewee 31)
>
> "We need those instructions to use as a kind of roadmap to move through the years… on the other hand, my opinion is that as long as you deliver on those key elements you as a hospital should have more freedom. Some areas are very detailed and that's because we are part of the regional authority and they have the money and power…" (Interviewee 32)

Informal coordination, supported by regular meetings, plays an important role and supports a sense of "family thinking": We are all in the same boat, let us help each other out. Discussion around the table to reach consensus and mutual understanding is an important tool. This is evident, for example, in the following quotes:

> "The management team of the region meets monthly with the managers of the hospital trusts; we discuss problems, for example waiting times. These are also informal… I think the model works; the mechanism of coordination

works but it is important that hospitals solve some of their problems by their own rather than bringing them to the region... We set the goals, for instance we set targets for waiting times, but we don't tell them how to reduce waiting times. They have the flexibility, and when the year is over they can see if they reached the goal and if they didn't we discuss what can be done in the following year to achieve these goals... (Interviewee 41)

"Three or four times a year the four regions meet with the department in the Ministry. We report and discuss in all the four regions. The CEOs of the regions also meet every month, but that's not a formal meeting; that's coordination... So from a national perspective, yes, there is a lot of coordination between these four regions. The reform had to do with this... there are also meetings between different functions with representatives of all the four regions... The purpose is to discuss national projects for instance, so there is a system of coordination, but it is an informal system—it's a club." (Interviewee 41)

Autonomy of Hospital Management

The 2002 hospital reform is now more than ten years old and though some changes have been made since the reform was adopted, the model is still in existence at the moment. Since it was proposed, there have been discussions about the implications of the reform and whether it has indeed reached a fine balance—as claimed—between central and regional coordination, on the one hand, and hospital autonomy, on the other hand. The regional level has been criticized by some for lacking political accountability, and in response, politicians were appointed in the board of trustees of RHAs a few years later. Others have questioned the need of the regional level, which may have increased bureaucracy and possibly deterred action from other more important goals, such as patient safety or quality. Central interference in some decisions that fall under the purview of the regions may further question the need for the regions (Magnussen, 2013). The Conservative government previously in opposition had long challenged some elements of the model and promised change should it come to office. Proposed changes focus on patient centeredness, reduction in unnecessary bureaucracy, quality and patient safety as well as strengthened central, political steering. A new hospital and healthcare plan is under development and some important changes are expected to be implemented.

Granting greater autonomy to hospitals was a main component of the reform model and it was seen as a means to improve hospital leadership and responsibility. The official documents emphasized that the reform was as much a responsibility and leadership reform as it was an ownership reform (Proposition 66). One of the criticisms of the previous hospital system arrangement was that too much political and administrative control was exercised on operational issues and too little on overarching issues concerning structure, strategy and priority setting. It was argued that what hospitals needed was to be empowered, to be more dynamic in their relationship with patients and each other. As health trusts, it was argued hospitals could choose between different solutions and create more room for innovation, lesson learning and positive competition. The change in hospital autonomy targeted a wide range of areas, including:

- The responsibility to manage personnel and capital;
- The right to decide on how financial resources should be used with the qualification that hospital trusts cannot go bankrupt and financial decisions need to be aligned with the contract framework and priorities established directly by the RHAs and indirectly by the state;
- The possibility to assume responsibility for all inputs, including labor;
- The discretion to choose an organizational structure that promotes effectiveness and efficiency.

Overall, it can be observed that much emphasis was placed on giving hospital management the possibility to make informed decisions and assume responsibility on a wide range of operational matters with little interference from above. The reform gave hospital trusts the possibility to decide *how* hospitals should be organized and run, but decisions on *what* services to provide and according to what standards were made by the RHAs or the central government through specific governance mechanisms. The law clearly underlines the public nature of the tasks to be carried out by hospitals, emphasizing that hospital trusts, though to some extent organized as a business, are not private, for-profit businesses. Similarly to the regions, hospital trusts are governed by a board composed of local politicians and other members of the community. The board members of hospital trusts are appointed (not elected) by the RHAs. Originally when the reform was designed, the structure of the board included no politicians but this was changed later following concerns about political accountability. Some scholars have assessed the autonomy of hospital trusts to be substantial: "...within the explicit boundaries imposed by the budget and the (more implicit) distribution of functions to hospitals, regional authority provides few limits or boundaries on the management of a hospital" (Magnussen, 2013, p. 21). Hospital management needs, however, to consider specific coordination instruments used by their owners and, in addition, hospital management decisions need to be approved by hospital boards. These tools are designed to ensure accountability and regional coordination. Norway's hospital system is considered to be "formally quasi-autonomous" in the sense that hospitals operate "within a centrally-set, broad structural and financial framework" (Magnussen, 2013, p. 21). Despite the high degree of formal operational autonomy introduced by the reform, in practice it is not excluded that central and regional coordination are more detailed and specific than originally designed, which may hinder wise local decision making (Magnussen, 2013. p. 21). The idea that hospital managers have sufficient discretion to make both operational and strategic decisions is also widely shared among the interviewees included in this research. This discretion, however, needs to be exercised within the "confines" of the, first, financial and, second, structural framework. The example below testifies to the empowerment of management in the new model:

> "I have a lot of autonomy as long as I am within the budget and keeping in mind the Norwegian model in which labor unions, for instance, have a lot of influence. But I could build some bonuses and financial incentives in the payment system if I want to, so there is quite a lot of autonomy... I get a lump sum of money and I can manage that in the way that I like. When it concerns investments, there are limits... I can buy equipment without going to my owner within a certain amount of money. I can make strategic decisions, like developing the new hospital. I have the freedom to think strategically and I have redesigned the work processes..." (Interviewee 31)

This shows that hospital managers can experience the freedom to exercise their leadership prerogatives in a wide range of areas, including, as shown below, the type of services that a hospital can provide within the existing framework:

> "Our investment here followed a bottom up process and we have a very close collaboration with our owner... I can decide on service organization as I wish but the provision of services is regulated to some extent—I cannot provide some services that I am not allowed to. Some high level services can only be provided in some specific hospitals in Norway... so this hospital can provide any service with these few exceptions... We get asked from the region to do things once in a while, e.g. build a certain specialty... everything that is in the assignment letter is first discussed so that when we receive the letter it is not a surprise to us." (Interviewee 31)

The key question that arises is whether hospital managers perceive regional coordination to be restraining, that is inimical to promoting hospital solutions and decision making. Here, the answer is not immediately straightforward as compared to the situation before the reform. The reform also aimed at central and regional coordination, whereas before the reform, the 19 counties owned the hospitals while hospitals could enjoy a high degree of discretion, whether for good or for bad:

> "Before the reform, the counties only thought of themselves and tried to manage by themselves and there was very little cooperation between the counties. The resources were not efficiently used and the patient waiting lists were growing and the budget balance was negative and they always tried to say that that was the state's responsibility…" (Interviewee 41)

There is clear evidence to show that the financial situation improved considerably, although it took a long time to achieve this goal. In the first seven years after the hospital reform, the RHAs had accumulated a combined deficit of 10 billion NOK—a significant amount relative to the combined yearly budget of 54 billion NOK allocated to the regions in 2002. An audit of the Office of the Auditor General concluded that "it is unacceptable that over many years the regional health authorities have failed to adapt to the annual financial framework adopted by the Parliament for specialist health services" (Office of the Auditor General, 2009, p. 1). This is a significant finding considering that cost control was one of the main goals of the reform. There was much turnover in the top finance and management positions in the health trusts. The Office of the Auditor General found that more than half of the health trusts replaced their chief executives during 2006–2008 and the vast majority of the health trusts—15 out of 19—appointed new directors of finance. For many years, hospitals had been used to a soft budget constraint—one that could be changed following a visit to the Parliament. The centralization reform tried to change that inclination but it proved ineffective in the first years after the reform. The audit report concluded that stronger central and regional control coupled with stronger internal financial control were absolutely necessary. The two forms of financial control were closely related: The hospitals did not take their financial responsibilities seriously enough as long as the soft budget constraint was not replaced by a hard, non-negotiable constraint (Office of the Auditor General, 2009, p. 2). Starting with 2009–2010, the RHAs and hospital trusts began to regain financial balance, with a few exceptions, and started to accumulate surpluses which the regions and hospitals could then invest in capital improvement projects. This positive financial trend has persisted, and in the meantime there have not been major systemic concerns. An important question for us to consider is the explanation of this significant change and the role of the hospital reform in influencing this result. To do this, we delve further into the interview material. First, a look at the financial situation in the public hospital sector before and after the reform does not reveal significant financial differences. However, if we look at the situation in 2010 and thereafter compare it with the situation before the reform, we can clearly see major differences. A second important aspect that needs to be considered is that the total budget allocated to the regions grew significantly in the first seven years after the reform: from approximately 54 billion NOK in 2002 to about 100 billion NOK in 2009. Since 2009, the increase has been relatively small, up to 112 billion NOK. Therefore, the positive economic results cannot be attributed to the reform: It is unlikely that health authorities would have managed to achieve financial balance if it had not been for this significant increase in resources. While this is true, there is evidence in the interviews that gives credence to the premise that the reform still had an important, supportive role, in reaching these financial goals. This assessment does not come from the medical world, but from that of management, finance and audit. The growing deficits preceding and following the reform were attributed to an increase in activity and poor understanding of the marginal cost of treatment, which did not keep up with the marginal income. The government did not only increase the budget, but it also adopted stricter and more determined financial and political control than earlier by, for example, putting a yearly cap on the DRG points, giving instructions and sending signals to the regions to keep costs under control:

> "It was the model itself, with an emphasis on cost control that helped balance the budgets as well as a strong political determination not to give more money to hospitals. It took some time for them to make the transition from a soft to a hard, non-negotiable budget." (Interviewee 46)

The reform increased financial control while improving and professionalizing hospital management. Some may consider this dual-goal to be ambivalent and contradicting, but interestingly, our evidence shows that policy makers skilfully managed to reach both goals. Coordination improved and hospital management autonomy increased and improved. Had one of them suffered at the expense of the other, then there would be ground to question the model on this basis. For example, if hospital managers perceived the region's coordination to be constraining (which they do not) then this would make hospital decision making difficult. On the other hand, had coordination worsened (which it had not) then again this would have made unhappy those who are in favor of coordination. Changes in autonomy and coordination are not the final referee when assessing the success of a reform. This is particularly the case in healthcare where other important values and outcomes, for example, patient quality and safety, ought to receive more attention and are ultimately the criteria by which to assess success. Nonetheless, if we take coordination and autonomy and think of them as too contradicting public values—the more of one the less of the other—then Norway's hospital reform does not provide credence to this assumption. Our evidence shows that in broad lines policy makers have achieved both. This is not to say that there have been no issues and unintended developments. As we show in the coming sections, improving both coordination and autonomy by focusing on cost control and internal organizational processes have been perceived as increasing bureaucracy. There are also strong voices claiming that patient quality and safety and patient focus more generally have come second only and the priority has been on cost control.

CASES AND PROBLEMS OF COORDINATION

Though coordination is widely perceived to have generally improved, when we discuss specific problems of coordination, we see that coordinating hospitals in Norway is not problem free. Using the four types of problems of coordination, as in the previous chapters, we see that duplication of services, contradiction and divergence are perceived to affect the quality of coordination of public hospitals. Omission is not perceived to pose significant challenges to effective coordination. In the case of Norway, our research inductively found two salient domains of coordination that often recurred in the course of the research: coordination of the hospital network, and particularly the case of the merger of the Oslo University Hospital, and coordination of information and communication technologies. Big hospitals in capital cities are often very difficult to rationalize, as also found that in Estonia. The media coverage, the money, the politics and the operations of the medical profession are all more intense in the capital. So in a sense, this is the hardest test of coordination.

Coordination of the Hospital Network

Assessing coordination after the reform, as compared to the situation before the reform, points to a clear general finding that coordination improved. By taking over the hospitals, the state through the regional health authorities has been more successful than before the reform in creating a systemic perspective of the hospital system as a whole. Hospitals work together much better today than was the case under the ownership of the 19 counties. Local politics and influence have remained strong but the coordination has become stronger and more effective than before. Under the previous system, the 19 counties emphasized local coordination whereas under the new system regional coordination gained center stage. There is not much disagreement concerning this general finding and is shared by interviewees with different affiliations and professional backgrounds. Much of this improvement in coordination is attributed to the work of the RHAs, which were tasked with improving coordination within their regional jurisdiction, as shown in the following quotes extracted from two of the interviews:

> "I worked with the 2001 reform as well but my view is that at that time there was barely any national coordination. The 19 counties owned the hospitals and the state had control over the two or three national hospitals. I think from the Ministry perspective that the reform led to better central coordination than before. It was hard at that time with 19 different owners to have good coordination, so it definitely improved..." (Interviewee 39)
>
> "The reason why coordination improved is that there is only one owner now: the Ministry of Health. The four regional authorities are doing a necessary job and make decisions that would be hard for the Ministry to make... the delegation system, the letter of assignment, has become better and better... I am not sure if there will be changes because the regional authorities are functioning well and I don't know if another model would be better." (Interviewee 43)

The regions have sought, and in general terms, have succeeded in fostering regional coordination by using both formal and informal coordination mechanisms: not only do they own the hospital trusts but they also provide for them. The family metaphor is again appropriate in this context:

> "There is competition between hospitals, they compare their performance but this happens within the family. Hospitals are part of the same family and there are rules they need to follow..." (Interviewee 43)

The key term here is hospital trust—that is a network of hospitals, not individual entities. Hospital consolidation has involved closing down or reorganizing hospital services. The creation of hospital trusts that included different hospital entities ultimately proved to be a smart and effective approach to hospital consolidation. National politicians have not been entirely immune to criticism for supporting the reorganization of the hospital network, but the two administrative layers in between the center and individual hospitals attenuated that public criticism. They could justify the decision on professional and managerial grounds and point the finger to the regions and the hospital trusts. Although the regions and the hospital trusts are in part governed by politicians, they are not political institutions and can make decisions that politicians would strongly prefer to avoid making.

Even though the regions have improved coordination more generally, situations of duplicating both clinical and support services have persisted. These redundancies are generally believed to lead to inefficiency and to affect quality, but data on both of these indicators are scarce. There is also uncertainty about whether integration of services, as compared to a more decentralized arrangement, increases efficiency and improves quality. There are also a number of justifications for the perceived duplication in the system, taking into account the specific natural characteristics of a country such as Norway as well as specific legal provisions that support local, decentralized organization of hospital services. These legal provisions clearly contradict national efforts to increase service consolidation. The quote below describes the nature of duplication and contradiction in the hospital system in Norway as a whole:

> "Redundancy is a very common issue in Norway. With some exceptions, all services are provided in all the regions and by law many hospitals need to provide the same type of service. For example in the western region four different hospitals, three hours apart, provide prostatic surgery. Quality would be better than it is now if this service were provided in only one place. But then you've got the Norwegian policies on decentralized health services and if you start to take away some services and regionalize provision then you lose the general function of the hospital as well... So today we have cases in which services of higher quality could be provided in fewer places but we

choose to have a decentralized structure and as a result these hospitals have got to have something to do. That's a core element of Norwegian health policy. This is especially a problem in the north where there are small and distant communities..." (Interviewee 40)

We see therefore that contradiction is intertwined with duplication: They can work hand in hand. Another reason for duplication is the need to develop a good enough level of quality, which is directly linked with the volume of service, on a planned basis in order to be able to ensure quality on an emergency basis. This is especially, though not exclusively, a concern for hospitals that are running large emergency departments. The argument here, as one interviewee put it, is that "we can afford some duplication," and in fact duplication, in the long run, may actually pay off. This may be true, but there needs to be a good amount of evidence to support this viewpoint, which at the moment does not exist:

"In the case of redundancy, I would not be doing services that other hospitals are able to do better, but, and there is a but here, it is necessary to do some services to keep the emergency staff prepared enough for different events... So if I am not doing these services on a planned basis then my performance will not be good in the case of emergency and we are one of the largest emergency hospitals in Norway. That's the trade-off I was talking about... To me it's about how to provide and improve services and I don't think so much about whether redundancy is a problem... in some cases this is a problem for doctors and the smaller the hospital is the more difficult this is... for us it is not a problem." (Interviewee 31)

There are also other examples of contradiction in the coordination framework. This takes the form, for example, of unrealistic expectations and signals that hospitals receive. The medical profession, in particular, claims that the expectations on the medical personnel have grown continuously without a proportional growth in human and financial resources. Medical personnel are expected to reduce paperwork and bureaucracy while at the same time reporting requirements, which add to paperwork and bureaucracy, have continuously grown. For these reasons, it is not consistent with the facts to argue that in a highly regulated healthcare system as in Norway, contradiction has no place. Too much regulation, even in a prosperous, consensual and high-trust Nordic welfare state, can have its limitations. Nevertheless, our evidence does not show that these contradictions constitute a major problem that endangers the provision of hospital ser-vices or the financial sustainability of the hospital system. It is something that players in the system have got used to and is considered a sort of "normal nuisance." For example:

> "I don't think omission is a common problem... Contradiction is a problem; healthcare, as a main pillar of the welfare state, is much regulated and there is contradiction between legislation... For example, sometimes the political signal is to increase service to a certain group of patients but that is impossible to do because there is not enough capacity to take care of that... sometimes the expectations from politicians are unrealistic... overall there is fairly good balance and is something you need to work with..." (Interviewee 31)

Unlike duplication and contradiction, omission does not appear to be a concern. The generous welfare state, supported by strong social and political values which favor access to services, is effective in addressing omission. Perceptions may slightly differ if we take into account the waiting times for certain types of elective care, but eventually, the service is still being provided, though it may be provided later than expected or desired. The clear mandate of the RHAs is also instrumental in addressing possible omission and the opening up of the public system to private and non-profit providers is also likely to improve access. This is one of the main advantages of the current, regionally coordinated system. Having a good regional perspective over the available capacity across a larger area can address possible gaps in services which exist in some smaller catchment areas, for either natural, economic or professional reasons. It is without doubt that the current system supports this idea, as this interviewee explains:

> "Within each RHA all services are available so it's coordinated within the region. If one hospital cannot provide it then another hospital in the region will provide it... this differs from one perspective to another; a hospital or patient may say that the service is not readily or easily available but the RHA can say that it is since all services are available in each region according to its mandate... we do not have gaps within each region but there are gaps in the hospitals." (Interviewee 40)

The following quote stemming from the Ministry of Health and Care Services also supports this same idea:

"Omission is not a concern because the regional authorities will ultimately ensure that a service is provided; they can use their hospitals or private hospitals. When it comes to capacity, that's different; if there is not enough capacity then the question becomes how they coordinate to get the right capacity. They could coordinate better within the regions; that's a common question we are dealing with, e.g. the case of MRI. We see cases when there is limited capacity and then the regions need to look at their total capacity and ways to coordinate provision. Sometimes we wish it were coordinated quicker. There have not been major concerns..." (Interviewee 39)

Coordination of Process versus Coordination of Quality

A second salient case of needed coordination pertains to information and communication technologies (ICT) used across different regions and hospital trusts. The general trend following the reform has been toward standardization of these systems and the development of integrated solutions, but despite this trend, there has been growing frustration about using ICT programs and devices that "do not talk at all with each other." Having the flexibility to decide on the purchase and use of systems in a specific hospital trust creates coordination problems across different hospital trusts as long as these systems are incompatible or different in some important way. At the same time, however, standardizing these systems involves changing patterns of use, which may be deep-seated, and as a result, they have increased the focus on processes and activities—typically seen as unnecessary bureaucracy by medical staff who are directly involved in patient care. This finding is supported by evidence, stemming from both interviews and secondary data, including a recent audit on electronic communication and coordination in healthcare (Office of the Auditor General, 2014). This study concluded that the exchange of communication between different healthcare institutions is characterized by "extensive use of paper" whereas "technical solutions that have already been developed have not been adopted by all the players and are not used in accordance with the intentions" (Office of the Auditor General, 2014, p. 1). The audit recognized "the fragmented division of responsibilities" and recommended a stronger enforcement of standardized tools across the system—not only within a health region but across the four main regions. This idea was also clearly expressed in one of the interviews:

"There has been an audit about this so there are different systems but hospital trusts have been reluctant to use the same system. The government has been working very hard to get it on track but it isn't on track yet. There will also be an open hearing in the Parliament because of this. These are very badly coordinated, see the audit also. This is related to the reform and especially the situation before the reform because before hospitals had different systems, sometimes even in the same hospital, except the region North which had the same system. It is taking a lot of time. If you've got a system then you want to stick to it and it's hard to change. And it's also because they were allowed to make decisions on this... So this is an uncoordinated area... it does play a role because it influences the efficiency of the treatment, especially patient information flows between primary and specialist care as well as between hospitals in different regions."

One interviewee, in favor of a stronger center more generally but also as far as ITC is concerned, has put it this way:

"I think the regions have coordinated the hospitals enough, for instance by merging hospitals and I think it is now the time to say thank you for the job that you've done and now the Department in the Ministry will take care of the whole system... there is coordination within the regions but less so between the regions: different ITC systems for instance and sometimes even different medical standards, so central coordination not only regional coordination should be stronger..." (Interviewee 30)

The question, however, is whether this growing coordination through the standardization of processes is acceptable locally and consistent with the autonomy inherent in the current reform model. In line with the 2002 healthcare reform, coordination so far has focused on fairly general aspects while giving the regions and, further down, hospital trusts the flexibility to develop and use different means to achieve those requirements. If stronger coordination, as suggested by some, involves the standardization of ITC systems, then it will also involve the coordination of how hospital trusts ought to reach certain goals. In this case, coordination would be not only about what requirements hospitals should meet but also about how those requirements should be achieved. This position could be legitimately criticized on both legal and, most importantly, professional, medical grounds. Even though improving standardization is still work in progress, it is not new, but thus far it has not been radical. However, medical personnel have increasingly claimed that bureaucracy has increased while patient care and safety have had to suffer as a result. Should a more radical standardizing approach be taken, whether it is about ITC or quality of care, then this may further add to and create growing frustration among the professionals who feel increasingly alienated from their primary calling—patient care. Those players in the system with a medical affinity or who take a patient-centered, rather than a process-centered approach, have openly criticized this increasing standardization. They have recommended the elimination of the regional administrative level and the hierarchical and complex decision-making structures and greater emphasis on patient care. In the language of coordination, if they want coordination at all, then they would prefer that coordination to be about quality and the patient— not about "the system"—as shown, for instance, in the following quotes. Some of these ideas have been taken on board by the new conservative government who has promised to make patient care, patient safety and quality the cornerstone of its policy:

> "Norway is only 5 million people and to have three layers running the hospitals leads to too much bureaucracy. To put it rhetorically, people are shifting papers, reading reports and not actually treating patients. So we want to take the administrative regions and their boards and put those people, put that competence, out where the interaction with the patient is... And this has to do with the structure of the hospital system and the organizational bodies... Reporting is not wrong, but it often ends up in the cupboard. Better quality is key—the patient in the centre, better quality for the patient, that's the key idea of this government, a focus on the patient and not on the system..." (Interviewee 36)
>
> "We want to develop clear quality and performance standards and targets, so in this sense we are using the new public management. These already exist but we want to develop them further... To me coordination is about developing standards and targets that apply all across the country, but these need to have the patient in focus, so not coordinating your own coordination of the system, but coordination of care to the patient. It is the result that needs to be coordinated..." (Interviewee 36)

This interest in the coordination of quality "across the country" by means of developing standards and targets in the Directorate of Health is still a form of standardization and it is likely to run against professional autonomy as well as the 2002 reform model more generally. The challenge is to find the appropriate balance between effectively developing quality indicators as a form of national coordination and ensuring that hospitals themselves own that process of coordination:

"Whether this is contradicting to the planning approach we are taking depends on how you do it. We want hospitals to improve quality, that's our responsibility so if we can get the Directorate of Health to develop criteria then hospitals are free to do what they want as long as they meet those quality criteria. So this is our thinking, they need to meet those criteria but if they do we give them freedom to organize and provide their services the way they want to. Public hospitals also have the freedom to buy services from private providers if that is going to increase quality. I don't think there is so much contradiction; we need to know at the central level that they can provide the quality." (Interviewee 39)

This, however, is an old argument. The problem may be that to get good quality results, it may be necessary to follow the best medical procedures, and these procedures have to be expressed in the form of a detailed process. This inevitably results in what some call 'bureaucracy', that is a detailed set of process instructions or guidelines. This statement recognizes the delicacy of maneuvering central coordination of quality and hospital autonomy, but it does not consider the increasing move toward process standardization, as in the case of ICT systems shown earlier. Not only are hospitals expected to deliver on quality, but they are also expected to organize their processes in a coordinated, standardized way. This is therefore different from giving hospitals the freedom to organize their processes as they wish as long as "they can provide the quality." National coordination of quality is also seen as an important means "to bring politics back in" once that many of the hard decisions about the structure of the hospital network have been made (by the regions rather than politicians):

"Some parties in the Parliament want more influence on the specialist health care. Some politicians have expressed that there is too little political influence and too many decisions have been made by bureaucrats and they want to come in and make decisions..." (Interviewee 39)

Explaining Coordination

The propositions derived from principal-agent theory are as follows:

1. Positive incentives designed by central institutions with a coordinating role enable hospital system coordination
2. Negative incentives designed by central institutions with a coordinating role enable hospital system coordination

3. Information asymmetry and imperfect monitoring hinder central hospital system coordination

4. Conflicting interests and goals between principals and agents hinder central hospital system coordination

The propositions referring to the hospital system culture include:

1. The interaction between health policy makers, medical profession, hospital management and patients influences central coordination of public hospitals

2. Mutual trust between health policy makers, medical profession, hospital management and patients is helpful to central coordination of public hospitals

3. Stakeholder compliance with ethical standards affects central public hospital coordination. Usually, high levels of compliance with declared standards will assist in the implementation of official attempts at coordination

4. Hospital system culture is one reason for the differences in coordination across the selected hospital systems.

The reform model has improved coordination considerably, but as part of the model, the autonomy of hospital trusts has given hospitals enough possibilities to decide how hospitals should be organized and managed. We have seen, for example, how the discretion to decide on ICT tools has posed challenges to adopting integrated ICT solutions and to coordination more generally. Presumably compatible ICT systems that "speak to each other" would improve regional and national coordination and possibly lead to improvements in patient processing—shorter queues, less duplication for patients in providing their information over and over again and easier access to information about hospitals. The cases of coordination discussed in the previous sections show that some aspects of hospital activity have continued to resist coordination. Nonetheless, the reform model alone, though instrumental, does not explain why the coordination of processes has prevailed over the coordination of quality. Similarly, it does not explain why some hospitals have been more successful than others in resisting coordination. In exploring the relationship between the key elements of the two theories and coordination of the public hospital system in Norway, we found that some explanations find more empirical support than others. We argue, on the one hand, that conflicting interests and goals help us explain the effectiveness (or ineffectiveness) of coordination of hospitals in Norway whereas incentives, information asymmetry and imperfect monitoring seem less consequential. On the other hand, we argue that certain aspects of the hospital system culture exert strong influence on the effectiveness of coordination in Norway's public hospital system.

Conflicting Interests and Goals

In the case of Norway, we suggest that differing interests and goals are helpful in explaining why in the context of the 2002 hospital reform and the changes that followed the reform, the coordination of processes, particularly finance, has prevailed over the coordination of quality. Although in the last few years, quality has taken center stage in hospital policy, this is a fairly recent change, the effects of which are yet to be determined. In emphasizing "sound economics," some have argued that patient treatment and quality will benefit in the future once hospitals have attained financial stability. Nonetheless, the growing discontent with "focusing on economics" among the medical professionals is readily apparent and constitutes one central theme in the interviews with the medical professionals as represented by the Norwegian Medical Association. This is contrasted with those views, stemming from health administrators and managers, who prefer to frame the matter in financial and managerial terms. It is of interest that the accusation that managers and politicians focus too much on economics comes even in Europe's richest economy, where healthcare spending is high by the standards of most of the rest of Europe. We argue that these two differing views are strong enough to influence the nature of coordination, and thus far there is evidence to show that overall the economic view has prevailed. Within the medical world, there have been initiatives taken by groups of professionals, such as Health Action, who are advocating for giving back power to the professionals in the face of perceived growing bureaucratization. They argue that the system is too regulated while decision making is burdensome and far from where it needs to be: close to the professional and the patient. For example, this point is evident in the quote below:

> "We have shifted focus from patient care to economics… the main parameters by which hospitals are governed now, in my view, are economic parameters. Regarding centralization and coordination, we believe that

coordination has clearly become more centralized, from a local focus to a central and regional focus. We believe that various levels of leaders have been created from the service level to the top which is the Ministry... this has had two effects: first, you have a strict line and it costs a lot of money and the information from the service provision to the top can be blocked. We see that information flow is very different and that's an effect of the 2002 reform. So it has definitely affected central coordination. Decisions are made further from the patient than it used to be the case before, in my view and then the effect of the decision does not reach the level where the decision was made." (Interviewee 40)

The argument, according to this view, is that coordination *increased* but it did not necessarily *improve*. The increase in coordination is associated with increased emphasis on administration at the expense of patient care and quality:

"It is clear to me that central coordination increased but then is that positive or negative? That was the motivation that we can't have 19 different systems and that we need to coordinate quality and so forth but the question is: has this change improved quality? We think that it hasn't. Central coordination increased but I am not sure that it has had the effect on quality that we want..." (Interviewee 40)

We can naturally expect medical professionals and their organizations to favor professional goals, which sometimes necessarily run in conflict with more systemic financial and managerial goals. For coordination to be effective, agreement between the main stakeholders is essential. These differences between stakeholders hinder coordination:

"Conflict perhaps is too big of a word but there are different interests in the hospital sector in Norway as in other countries. Doctors are very autonomous; they have a certain position and it's difficult to have the medical profession to do stuff if they don't agree with it. They have the patients' interest in mind but they may not always have the broad perspective in mind. What we see concerning guidelines is that when the medical profession agrees with them and when they are consulted they are more easily implemented... For example, waiting times are an important goal to us but not everybody agrees that that is the most important thing but here we focus on patient rights: access to information, access to treatment, etc whereas a doctor might be more interested in the final result of the treatment so it's a kind of a different goal." (Interviewee 39)

This finding, however, is not supported only by representatives of the medical profession, but also by voices outside of the world of hospitals:

> "In terms of motivation, from the hospital side I think many doctors and some hospital administrations have claimed that there are too many decision levels in the system and there has been a bit of a complaint about that and everything that has gone wrong has been pointed at the regional health authorities. They had to make a lot of hard decisions which made them unpopular and this has helped the Ministry because otherwise we would have had to make all those decisions." (Interviewee 39)

Some hospital managers have also underlined this same central finding. For example:

> "Another area is that they should be stronger in developing quality indicators and be more interested in the way I am building or running my hospital. How is the population doing? Am I doing all right? So there should be more focus on quality and patient safety and less on how I organize the services... This already exists and we publish these indicators already but it needs to be developed more. The process, however, has been slow." (Interviewee 31)

International rankings of healthcare systems in the OECD countries support the finding that Norway, though it has one of the largest health expenditures per capita, produces only average performance. Furthermore, quality of care seems to be the Achilles heel. A recent set of international health performance scores indicate that out of 11 OECD countries, Norway is ranked the 11th in three indicators grouped under quality of care: effective care, safe care and patient-centered care. In terms of coordinated care, Norway is ranked 7th (Davis, Stremikis, Squires, & Schoen, 2014). The process of prioritizing quality of care has been slow because the concerns about cost control dominated the policy agenda for a number of years and seemingly crowded out systematic support of other policy goals. This has occurred in the context of an unusually well-resourced country, both in terms of financial and human resources, which receives major inflows of medical personnel from other countries, unlike Estonia and Romania:

> "The Ministry has been very strict and politically it has been very important to ensure that budgets are balanced. Now they discuss patient rights, security and quality since the budgets are balanced and I think that's very good. You don't have to have these discussions now all the time about budgets, budgets..." (Interviewee 38)

Because of the emphasis on cost control, medical professionals have thus far primarily reacted to this concern and less so to another parallel development which has slowly taken shape—the managerial approach to quality of care. The hospital reform has sought and, to a good extent, has succeeded in professionalizing management, which started to confidently challenge what used to be a "no manager's land." Our data do not show any systematic opposition to this development but this may be explained by the fact that it is relatively novel or, again, by the predominance of cost-control thinking:

> "In the old system, management was not seen as something important because it was the doctors who were always in charge and were making fun of the management of that time. It was in fact the professors who were in charge… the manager was someone who would help the doctors get more money from the authorities, so managers were helping them along… Since 2002 we can say that there have been major efforts to make the leadership more professional." (Interviewee 33)
>
> "You could see a larger trend in other sectors towards increased professionalism in the public services. Doctors at that time had pretty much all the positions in the hospital and the first thing I did when I came here in 2002 was to say: OK in order to develop this hospital we cannot have doctors in every leadership position… This process was tough at first for about one year and a half, but month by month they could see the improvements and with the support of the board it worked." (Interviewee 32)

In a generally consensual, high-trust hospital culture, in which compliance with ethical standards and regulation is among the highest in the world, it may be surprising to argue that conflicting interests and goals are sufficiently strong to influence the coordination of hospitals. One can argue that the different views between the principals and the agents, though they exist, are somehow rendered powerless by a culture that ultimately has the patient's interest in mind. As a result, any likely differing view will somehow be reconciled or addressed in such a way that remains inconsequential for coordination. There is some support for this view in the primary data collected in the course of the research. However, we find the argument unconvincing. In our view, it does not offer the best explanation of the coordination problems identified earlier in this chapter. The analysis of conflicting interests and goals in Norway admittedly may seem a little artificial at first. But even in a wealthy Nordic welfare state, cost control in the hospital sector and public hospital consolidation took precedence over other goals and for many years represented the main goal of state policy. It certainly occurred in a culture that is relatively high-trust and compliant with ethical standards and the principles of the welfare state, but there have been struggles to reconcile the differing interests between powerful actors in the system, particularly between central policy makers, regional administrators, the elite medical profession and local stakeholders. Even if we assume that the hospitals (the agents) share both the interests and the goals of their direct principals (the regions)—which has not always been the case—we can question whether this agreement includes various details of the relationship, such as sub-goals and means to achieve those sub-goals. For coordination to be effective, we would argue it is necessary to agree not only about abstract principles, but also about concrete aspects, such as for instance agreeing on what information tool to use. Furthermore, both the principal and the agents may agree that quality of care is highly important, but this does not necessarily imply that there is agreement over how quality of care ought to be improved or about what "quality of care" means in practice. For these reasons, it is possible that disagreement, even in a generally consensual and favorable culture, can make coordination difficult.

The Elite Medical Profession

Although actor-oriented interests and goals influence the effectiveness of coordination, the culture of the hospital system exercises influence on the ability of the coordinating agencies to foster a working together of the system of public hospitals as a whole. In general terms, the hospital system culture in Norway is conducive to and facilitates coordination. Embedded in a larger administrative system, in which coordination is a key element, public hospitals are part of a system that has been increasingly governed in such a way as to promote coordination. We have seen earlier in the chapter how one of the primary aims of the 2002 hospital reform was to improve regional coordination through the creation of the regional health authorities, on the one hand, directly owned by the central government. On the other hand, the creation of the hospital trusts, owned by the regions, led to hospital consolidation and the creation of hospital networks within and between the different hospital trusts. This has included in 2007 the largest merger in the healthcare sector in the recent history of the country: the merger of the South RHAs and the East RHA and the creation of the South-East region which is by far the largest regional health authority, making up 50 % of the entire hospital sector. In the context of the merger, four different hospitals in Oslo, two of which previously belonged to different regions, were merged to create one of the largest hospitals in Europe, Oslo University Hospital. This operation receives detailed attention in this section, and it shows how a hospital system culture can resist the strongest efforts to enact hospital consolidation.

The strength of coordination for the purpose of consolidating the network of public hospitals in Norway has proved effective overall. The state and the regions have made use of legal prerogatives and governance mechanisms to restructure the network of public hospitals and the organization and provision of hospital services. In most of these cases, coordination proved effective enough to overcome local resistance. The number of hospital entities dropped significantly and mergers stimulated networked organization and provision of services within and between the hospital trusts. There have been a number of high-profile cases in which there was systematic local resistance against the planned consolidation, but despite public demonstrations, the decisions were finally implemented. One example is the case of emergency services in Telemark Hospital. Despite public protests in front of the Parliament building in Oslo, supported by thousands of people, the decision to close those services was finally adopted and motivated on both quality and economic grounds. It was first decided by the hospital board, then by the regional board and finally the minister explained the decision in the Parliament. Another salient case includes the reorganization of neurosurgery in the Western region between the Bergen and Stavanger hospital trusts. Both hospitals wanted to develop neurosurgery on their own premises but to improve quality, the decision was made to consolidate these services in the university hospital in Bergen, which is the largest in the Western region. Although at first, the management of the hospital in Stavanger made the decision to develop a neurosurgical department in Stavanger, later on it had to comply with the decision of the region. The strength of regional coordination again prevailed over local ambitions:

> "There are conflicting views, I am sure about it, but governance is hierarchical and strict and there needs to be compliance. It is regulated by law. Leaders are fired if they don't comply and this has happened especially in the case of economic matters…" (Interviewee 40)

The strength of regional coordination in general counteracts hospital divergence and reduces the risk of uncoordinated hospital behavior:

> "In terms of divergence this happens with the large university hospitals which want to grow bigger and bigger and be the best which is not bad but it is more difficult to coordinate them and that's why the regional level is important. Smaller hospitals would be happy to be the little brother if the big brother is taking care of them but that doesn't happen all the time so the regional authority then can intervene... Divergence in the sense of non-compliance with central or regional instructions can happen but the regions can change the board of the hospital so they can't go that far out. They are their own entities but they are quite influenced by the regional authorities... divergence is there it not too much room for it; freedom only goes to a certain extent." (Interviewee 39)

However, there have been exceptions and the most salient one has undoubtedly been the case of the merger of the Oslo University Hospital. We now turn to this case. The merger of the Oslo University Hospital was preceded by the merger of the South and East RHAs, which were merged with the aim of integrating the different hospitals in Oslo, some of which belonged to the two different regions, the south and the east. This operation, effective since January 1, 2009, led to the administrative merger of four different hospitals: Aker University Hospital, Rikshospitalet University Hospital, the Norwegian Radium Hospital and Ullevål University Hospital. The aim of the merger was to improve the hospital structure in the city of Oslo by unifying regional functions, strengthening the role of local hospital and establishing good pathways of patient care (Oslo University Hospital, 2013). Within a relatively small geographic area, some of the four hospitals offered the same treatment and health services. It was believed that creating a unique administrative structure, directly accountable to one regional authority, would lead to an efficient use of human and financial resources and ultimately improves patient care and treatment. The university hospitals in Oslo have traditionally been considered the foremost medical centers in the country and have developed a specific elite medical culture—half of the medical research in Norway, for example, is carried out at the Oslo University Hospital. The hospital also has nationwide responsibility for a series of national and multi-regional centers of competence and provides very specialized, high-profile treatment comparable to other large university hospitals in Europe. Despite the good reputation of the elite hospitals in Oslo, both the process and the results of the merger have been seriously contested. The process, to start with, was characterized as "difficult for everyone involved: employees, managers, the regional level and the political level" (Ministry of Health and Care Services, 2014b, p. 3). This same report concluded that "we have spent very much effort on structure" and the time has come to harvest some of the benefits of this massive reorganization. The reorganization in the Oslo metropolitan area has also been costly financially—the total bill of the RHA South East is estimated at 7 billion NOK (Ministry of Health and Care Services, p. 4). Two audits have critically evaluated the process and results of the merger and found little payoff thus far (Office of the Auditor General, 2012, 2013b). The auditors argued that the South-East RHA stands out among the four regions for being relatively passive in conducting its ownership role. The same criticism was cast on the Ministry of Health and Care Services as the central authority in the hospital system:

"Challenges such as poor-quality buildings, scattered localities, the fragmented frameworks for the health enterprise and fragmented and different ICT solutions, have in particular impacted Oslo University Hospital's ability and opportunity to complete the reorganization task. The South-East Regional Health Authority was familiar with the challenges before the task was assigned. The consequences for Oslo University Hospital's implementation ability and treatment of patients were not sufficiently assessed or taken into consideration by the region. Due to this, the South-East RHA has contributed to creating unrealistic expectations..." (Office of the Auditor General, 2012, pp. 2–3)

This, however, was not the only fault that was found. In seeking to explain why the merger has not produced significant results so far, there was something more difficult to change than "simple" organizational operations. To be fair, a few years are nowhere near enough time fully to rationalize a set of scattered buildings and complex, interdependent services. It may be a long time in politics but it is a short time in bricks and mortar, and in the process of changing cultures and local loyalties. However, organizational merger may have created the potential for doing those things over the longer term, something that would never have happened while they were separate institutions:

"Although progress has been seen in some areas, the restructuring of OUS has not provided clear improvements to date in treating patients or utilization of resources... OUS has persistent challenges marked by bottlenecks, waiting times and failure to meet deadlines. Introducing more effective treatment chains still remains for several forms of treatment and there is significant potential for utilizing expertise and working methods of the previously separate medical disciplines..." (Office of the Auditor General, 2013b, p. 2)

"After the merger of the Oslo University Hospital there have been a lot of problems and media interest... the complexity of the hospital is unusual for Norway and maybe we did not foresee all the possible problems that could occur following the merger... maybe as we look at it today we could have done the merger in a different way, big but not so big. Perhaps we could have merged Ahus to Akershus rather than to Oslo University Hospital. There have been problems but there are not so many today compared to three years ago so the situation is changing." (Interviewee 41)

The interviews provided further insights into why the reorganization has not yet produced the expected results. We argue that together with practical logistic considerations, such as the multi-site structure of the hospital that takes massive investment and time to change, resistance from certain elite medical specialties help us shed light on these findings. Thoracic surgery and neurosurgery, which are typically found on the top of the medical hierarchy when it comes to reputation, have traditionally fallen under the responsibility of both Rikshospitalet and Ullevål Hospital—two of the merged hospitals. Although there is only a short distance between the two facilities, both hospitals have historically developed significant competence into these highly esteemed specialties and were perceived as competing rather than collaborating. The merger has sought to centralize these specialties, as well as others, but resistance from medical professionals has prevailed despite sustained efforts thus far. Other specialties, such as ear, nose and throat, agreed to the proposal of centralization, but not neurosurgery and thoracic surgery:

"Before the merger it was considered a problem that the hospitals did not cooperate though they were physically close. Resources were not used in the best possible way. The idea was to merge in order not to duplicate: both support and the medical specialties, which were competing with one another... After the merger it takes time to change the previous culture... I think there is better utilization of resources after the reform, depending on medical specialty—some still don't work together." (Interviewee 46)

As one interviewee plainly put it:

> "When the doctors want it, you can do it but when the doctors don't want it, it takes a lot more time and a new building." (Interviewee 33)

However, it is not any doctors, or all doctors, but those who are at the top of the medical hierarchy whose position may change and who may desire to pay little attention to "simple and perhaps useless administrative stuff." This following quote provides an inside and helpful view of the tension inside the neurosurgery and thoracic surgery departments of the two elite hospitals:

> "The doctors are still in charge and you can see that in the case of our merger here in Oslo... we had to merge these because within two kilometers you had two hospitals performing similar high-tech services, like neurosurgery and thoracic, heart surgery... this normally should have happened earlier. These were the two specialized departments in the case of which there was agreement that it was possible to have only one department. The merger was successful in the case of ear, nose and throat and ophthalmology but long before the merger it was agreed to gather all ophthalmology at Ullevål and ear, nose and throat at the Rikshospitalet. And that was very dramatic because those from Rikshospitalet did not want to come and work at Ullevål and some even quit while those from Ullevål agreed to go to Rikshospitalet—they thought it was a good idea. You know there is medical hierarchy and on top are some of those specializations that did not agree to merge such as heart surgery and neurosurgery..." (Interviewee 33)

Despite a regulated hospital system with generally clear lines of coordination and ownership, we see that in some salient cases, elite medical opposition can resist coordination efforts. It took a merger of two regional authorities and a merger of four different hospitals to seek to unify two medical departments, and in spite of this large-scale organizational change, deeply seated medical cultures prevailed. This resistance may be temporary only but it has already endured a good number of years and testifies to the power of elite medical professionals in the face of organizational change.

The most important theoretical question is what theoretical lens can best explain these differences between stakeholders—the cultural perspective inspired by sociological institutionalism or the differing interests and goals based on principal-agent theory? We argue that both theories contribute important insights to explaining the differences between the main hospital stakeholders in Norway. A first point to reiterate is that differences between stakeholders hinder coordination. The greater the difference the more difficult coordination is. What factors contribute to these differences is a related question and to answer this question, we suggest that we need to draw not on one but on both perspectives—both the actor-oriented interests and goals and the cultural factors stemming from the different norms and values that characterize the different professions. These values and norms are cultural, institutional factors, a result of socialization processes that go beyond the rational interests and goals of powerful actors. The different norms and values shape the interests and goals of the actors. However, this, we suggest, does not necessarily cancel the fact that the elite medical profession, central policy makers and local politicians possess their own set of interests and goals. These are culturally contingent but, nevertheless, they are still interests and goals that differ from one actor to another. It is for these reasons that we suggest that the hospital system culture, seen through the lens of sociological institutionalism, combined with the interests and goals of key stakeholders provide the best explanation for coordination problems. It is not only culture that matters—examples of coordination problems can occur and have occurred in one of the most high-trust, consensual and compliant hospital systems.

BIBLIOGRAPHY

BBC News. (1999, March 19). UK politics, all aboard the third way. Accessed October 22, 2014.

Davis, K., Stremikis, K., Squires, D., & Schoen, C. (2014, June). *Mirror, mirror on the wall; how the performance of the U.S. health care system compares internationally.* New York: The Commonwealth Fund.

European Observatory on Health Systems and Policies. (2014). *The health systems and policy monitor, Norway.* Available online. Accessed September 23, 2014.

Johnsen, J. R. (2006). *Health systems in transition: Norway.* Copenhagen: WHO Regional Office for Europe on behalf of the European Observatory on Health Systems and Policies.

Lægreid, P., Opedal, S., & Stigen, I. M. (2005). The Norwegian hospital reform: Balancing political control and enterprise autonomy. *Journal of Health Politics, Policy and Law, 30*(6), 1027–1064.

Magnussen, J. (2013). Hospital sector governance in Norway: Decentralization and the distribution of tasks. *Eurohealth Observer, 19*(1), 19–22.

Magnussen, J., Hagen, T. P., & Kaarbøe, O. M. (2007). Centralized or decentralized? A case study of Norwegian hospital reform. *Social Science and Medicine, 64*, 2129–2137.

Ministry of Health and Care Services. (2009). *The Coordination Reform: Proper treatment at the right place and right time*. Summary in English Report No. 47 (2008–2009) to the Storting. Oslo: Ministry of Health and Care Services.

Ministry of Health and Care Services. (2014, September 1). *South-East regional health authority, field trip report*. Oslo: Ministry of Health and Care Services.

Office of the Auditor General. (2009). *Investigation into the financial management of the regional health authorities and health trusts*. [Document 3:3 (2009–2010)]. Oslo: Office of the Auditor General.

Office of the Auditor General. (2012). *Efficiency and financial performance in state-owned companies should be followed up more closely*. [Press release]. Oslo: Office of the Auditor General.

Office of the Auditor General. (2013b). *Execution of state ownership must be bolstered*. [Press release]. Oslo: Office of the Auditor General.

Office of the Auditor General. (2014). *Investigation of electronic messaging in the health and care sector*. [Document 3:6 (2013–2014)]. Oslo: Office of the Auditor General.

Oslo University Hospital. (2013). *Oslo University hospital presentation*. Oslo: Oslo University Hospital.

Ringard, Å., Sagan, A., Sperre Saunes, I., & Lindahl, A. K. (2013). Norway: Health system review. *Health Systems in Transition, 15*(8), 1–162.

Statistics Norway. (2014). Online database. Oslo: Statistics Norway. Accessed September 04, 2014.

CHAPTER 8

Discussion and Conclusions

This study of organizational reform in public hospital systems and central coordination in Estonia, Norway and Romania has brought to the surface a number of key findings. In this concluding chapter, we first summarize the content of the reforms that were investigated in this research, followed by a comparative evaluation of the reforms in the three country cases as it pertains to coordination. Theoretically, we aim to explain the relationship between organizational reform and central coordination across the three cases building on the theoretical discussion in Chaps. 5–7. Finally, we reflect on the choices made in designing the research and draw implications for practice.

ORGANIZATIONAL REFORM AND COORDINATION IN PUBLIC HOSPITALS

We have seen that organizational reform in public hospitals has constituted an important component of healthcare policy in all three countries in the past 10 to 15 years. All three countries have experimented with structural reform (including decentralization or centralization) and have grappled with granting management autonomy to public hospitals while seeking to solidify policy making and coordination capacity at the center of government. Importantly, this administrative change across the three hospital systems has not been marginal only—it has involved major

© The Author(s) 2017
S. Dan, *The Coordination of European Public Hospital Systems*,
DOI 10.1007/978-3-319-43428-5_8

resources and has received considerable attention from different stakeholders. Although hospital decentralization and autonomy reform constitute on-going processes that may constantly undergo some degree of change, we have observed that in two of our three cases, Estonia and Norway, the reform model proposed more than 10 years ago has essentially endured to the present. While ideas for change to the model have been put forward, in Norway, for example, it is unlikely that this change would radically reshape the type of reform model adopted years ago. Romania, while clearly experimenting with the same types of international ideas, has thus far only implemented decentralization. Granting greater autonomy to hospital management is still an idea that is being considered by central policy makers in Romania, but it is uncertain if, when and how it will be implemented. For example, the latest healthcare strategy, *the National Health Strategy 2014–2020*, includes a few "strategic action points" aiming at increasing the flexibility of hospital management in areas such as human resources, the use of modern managerial tools and performance and quality assessment (Ministry of Health, 2014, pp. 57–63). Thus, reform of hospital management autonomy is very much work in progress. However, decentralization—the transfer of ownership of public hospitals from the central government to local public authorities (i.e. municipalities and county councils)—was implemented on a large scale. Pro-decentralization proponents, of whom there are many in Romania, managed to get reform all the way through implementation. This has not been the case with hospital autonomy which has undergone systematic internal resistance. Unlike hospital autonomy, hospital decentralization is less contested and is, in fact, one instance of a larger trend in public administration reform which has favored decentralization both internally and externally (see e.g. the EU's support to "hasten" the long-lasting process of decentralization).

Of all three countries, Estonia adopted the most decentralized and autonomous model as a result of the creation of legal hospital forms rooted in private law, foundations and limited-liability companies, coupled with political decentralization. Adopted in the early 2000s, the reform model has ultimately been endorsed by parties across the political spectrum. What is particularly interesting in this case is that there is little interest in changing these fundamental principles of the system which are taken as a given to which further change can then be applied. For example, reorganizing the hospital network and creating networks of hospitals to improve coordination have recently been confidently pursued, but these do not change, however, the basic model which is still based on autono-mous hospitals operating under private law and political decentralization. In the past 10 to 15 years, Norway moved toward centralization of hospi-tal ownership, unlike Estonia and Romania, combined with the creation of autonomous hospital trusts. A distinctive feature of the hospital reform in Norway was the creation of the regional health authorities which own the hospital trusts and are in turn owned by the central government. These regional authorities are autonomous entities operating under the financial and structural framework of the state. For this reason, the centralization of ownership can also be described as regionalization capitalizing on the geography and history of the country which have traditionally included strong regional and local preferences. Unlike Estonia, however, the struc-ture of the hospital system has been more seriously contested, especially by parties with conservative affinities and by the medical profession. Eliminating the regional health authorities and replacing them with more centralized responsibilities in the Ministry of Health and Care Services and/or the Directorate of Health has been one recommendation but it is yet uncertain what the final arrangements will include and how different they will be from the model proposed in the early 2000s.

In the face of organizational reform, the state capacity to coordinate the decentralized and autonomous hospitals has been put to the test. At a more general level, we see different mechanisms of coordination in the three public hospital systems. In spite of these different general mecha-nisms of coordination, there are a number of similar patterns that can be observed. We have observed a reconsideration of the role of central institutions, most notably the ministries of health, but also health insur-ance funds in social insurance systems or other central bodies in tax-based systems. There have been two major trends in this respect and these have followed a fairly sequential order. First, before the reforms, we can notice a change in the role of the ministries of health from that of hospital admin-istrators which owned and closely coordinated and controlled the public hospitals to one of "steward" of the healthcare system. Though we should also remember that in this earlier era when the center, theoretically, was intensively coordinating, there were many symptoms that suggested that coordination was not working. Structural and hospital autonomy shaped this shift which can most clearly be observed in the case of Estonia and to some extent in the case of Norway. In the latter case, though it can be argued that the 2002 hospital reform recentralized hospital owner-ship, this did not, however, involve a major change concerning the central administration of hospitals. The reform did not turn the state into an administrator of hospitals. Hospitals, in fact, gained a new legal form and were organized as trusts owned not directly by the state but by the regional health authorities. As far as this aspect is concerned, however, the case of Romania stands out. In this case, there has been growing interest to redefine the role of the Ministry of Health following international trends. Nonetheless, the Ministry of Health still has an important administrative role, especially in the case of those hospitals that did not undergo decentralization. The Ministry of Health aspires to be a steward of the healthcare system, but in reality, it still maintains "tight" hands on the public hospitals. This does not come as a great surprise considering that hospital autonomy is limited in the case of Romania.

A second more recent trend has been a reconsideration of the role of the center in the sense of strengthening coordinating, regulatory and policy making capacity at the center of government. In Estonia, for example, we have seen pressure on the Ministry of Social Affairs to improve its regulatory capacity by coordinating the purchase of expensive medical equipment, reorganizing the hospital structure (the master plan) and improving the coordination of the quality of care. Similarly, in Norway, the center of government (rather than the regional health authorities) has followed similar trends in recent years. Standardization of processes, such as ICT tools, and the standardization of the quality of care have been two of the most recent policy trends. As in Estonia, there has been pressure on the center to assume a more direct role in the governance of these domains and pressure to "bring politics back in."

We notice therefore a pendulum moving back and forth with some alterations in what is considered to be ailing, but this process does not necessarily involve radical change to the reform model. It is an approach that is more likely to be politically and socially feasible and that incrementally addresses the problems identified in the system. The health insurance funds in social insurance systems are a second type of central institutions that proved influential in hospital policy. The traditional role in this case has been that of a "mere" reimbursement agency that processes invoices and, in return, refunds healthcare providers—little interest in policy, strategy or quality of care. Our empirical research has not identified a significant change concerning the role of the National Health Insurance House in Romania. Problems have been identified both with the insufficient amount of financial resources and the ailing DRG system, but a change in the role of the fund has not yet gained saliency. This is not the case, however, with the Estonian Health Insurance Fund. In this case, the fund, in fact, is perceived to play the most important role in the hospital system and has gained a position as a stand-alone institution that works alongside the Ministry of Social Affairs. Although not *officially* a policy institution, the fund's policies can have an instrumental role in influencing hospital behavior. The funding system, and more importantly the financial incentives embedded in the funding mechanism, plays a role in the type and the amount of services that some hospitals provide. Hospitals have learned to react to these incentives and have become more financially interested than before the reform. These incentives may not necessarily reflect a certain policy position that the fund is taking, but they do not remain inconsequential for hospital behavior, as the case of oncology has shown. Furthermore, the fund has been one of the proponents of focusing on and improving the assessment of quality of care. Its role, however, has been limited by virtue of not being officially a policy institution. Nevertheless, the fund is putting pressure on responsible policy institutions to develop and use comparative quality and performance indicators and assessments in the hospital system.

At the outset of the research, we posed the following research questions, which for convenience, we list below:

Step 1
RQ1: Has hospital autonomy changed national coordination of the system of publicly owned hospitals in Estonia, Norway and Romania?
RQ2: Has decentralization changed national coordination of the system of publicly owned hospitals in Estonia and Romania?
RQ3: Has recentralization changed national coordination of the system of publicly owned hospitals in Norway?
Step 2
RQ4: What theory best explains similarities and differences in coordination problems between the selected cases?

In what follows, we take each research question in turn, summarize the findings from Chaps. 5–7 and then comparatively discuss the findings. First, we discuss the relation between hospital autonomy and central coordination. On the basis of existing literature on the autonomy of public sector organizations and coordination in the public sector, we hypothesized that the autonomy of hospital management affects central coordination. The more autonomous hospitals are the more difficult it is for national institutions to coordinate the system of hospitals as a whole. Similarly, the more independent hospitals are the more difficult it is for them to work together as a system—it is expected that autonomous hospitals are more likely to be concerned with organizational interests and goals than with systemic desiderata. Our classification of cases has indicated that public hospitals in the three countries are characterized by different degrees of autonomy: Estonia displaying the most autonomous arrangement, followed by Norway and, finally, by Romania. Therefore, we would expect central coordination to be most difficult to enact in Estonia, followed by Norway and Romania.

In comparing the results across the three cases, we can conclude that hospital autonomy has overall posed serious challenges to the central coordination of autonomous hospitals in Estonia, much more so than in the case of Norway and Romania. The collected evidence in the case of Estonia has shown how, for example, some ambitious hospitals have diligently and effectively used their status grounded in private law to develop their own strategies that do not always or necessarily align with the expectations of central coordinating institutions. Furthermore, in analyzing the interview material and comparing it across the three cases, it is more likely that the discretion of hospitals in Estonia is perceived to pose challenges to coordination than in the other cases. While our research supports this general result, the autonomy of hospitals is not the only factor that affects the effectiveness of coordination. Moreover, hospitals that enjoy a lower degree of autonomy, as in Romania, for example, are not necessarily more effectively coordinated than hospitals that enjoy a high degree of decision-making discretion.

When we get to specific details and cases of coordination, then it is more likely that the picture becomes more nuanced, and this, we would argue, is one of the merits of the approach we have taken in this research. We did not restrict the study to one or two pre-determined domains of coordination, such as medical personnel or finance, as important as these may be, but we inductively allowed the investigation to reveal areas which are in need of coordination. We have seen in this way how in Norway, for instance, coordination problems exist in more specific areas of ICT and in the case of elite medical specialties in the Oslo University Hospital. Overall, coordination in Norway has significantly improved following the 2002 hospital reform, but this does not necessarily mean that coordination in the public hospital sector is problem-free. The research design did not allow assessing the individual effect of autonomy on coordination while keeping other possible factors constant. That was not the intention of the research, but in exploring the relationship between hospital autonomy and central, vertical coordination in different cases, we have explored other factors at play. If we look again at Estonia and Norway, we see that not only are hospitals more autonomous in Estonia than in Norway, but central coordination in Estonia is much weaker than in Norway. Though hospitals in Norway enjoy a good degree of autonomy, autonomy does not seem to hinder hospitals from strategic thinking. One can think strategically as long as one has a clear and fairly stable set of rules. The highly regulated hospital sector in this country generally ensures effective coordination. This is achieved both formally through the financial, structural framework and the annual letter of instruction as well as by means of informal coordination such as regular meetings throughout the year. In Estonia, central coordination proved insufficient not only because of the autonomy of hospitals but also because of weak central coordination which includes inadequate regulation concerning the purchase of expensive medical equipment and the reorganization of the hospital network. For these reasons, we may question the contention that a high degree of autonomy necessarily leads to coordination problems. It is only one part of the equation. The case of Romania is a case in point. We have argued that autonomy reform in Romania has not yet been implemented and that hospitals perceive their autonomy to be limited. Therefore, if we were to follow the previous argument, we could expect central coordination to be effective in this case. However, there is no evidence that this has been the case and, furthermore, the limited autonomy has caused frustration among the hospital managers who perceive that coordination in fact takes the form of control. This control, on the Ministry of Health side, however, is deemed necessary to address serious ethical problems and corruption. If coordination of hospitals is an important policy goal, then it is not enough to cut down on hospital autonomy—effective coordination mechanisms and instruments are essential.

Second, we considered the relationship between decentralization of hospitals in Estonia and Romania, recentralization in Norway and central coordination. Decentralization involves the transfer of ownership from a higher, central level of authority, most typically the ministries or departments of health, to a lower level of authority such as county councils or municipalities. Recentralization is the opposite phenomenon resulting in ministries of health becoming, directly or indirectly, the owners of public hospitals. Although we agree that hospital autonomy and decentralization may follow similar processes and trajectories that ultimately result in power being dispersed from one entity to a number of different entities, we chose to treat these two reforms separately, as argued earlier. These reforms may follow similar trajectories but this is not always or necessarily the case. It has been the case in Estonia, but not in Norway and Romania. In Norway, for example, the 2002 hospital reform included both recentralization of ownership and the creation of hospital trusts. In Romania, decentralization and hospital autonomy have been considered within the same program of hospital reform, but whereas decentralization was implemented, hospital autonomy has not yet been adopted. For these reasons, we argued that it is best for the purposes of this research to treat them as two inter-related, but separate types of organizational reform. In terms of the relationship between decentralization of hospitals and central coordination, we have found significant differences between Estonia and Romania. As we discuss these differences, we need to keep in mind the other factors that play a role such as the autonomy of hospitals and the effectiveness of central coordination.

There are also differences in these respects, as argued in the previous paragraph. The research has shown that political decentralization in Estonia combined with a high degree of hospital autonomy and insufficient central coordination, challenged a systemic approach to hospital governance. Considering that most hospital boards consist of local politicians, and that there is little influence from the center, local politics expressed through local interests and goals that are different from those of central authorities, proved effective in resisting central coordination. In this sense, political decentralization turned out to make a difference. Had the national, systemic perspective been supported by the hospital boards, then central coordination may have become effective. In the hospital system in Romania, the large-scale 2010 decentralization reform has covered most public hospitals, but our research has shown that de facto decentralization has not yet been entirely institutionalized. Furthermore, the Ministry of Health acting through its de-concentrated public health authorities is still exerting important influence on both the decentralized hospitals and those hospitals that remained under direct central coordination. It is not clear whether decentralization has yet had any significant impact on the ability of the Ministry of Health to coordinate the system of public hospitals as a whole. This finding can be explained by the limited de facto decentralization and by the low degree of hospital autonomy, given the fact that hospitals are in reality still budgetary institutions operating under the framework of the state budget.

Recentralization in Norway has generally made it easier for the state to coordinate the hospital network and enact cost-control measures than it was the case before the reform when hospitals were owned by the 19 different counties. In this respect, recentralization led to improvements in coordination, despite the creation of hospital trusts enjoying sufficient autonomy to make local decisions. A critical factor here was the creation of the formalized regional health authorities which have generally been effective in carrying out their mandate to ensure regional coordination within their jurisdiction. In working closely with a limited number of hospital trusts, following the process of hospital mergers, the regions were typically able to enact coordination and make tough decisions which would have been difficult for national politicians to make. Acting as administrative bodies, though partly governed by politicians, the regional health authorities have gradually played a key role in improving coordination of the hospital sector as a whole.

An important element of the analytical framework of the book was the different types of coordination problems. In choosing to focus on specific problems of coordination—duplication, omission, contradiction and divergence—we sought to make the analysis more specific than it would have otherwise been possible by adopting a more general framework of assessing coordination. Looking across the three cases, we can conclude that omission seems less prevalent than the other types of problems. The exception in this case is waiting lists for elective care, a common concern internationally, but though this situation leads to no service being provided temporarily, the service will eventually be provided. For this reason, we did not treat waiting times in detail and the subject is broad enough to warrant a more specific study of its own. Nevertheless, lack of coordination can arguably be a factor affecting omission and waiting times—better coordination between hospitals horizontally, for example, can lead to shorter waiting times and can possibly be a solution to situations of omission. In other words, it is possible that poor coordination leads to no service being provided, but we did not find sufficient evidence that would systematically point in this direction in any of the three hospital systems.

Concerning the other types of coordination problems, we have documented specific cases in one or more of the three countries, such as for example divergent behavior of the East Tallinn Central Hospital and the Oslo University Hospital. The key point is that by looking at specific problems of coordination, we can readily show that although coordination generally improved, as it has in Norway, there are still specific domains in need of improved coordination. It is true that big hospitals in capital cities are typically the most difficult to coordinate and enjoy a certain status by means of their medical and scientific reputation. One therefore could argue that they are exceptions to the rule. While this may be true, it is primarily these leading hospitals that may be in need of coordination as they use large amounts of resources and are in a position to influence the network of hospitals as a whole. An important question is whether these four types of coordination problems are indeed problems or rather simple administrative "glitches"—something with which hospitals and coordinators need to learn to live with that does not pose serious problems to the efficiency, financial sustainability or quality of care of hospital systems. We would suggest that these problems may challenge one or more of these systemic goals, but the evidence is limited. This was evident in the interview material in all the three countries: some interviewees perceive this to be the case but they provide little evidence. In those cases in which specific studies have been conducted about the financial sustainability of the current hospital network and the purchase of expensive medical equipment, as in Estonia, these do not cover the coordination problems as understood in our research. We have seen how they struggled to tackle one or more of these problems, failing in some cases and succeeding in others. The drive toward merging hospitals and creating formal or informal hospital networks that work together is one clear sign of this growing interest, which is typically motivated by the need to improve efficiency and quality of care. Whether these goals of improved efficiency and quality stemming from integration have been obtained is an interesting research avenue, and it is debatable whether this has been the case. Therefore, we suggest that problems of coordination are not mere administrative glitches and may lead to inefficiencies, and sub-optimal quality of care. At the same time, however, our research suggests that it is not necessarily hospital autonomy and decentralization which have caused these problems. They are certainly not new to hospital systems and a state-owned and controlled system does not necessarily guarantee problem-free coordination. We suggest, nonetheless, that these types of reform tend to reinforce coordination problems insofar as central coordination is inadequate. They need to be understood as part of the larger governance arrangement.

   In the case of Estonia, we emphasized that, in spite of reinforcing coordination problems, decentralization and hospital autonomy have also produced a number of positive effects. These have generally included improved management capacity and professionalism, orientation toward the patient and, relatedly, growing interest in the quality of healthcare services, and a drive toward modernization, change and innovation more generally. Furthermore, the empirical evidence has clearly shown that the vast majority of interviewees, regardless of institutional affiliation, while highlighting certain problems, have generally perceived the reform to have had positive effects when compared to the situation before the reform. This is useful in showing that improved coordination is but one desideratum that policy makers may want to achieve when promoting a new policy.

Turning to Romania, in this case, the 2010 decentralization thus far has partly achieved its goals and there is evidence suggesting that those local authorities that had sufficient administrative and financial capacity have contributed financially and managerially to the governance of the newly decentralized public hospitals. There is evidence therefore that things are moving in the right direction and decentralization is one of the factors explaining this improvement. Nonetheless, though decentralization and hospital autonomy, in our view, are desirable, reaping the benefits of these types of reform has thus far been unequal. Not all local authorities possess the capacity and resources to assume the new responsibilities and central policy makers did not take sufficient interest in adapting the provisions of the reform to the local context. The pilot project could have included a few small local authorities from each region rather than only two well-resourced and large municipalities. On the basis of this limited pilot project, the reform proponents drew hasty conclusions that did not entirely reflect the reality on the ground. The reform was seen as a needed step forward, however, and was pushed forward to resist opposition even though not all reform pre-requisites were in place. In a turbulent financial context and great variation in financial and administrative capacity from one local authority to another, we ask whether it is realistic to wait until all pre-requisites are met before hospital decentralization is implemented. Moreover, the decentralization process has already been postponed—following an incremental approach—for many years. However, policy makers, following a systematic evaluation, could have included in a first phase only those local authorities that possessed enough capacity, followed at a later stage by the local authorities that seemed to be in need of greater capacity before undergoing decentralization. Not being sensitive to the local context meant that the benefits of a good idea were not entirely taken advantage of. This leads us to suggest that inherently decentralization and autonomy can address some of the deep-seated problems of the hospital sector in Romania, but the context needs to support, rather than hinder, reform. This has not been the case throughout the extensive and complex healthcare sector.

The 2002 hospital reform in Norway has facilitated cost control and overall improved regional coordination of hospital services. It also facilitated the reorganization and modernization of the public hospital network and created the premise for improving quality of care and patient safety. We argue that the 2002 reform had an instrumental role in improving coordination through the creation of the regional health authorities which were given specific coordination responsibilities. Similarly, hospital trusts which bring together different hospitals under the same general management, generally responded positively to the regional coordination efforts. Nonetheless, medical professionals in particular have drawn attention to increased red tape and administrative burden, an alleged focus on "economics" at the expense of patient treatment and care, and a general emphasis on processes rather than patient outcomes. Therefore, the 2002 hospital reform and the creation of the regions were blamed for these unintended consequences and proposals for change have been put forward, which may involve a change in the coming years to the model adopted years ago.

EXPLAINING COORDINATION: CONFLICTING INTERESTS AND GOALS AND HOSPITAL SYSTEM CULTURE

In order to seek to explain the relationship between reform and coordination problems, the book derived a list of theoretical propositions from each of the two theories and confronted them with the empirical evidence collected in the course of the research. Chapters 5–7 provided an extensive discussion for each case and proposition. In this concluding chapter, we first summarize the main theoretical findings for each case and then compare the three cases, and end the section with a discussion of theoretical implications. In explaining the effectiveness of central coordination, we found that some of the key insights of principal-agent theory are more useful than others. In this respect, there are differences between the three hospital systems. First, positive incentives employed by the principals to coordinate the activity of the agents play a more important role in the case of Estonia than in Norway and Romania. We have emphasized that financial incentives embedded in the financing system in Estonia incentivize hospitals to develop and provide cancer treatment that gives hospitals a bigger margin over their costs than other services, such as intensive care, which is generally unprofitable. These incentives have thus stimulated discoordination. Rather than support central coordination, they have hindered it.

Some hospitals, most notably East Tallinn Central Ltd., have responded to these incentives and developed divergent behavior which turned out to be difficult to govern, thus eschewing central coordination. While this case is prominent, we have not identified similar examples in the other two hospital systems. The two regional hospitals, Tartu University Hospital and North Estonia Medical Center in Tallinn, which are the two major cancer treatment centers, have developed cancer services that have been in line with national strategic plans. We therefore suggest that positive incentives play an important but limited role in influencing the effectiveness of coordination. They have been important in the sense that they have influenced the behavior of major hospitals thus possibly also affecting other public hospitals. They have, however, been limited in the sense that only some hospitals have reacted to these incentives in ways that contradicted national strategic plans. Negative incentives (or sanctions and penalties used by the center to coordinate hospital behavior), on the other hand, appear influential in the case of Romania where in recent years, budget cuts led to a reduction in salaries in the public sector, thus affecting the coordination of the ailing public finances and, as a consequence, hospital finances, specifically. These negative incentives—taking the form of budgetary cuts—exacerbated the contradiction between state policy goals and the achievement of those goals by hospitals.

The financing mechanism, based on the DRG system, further affects the coordination of financial resources as a result of a major disconnect between the reimbursed prices and the actual costs of treatment. This difference further reinforces lack of transparency, unethical behavior and various forms of corruption—recurring characteristics of the hospital system culture in Romania. Second, we considered a second component of the principal-agent theory: information asymmetry and imperfect monitoring. Information asymmetry lies at the core of the principal-agent relationship and is one key factor why the principal needs to develop incentives to align the interests and goals of the agents to his. Imperfect monitoring is different in that it consists of the process through which the principal gathers information to address the asymmetric relationship. However, ultimately both the aim of collecting information and of monitoring is to provide the principal with the missing and needed information to enact coordination.

Information asymmetry is a condition of the principal-agent relationship. Given this condition, the principal is interested in gathering information through monitoring that would help, at least in part, to address the asymmetric relationship. This does not imply that the principal will or can necessarily obtain sufficient information to change the asymmetric relationship, but it does imply that he is interested in doing so. The existence and use of monitoring tools show the interest of the principal in improving the information at his disposal. Therefore, this proposition contends that it is the lack of information that hinders coordination. In this case, we have found similarities between the three hospital systems and suggest that information asymmetry play a minor role only in hospital coordination. Certainly the drive for more and accurate information lies behind the trend toward the development of ICT systems, digital governance and e-health solutions. These are meant to improve the accuracy, availability and transfer and communication of information across different institutions and players in the healthcare sector both vertically and horizontally.

We have also seen how in the case of Norway the coordination of ICT has met with resistance and has been painfully slow, despite sustained effort to promote the introduction and use of systems that "talk to each other." These problems may have occurred because players were afraid of a big brother central coordinator or they may have occurred because different actors already had their own systems that they were used to and did not want to take the time, energy and money to change. Regardless of the reason, by not changing as expected, they hindered central coordination efforts. We have also seen in all three cases the need for performance and quality information that can support a greater emphasis on the coordination of clinical outcomes, rather than just the coordination of process. Nonetheless, we argue that in all three cases, central coordinating agencies have possessed sufficient information on areas that need coordination but despite this information, they were not able to improve coordination. This suggests that there are other factors that can explain the ineffectiveness of coordination. Examples in support of this finding abound across the three systems. For instance, Estonian central policy makers are well aware of the hospital network in need of reorganization and of the divergent behavior of East Tallinn Central. The same is the case for the coordination of quality of care in Norway, coordination of ICT tools and the situation of the merger of the Oslo University Hospital—the rivalry between the two neurosurgery and thoracic surgery units at Rikshospitalet and Ullevål Hospital was no secret. Likewise, the general problems of the

Romanian hospital sector are well-known, as clearly evidenced in the different healthcare strategies developed in recent years (Ministry of Health, 2010; Ministry of Health, 2014). The key point, we argue, is that despite this information, policy makers failed to act in such a way as to effectively address these problems.

Why this has been the case needs a more convincing explanation, to which we now turn. We argue that a third component of principal-agent theory—the role of conflicting interests and goals—combined with the hospital system culture derived from institutional theory best explain coordination across the three cases. This is not to say that the three hospital systems possess the same hospital culture, which is not the case as shown earlier, but the influence of the hospital culture itself proves illuminating and is an additional causal factor. The same is the case for the conflicting interests and goals. We do not necessarily suggest that the same stakeholders are at odds with each other in all cases or that the interests and goals differ with the same intensity in all countries at all times. However, whether outright conflict or differences in opinions, goals or methods to achieve a certain goal, the key point is that these are influential enough to hinder or prevent coordination from being enacted. We have found considerable evidence in support of this explanation in the three cases. In Estonia, for example, we highlighted that the interests of local politicians, who govern most hospital boards, differ from those of central policy makers who are in favor of central coordination. Had there been consensus, we would argue coordination would have been much easier to implement than it has been the case so far. Furthermore, hospital management, endowed with a high degree of autonomy, follows an individual or local organizational logic whereas national policy makers favor a systemic perspective—the efficiency and financial sustainability of the hospital sector in its entirety. As the saying goes: "where you stand depends on where you sit." Again, the alignment of these goals, unrealistic though it may seem, would facilitate coordination.

Likewise, in Norway, though a high-trust culture that is compliant with ethical standards, we documented that differing interests and goals do exist, as in the case of Oslo University Hospital, but also more generally between the different administrative layers and professions—the medical profession is supporting patient care, investment in high tech medicine and treatment whereas administrators are favoring cost control and a managerial approach to quality assessment. Intertwined with actor-centered interests and goals is a hospital system culture that resists coordination.

The medical profession has traditionally occupied a central role, and stood against NPM-type reforms, which at least to some extent favored management, cost control and performance assessment and which challenged deep-seated professional practices. We have seen how the medical professionals in Estonia and Romania, in particular, have increasingly made use of international professional mobility and created unrest and unpredictability in human resource policy. Similarly, elite medical specialties, such as neurosurgery, thoracic surgery and oncology, have challenged the integration of these specialties into more systematic and coordinated organizational arrangements and fought to preserve the status quo, despite sustained coordination efforts.

Similarly, in Romania, there is evidence suggesting that the elite medical profession—"the law makers"—are in fact "running the show" in health policy and have eschewed forms of governance that would undermine their position. Characterized by "old-school" attitudes, this elite medical profession is likely to disqualify management attempts to coordinate performance and quality and introduce change to the system. Therefore, we argue that it is especially the elite medical profession, rather than the medical profession as a whole, that acts as a nucleus against central coordination. The status of the medical profession is deep-seated and long-standing, and not a product of decentralization and hospital autonomy reform. These types of reform have challenged but not changed the hospital system culture. In addition to the medical profession, the hospital system culture resisting coordination also comprises management professionals who do not necessarily agree with being centrally coordinated. Especially in a context of hospital management autonomy in Estonia, and to a much lesser extent in Norway and Romania, we have seen how a business and market mindset penetrated the new hospital culture. Supported by a larger culture in favor of business and the market and inter-sectorial mobility, hospital managers in Estonia felt especially empowered finally to start managing. This involved the introduction of business techniques, the use of which in some cases challenged government coordination. The case of Estonia clearly shows that it is not only the medical profession that may hinder central governance, but that hospital management itself may act in such a way as to hinder it.

These findings give rise to a number of theoretical implications. Our research shows, first, that incorporating insights on conflicting (or differing) interests and goals from theories such as principal-agent is useful in explaining the effectiveness of coordination. Of all the elements of principal-agent theory, conflicting interests and goals proved the most relevant and consistent with the empirical evidence. This finding supports one aspect of the principal-agent theory, but less the other propositions—information asymmetry, imperfect monitoring and the use of incentives for coordination purposes. Principal-agent theory proved only partially useful. Furthermore, it is important to note that the influence of conflicting interests and goals in political processes was not an original discovery of principal-agent theorists. These were part of mainstream political science before principal-agent theory became popular. This implies that other theories in the social and political sciences that incorporate differing interests and goals can help in explaining coordination in public hospital systems. It is a merit of principal-agent theorists, however, that they built upon and popularized this set of ideas in a way that is clear and relevant not only in business but also in healthcare policy and management.

Second, we argue that the concept of hospital system culture, derived from, but not equal to the whole of, sociological institutionalism, helpfully complements the actor-centered interests and goals and exerts influence on central coordination. It is not only the differing interests and goals of the key stakeholders that hinder central coordination, but also their different values, norms and behavior patterns that stem from those different values and norms. These factors are cultural in an institutional sense and shape stakeholders' interests and goals. Within the hospital system culture, the elite medical profession, local politicians and powerful management stakeholders play an important role. The dynamic interaction between these stakeholders affects the effectiveness of central coordination.

Thus, we suggest that conflicting interests and goals and the proposed hospital system culture offer complementary rather than competing insights into organizational reform and public hospital coordination. Both are needed and useful—actors do play a role but so does cultural norms and value which shape actors' interests and goals. We did not find evidence against a specific theory, say principal-agent, and at the same time in favor of the second competing theory, in this case sociological institutionalism. Had we found such evidence, we could have concluded that a competing approach is most consistent with the available evidence. However, while we do not dismiss either of the two theories as a whole, in the case of principal-agent theory we did find more support for certain elements of the theory than for others. Admittedly, our treatment of sociological institutionalism was limited, in that we only looked at culture, and excluded other interesting ideas that are part of the richness of the new institutionalism. The complementarity between conflicting interests and goals and the hospital system culture leads to a consideration of the relationship between these two sets of ideas. They are broad enough to cross the boundaries of a particular theory, as already shown, and that applies to both principal agent and sociological institutionalism. Neither of these was the first to "invent" the concept of conflicting interests and goals, on the one hand, and culture, on the other hand. In this book, we emphasized the impact of conflicting *interests and goals,* as derived from principal-agent theory whereas in the case of culture the emphasis was placed on different *values and norms.* What both theories have in common is the *differing* aspect of these factors. Whether values, norms, interests or goals, the crucial finding is that they differ. The more different and con-flicting they are, we suggest, the more difficult it is to enact coordination.

Arguably, values and norms shape behaviors and routines, and may thereby indirectly influence the interests and goals of actors. One can thus suggest that the differing interests and goals of hospital stakeholders are themselves contingent on cultural factors. As long as the concept of cul-ture can be stretched to mean almost anything that may be true. However, in keeping with the distinction in political science between structure and institution, on the one hand, and agency and behavior, on the other hand, we emphasize the difference between culture in an institutional sense, and actor-oriented goals and interests. They may be mutually shaped but they are not the same. Hospital stakeholders do not only have certain values and norms as a result of specific socialization processes and develop certain attitudes and behavior patterns as a result of the values and norms, but they also possess specific interests and goals. Though they are shaped by different cultural values and norms which in turn determine the goals and interests to be different, but this influence does not necessarily cancel the role of interests and goals. In emphasizing actors' differing interests and goals, principal-agent theory, we suggest, can contribute useful insights into public sector coordination.

Third, a criticism of principal-agent theory applied to complex public policy is that the theory proves useless when multiple principals and agents are involved. However, we have shown earlier that the theory has in a few instances been applied in healthcare and deemed useful. In our case, we paid particular attention to the key insights of the theory and applied principal-agent as a framework between the coordinating actors and the coordinated hospitals. We treated multiple principals and paid particular attention to the role of the ministries of health and the health insurance funds as the key central governing bodies. Likewise, we were interested in the coordination of public hospitals as a system but paid particular attention to cases that would stand out, such as the cases of divergent hospital behavior. Overall, we did not find inconveniences in using the insights and the principal-agent framework to a sector involving multiple principals and agents. At the same time, it needs to be acknowledged that this work did not use explicit theoretical or modeling tools that would test the relationship between one or more principals, on the one hand, and multiple agents, on the other hand. Future research using principal-agent theory in healthcare policy and governance could aim to test this relationship, although the operationalization would be very challenging.

A fourth implication concerns the debate on NPM and post-NPM. In choosing two types of reform that are usually included under NPM, we draw implications for NPM theory more generally while keeping in mind that the reforms that we investigated were decentralization and hospital autonomy only (not performance management, contracting out and other similar reforms). In choosing different cases, some of which better resonate with NPM than others, we can draw implications of the effects of NPM reform on central coordination. Estonia, as explained in Chap. 3, is for our purposes a NPM case characterized by a high degree of hospital autonomy and decentralized hospitals, Norway is a mixed case defined by high autonomy and centralized ownership. Romania consists of a mixed case with decentralized hospitals and low autonomy, and a non-NPM case characterized by low autonomy and centralized hospital ownership. The question is whether in a strong NPM case, coordination has been more challenging, as typically claimed, than in a case that displays less of a NPM character. According to this proposition, coordination is more difficult to enact in Estonia, than in Norway and would be the easiest to achieve in the least NPM case. Following the same logic, we would expect differences between the coordination of decentralized hospitals in Romania and those that did not undergo the process of decentralization. However, in this latter case we did not find any significant differences. Although the ownership of hospitals changed, the autonomy of hospitals did not undergo significant change and the Ministry of Health has continued to exert control on both the centralized and decentralized hospitals. Not only are decentralized hospitals coordinated locally, but they have continued to be centrally controlled. Looking across the three hospital systems more generally, we have found central coordination to be more difficult in Estonia than in the other two cases.

Nonetheless, we have argued that a high degree of hospital autonomy and a decentralized arrangement do not necessarily make coordination ineffective. There are other factors that need to be considered. Conversely, centralized and low-autonomy hospitals are not necessarily more effectively coordinated than high-autonomy and decentralized hospitals. Romania is a case in point here. In conclusion, while we see a relationship between NPM-type reform and problems of coordination, decreasing the autonomy of hospitals or centralizing ownership does not necessarily lead to improved coordination. Furthermore, policy makers need to consider possible trade-offs that may arise from tightening control keeping in mind that improved coordination is but one goal they may want to achieve. Policy makers need to be aware that *more* coordination does not necessarily involve *better* coordination. What they need to aim for is better not greater coordination. Too much coordination may create or reinforce a focus on process rather than outcome, which will be difficult to sell in today's environment where politicians, patients and citizens increasingly expect results and not only due process. Therefore, an acceptable balance needs to be found between the coordination of process and the focus on outcomes. The former may improve the latter but it may also stifle it.

A fifth implication concerns the case selection and the implications for comparative research in healthcare policy and public policy and management more generally. In choosing one Nordic hospital system and two former communist states, the selection of cases is unusual. Most of the comparative empirical research has treated reform in Western and Northern Europe apart from reform in Central and Eastern Europe. The multitude of differences, it is argued, is likely to render such comparisons useless. The use of a most similar research design, the typical approach, is therefore not readily applicable. Underlying this design is also the assumption that variables can be held constant and the control for extraneous variance, other than the independent variable of interest, is exercised by selecting most similar cases (Peters, 1998b). Alternatively, a most different design considers different cases and looks for explanation why a similar outcome is observed. However, it is difficult to find in reality situations in which the requirements of any of these two designs are satisfactorily met in political science research (Peters, 1998b).

For the purposes of this research, we selected similar types of organizational reform that were implemented in different countries and were interested in explaining the relationship between reform and coordination in different countries. The assumption here, which turned out to be supported by the data, is that the differences between the three hospital systems do not necessarily explain the effectiveness of coordination. For example, certain socio-economic characteristics do not necessarily explain why coordination fares better in a country than in another. A resourceful hospital system, as in Norway, does not guarantee effective coordination. Comparing Estonia and Romania, for instance, we can reach the general conclusion that though the socio-economics are more favorable in Estonia than in Romania, this does not seem to have resulted in improved coordination. Similarly, if we consider the size of the system (much lower in Estonia) we would be inclined immediately to expect coordination to be easier when compared to a larger system. However, this has not been the case. These differences may affect coordination, either by facilitating or hindering it, but they do not explain its effectiveness. The same is true concerning the elements of the hospital system culture analyzed in the course of this research. A generally high-trust culture that is compliant with ethical standards does not necessarily imply that no coordination problems can occur. The case of Norway is a case in point. Coordination problems can and have occurred, as shown in this research, in one of the most coordination-favorable cultures. Granted, the scale and intensity of coordination problems between the three cases is different, and in general the case in Norway has revealed better coordination than in the case of Romania, but the key point, we suggest, is still valid. The implication therefore is that we can aspire to compare the coordination of hospitals in different countries rather than restrict to those that appear to be most similar.

Implications for Practice

This research also leads to a number of implications for practice. First, at the center of this book lies the relation between central coordination and local autonomy, which has given rise to controversies both in theory and practice leading to on-going experimentation with finding the right mix between these two values (Pollitt & Bouckaert, 2011). The assumption underlying this debate is that more local and organizational autonomy means less, and presumably less effective, central coordination. Therefore, policy makers have considered finding the proper balance knowing that there is a trade-off at stake, and that they cannot expect the best of both worlds. While we find support for this hypothesis, we suggest that there are innovative ways in which reformers can grant significant decision-making autonomy to public hospitals while maintaining a coordinated approach to the entire public hospital system. A general assessment of our three cases reveals two extreme cases: Estonia and Romania. Hospitals in Estonia benefit from a high degree of autonomy but this arrangement can be criticized for lacking central coordination. By contrast, Romanian public hospitals enjoy little decision-making autonomy and central coordination has remained tight and in some areas has in fact increased in recent years (see e.g. the case of centralized public procurement).

As far as hospital autonomy and coordination are concerned, we argue that policy makers in Norway have managed to find an acceptable balance. Central and regional coordination while generally effective leaves ample room for hospital decision making. Hospital managers do not experience coordination to restrict their discretion which, in general, has meant that coordination, with a few exceptions, has been acceptable and followed through. The case of Norway does certainly not portray a perfect picture but the 2002 reform and the creation of regional health authorities and hospital trusts, we argue, greatly facilitated coordination while preserving hospital autonomy. An implication of this finding is that policy makers in other countries may want to consider an arrangement—whether regional or more local—to improve coordination over large catchment areas, which presumably can then be easier to govern nationally.

This arrangement needs to ensure that hospitals are given the authority to make decisions within the national and regional/local structural and financial framework. Within these catchment areas, hospitals need to be encouraged to cooperate in order to reduce coordination problems such as duplication and omission. Being part of the same region is likely to improve collaboration and can gradually create or reinforce a sense of regional identity which can be supportive of cooperation within the same region. The challenge will remain to ensure that this regionalization is still consistent with a national, systemic perspective. It is possible that regions or the local authorities may develop regional interests and goals that misalign with the national perspective. A strong center therefore is necessary to counteract this tendency if national coordination is to be improved. These ideas have gained momentum across Europe supported by a trend toward network thinking and the need to specialize and integrate high-level specialties and medical services to improve quality and increase efficiency. We have observed similar developments in Estonia and Romania, but they need to be sustained and implemented in practice, which has not yet been the case in either of these countries. The organization of hospitals as foundations or hospital trusts is a step forward compared to an arrangement based on budgetary institutions. This arrangement is conducive to fostering a sense of organizational responsibility and is more likely to facilitate the professionalization of management. Furthermore, it involves an increase in decision-making autonomy which, supported by a fitting context, can improve the organization and provision of services. These foundations, however, need to be integrated into a larger area, as suggested earlier.

Hospital reform, as a case of public sector policy more generally, is inherently complex and gives rise to a host of effects, some of which are intended while others are unintended and difficult to predict (Margetts, 6, & Hood, 2010; Pollitt & Bouckaert, 2011). Therefore, policy makers need to take into account the possibility that a reform may at least to some extent achieve its goals, for example, improved coordination, but at the same time that same reform is likely to make some things worse. As much as possible, reformers need to consider before designing the reform who will be affected and how, for example, medical professionals, local authorities, hospital managers and so forth. In all three cases, but especially in Estonia and Norway, we have found unintended consequences at play which have subsequently triggered a reconsideration of the model of the reform previously adopted. A further implication of this finding is that policy makers need to ensure they have the capacity to monitor reform regularly and identify any areas that may need change along the way. This needs to be reconciled with the reality on the ground, which involves an accurate understanding of this reality, as well as the need to let reform develop its course to prevent reform from being prematurely stifled.

BIBLIOGRAPHY

Margetts, H., 6, P., & Hood, C. (Eds.). (2010). *Paradoxes of modernization: Unintended consequences of public policy reform.* Oxford: Oxford University Press.

Ministry of Health. (2010). *National strategy for hospital rationalization.* Bucharest: Ministry of Health.

Ministry of Health. (2014). *National health strategy 2014–2020*. Bucharest: Ministry of Health.

Peters, G. B. (1998b). *Comparative politics: Theory and methods*. New York: New York University Press.

Pollitt, C., & Bouckaert, G. (2011). *Public management reform: A comparative analysis—new public management, governance and the Neo-Weberian state* (3 ed.). Oxford: Oxford University Press.

APPENDIX

I. INTERVIEW QUESTIONNAIRE: CENTRAL HEALTHCARE INSTITUTIONS (ENGLISH VERSION)

1. How would you describe current activities taken by national-level health policy institutions to coordinate the system of publicly owned hospitals in Estonia/Norway?

Note: Coordination means the activity taken by national policy institutions such as ministries of health to ensure that public hospitals work as a whole system.

2. Compared to a few years ago, how would you characterize the activities taken by national-level health policy institutions to coordinate the system of publicly owned hospitals in Estonia/Norway?

• What trend do you observe in this respect?
• What could best explain this trend?

3. What changes (if any) with the aim to coordinate the system of publicly owned hospitals in Estonia/Norway have been made in recent years?

• In your view, what reasons could best explain these changes?

© The Author(s) 2017
S. Dan, *The Coordination of European Public Hospital Systems*,
DOI 10.1007/978-3-319-43428-5

243

4. How do you see the ability of national health policy institutions to coordinate the system of publicly owned hospitals in the following areas:

• Human resources
• Finance
• Service organization
• Service provision

5. Thinking about the system of publicly owned hospitals in Estonia/ Norway as a whole, do you encounter the following problems concerning the coordination of the system by national health policy institutions?

i. When, for example, two different hospitals perform the same task that could be performed more efficiently and effectively in one place only [duplication]
• Please provide some examples of situations when you experienced this problem

ii. Gaps in performing a needed task so that a task ultimately ends up not being performed by any hospital [omission]
• Please provide some examples of situations when you experienced this problem

iii. Differences in policy, legislation or regulations governing hospitals that contradict one another [contradiction]

• Please provide some examples of situations when you experienced this problem

iv. Self-interested action by a particular hospital that affects the system of hospitals as a whole [divergence]

• Please provide some examples of situations when you experienced this problem

6. Of the four types of problems discussed earlier, which do you think are most frequently encountered?

- What can explain this situation?

7. Thinking about the reform to decentralize (for Estonia) or recentralize (for Norway), in your view, in what ways has this reform affected the national coordination of the system of publicly owned hospitals in Estonia/Norway?

8. Would you say that national coordination improved, deteriorated or did not change significantly as a result of decentralization (or recentralization in the case of Norway)?

9. Thinking back about the reform to create self-governing public hospitals—that is publicly owned hospitals that have greater power to make decisions—in what ways has this reform affected the national coordination of the system as a whole?

10. Would you say that national coordination improved, deteriorated or did not change significantly as a result of giving a high degree of autonomy to hospitals?

11. When thinking about the culture of the Estonian/Norwegian healthcare system, in what ways do you think that this culture is different (if it is different) from the culture of healthcare systems in other EU countries?

II. Interview Questionnaire: Hospitals (English Version)

1. How would you describe current activities taken by national-level health policy institutions to coordinate the system of publicly owned hospitals in Estonia/Norway?

Note: Coordination means the activity taken by national policy institutions such as ministries of health to ensure that public hospitals work as a whole system.

2. Compared to a few years ago, how would you characterize the activities taken by national-level health policy institutions to coordinate the system of publicly owned hospitals in Estonia/Norway?
3. What changes (if any) in health policy in the past years in Estonia/Norway would you say have had the greatest impact on the coordination of your hospital by national health policy institutions?
4. How would you characterize the discretion of hospital management to make decisions concerning the administration of the hospital you work for?

• What trend do you observe in this respect?
• What could explain this trend?

5. Should national health policy institutions coordinate the system of publicly owned hospitals in the following areas?

• Human resources
• Finance
• Service organization
• Service provision

6. Would you say that national level coordination of your hospital in these specific areas improved, deteriorated or did not change significantly as a result of management reforms in the hospital system?

• Why do you think so?
• What other evidence exists to support this view?

7. When thinking about the culture of the Estonian/Norwegian healthcare system, in what ways do you think that this culture is different (if it is different) from the culture of healthcare systems in other EU countries?

III. Interview Questionnaire: Central Healthcare Institutions (Romanian Version)

1. Cum a-ţi descrie la acest moment activităţile Ministerului Sănătăţii şi a altor instituţii cu rol de coordonare în ceea ce priveşte coordonarea sistemului de spitale publice din România?

Notă: Prin coordonarea sistemului de spitale publice înțelegem desfășurarea acelor activități cu scopul de a asigura că spitalele publice de diverse tipuri lucrează ca un întreg, ca un sistem în ansamblul său.

2. Comparativ cu acum câțiva ani, spre exemplu 5 ani, cum a-ți caracteriza activitățile Ministerului Sănătății și a altor instituții cu acest rol în ceea ce privește coordonarea sistemului de spitale publice de la noi din țară?

- Ce tendințe observați în această privință?
- Ce factori credeți că explică aceste tendințe?

3. Ce schimbări semnificative (dacă este cazul) au fost făcute în ultimii ani ce au avut ca scop coordonarea de către instituțiile centrale a rețelei de spitale publice din România?

- În opinia dvs. ce factori au condus la aceste schimbări?

4. Cum evaluați capacitatea Ministerului Sănătății și a altor instituții cu rol de coordonare a spitalelor publice în următoarele domenii:

- Resurse umane
- Resurse financiare
- Organizarea servicilor medicale furnizate de spitalele publice
- Furnizarea servicilor medicale de spitalele publice

5. Referindu-ne la sistemul sau rețeaua de spitale publice din România ca și un întreg sistem, considerați că există în sistem următoarele probleme de coordonare?

i. Spre exemplu situații în care două sau mai multe spitale publice indiferent de tip furnizează același serviciu medical care ar putea fi furnizat mai eficient și cu rezultate medicale mai bune doar în unul sau unele din aceste spitale publice

- Puteți să-mi dați exemple de astfel de situații?

ii. Situații în care există lacune în a furniza un anumit serviciu medical astfel încât acest serviciu nu este furnizat de nici un spital public din județ sau din țară

- Puteți să-mi dați exemple de astfel de situații?

iii. Situații în care există diferențe între diverse legi sau politici din domeniul coordonării rețelei de spitale publice din țară astfel încât acestea se contrazic între ele
- Puteți să-mi dați exemple de astfel de situații?

iv. Acțiune unilaterală a unui spital sau grup de spitale publice care afectează sistemul de spitale publice în ansamblul său
- Puteți să-mi dați exemple de astfel de situații?

6. Dintre cele 4 tipuri de situații de mai înainte pe care le-ați întâlnit cel mai des până acum în activitatea dvs.?
- Ce factori credeți că explică acest lucru?

7. Referindu-ne acum la reforma descentralizării majorității spitalelor publice de la noi din țară, în opinia dvs. în ce fel a influențat ea coordonarea rețelei de spitale publice în ansamblul său?

8. Cum a-ți evalua coordonarea spitalelor publice în urma descentralizării? Considerați că această coordonare s-a îmbunătățit, s-a înrăutățit sau nu s-a schimbat semnificativ?
- De ce credeți asta?
- Ce date există în acest sens?

9. Referindu-ne acum la reforma de a crea spitale publice autonome—adică spitale publice în care managerii de spital au un grad mare de libertate în a lua decizii—în ce fel credeți că această reformă a afectat sau ar afecta coordonarea rețelei de spitale publice în ansamblul său?

10. Cum a-ți evalua coordonarea spitalelor publice în urma acestei reforme de a crea spitale publice autonome? Considerați că această coordonare s-a îmbunătățit, s-a înrăutățit sau nu s-a schimbat semnificativ?

11. Gândindu-ne la cultura sistemului sanitar din România (în sens de mentalitate, adică la moduri de gândire și comportament ce definesc un anumit domeniu) cum a-ți caracteriza-o pe scurt? Ce trăsături caracteristice o definesc după părerea dvs.?

IV. Interview Questionnaire: Hospitals (Romanian Version)

1. Cum a-ți descrie la acest moment activitățile Ministerului Sănătății și a altor instituții cu rol în domeniu în ceea ce privește coordonarea sistemului de spitale publice din România?

Notă: Prin coordonarea sistemului de spitale publice înțelegem desfășurarea acelor activități cu scopul de a asigura că spitalele publice de diverse tipuri lucrează ca și un întreg, ca un sistem în ansamblul său.

2. Comparativ cu acum câțiva ani, spre exemplu 5 ani, cum a-ți caracteriza activitățile Ministerului Sănătății și a altor instituții cu acest rol în ceea ce privește coordonarea sistemului de spitale publice de la noi din țară?
   • Ce tendințe observați în această privință?
   • Ce factori credeți că explică aceste tendințe?

3. Ce schimbări semnificative (dacă este cazul) întreprinse în ultimii ani în sistemul nostru sanitar au avut cel mai mare impact asupra activității spitalului dvs.?

4. Cum a-ți caracteriza autonomia spitalului de care aparțineți în sensul de libertate de a lua decizii privind activitatea de zi cu zi a spitalului și libertatea de a lua decizii strategice pe termen mediu și lung?
   • Ce tendință observați privind autonomia spitalului pentru care lucrați?
   • Ce factori credeți că explică această tendință?

5. Cum evaluați capacitatea Ministerului Sănătății și a altor instituții cu rol de coordonare a spitalului de care aparțineți în următoarele domenii:
   • Resurse umane
   • Resurse financiare
   • Organizarea servicilor medicale furnizate de spitalele publice
   • Furnizarea servicilor medicale de spitalele publice

6. Cum a-ți evalua coordonarea spitalului dvs. în urma descentralizării? Considerați că această coordonare s-a îmbunătățit, s-a înrăutățit sau nu s-a schimbat semnificativ?
- De ce credeți asta?
- Ce date există în acest sens?

7. Gândindu-ne la cultura sistemului sanitar din România (în sens de mentalitate, adică la moduri de gândire și comportament ce definesc un anumit domeniu) cum a-ți caracteriza-o? Ce trăsături caracteristice o definesc după părerea dvs.?

V. Program of Interviews: Estonia

1. Preliminary interviews

Title	Affiliation	Date of interview
HealthIN Ltd	Praxis Center for Policy Studies	13.08.2012
Budgeting and Contracting Unit, Department of Healthcare	Estonian Health Insurance Fund	14.08.2012
Manager	World Health Organization	15.08.2012
Management board	Tartu University Hospital Foundation	16.08.2012
Audit Manager	National Audit Office of Estonia	17.08.2012

2. Main interviews
A. Hospital management representatives

Title	Hospital	Type of hospital	Date of interview
Management board	Tartu University Hospital Foundation	Regional	08.08.2013
Management board	Pärnu Hospital Foundation	Central	09.08.2013
Management board	South Estonia Hospital Ltd.	Local	19.08.2013
Management board	Tallinn Children's Hospital Foundation	Regional	21.08.2013
Management board	Läänemaa Hospital Foundation	Local	17.08.2013
Management board	Viljandi Hospital Foundation	Local	28.08.2013

(continued)

(continued)

Title	Hospital	Type of hospital	Date of interview
Management board	West Tallinn Central Hospital Ltd.	Central	29.08.2013
Management board	Ida-Viru Central Hospital Foundation	Central	30.08.2013

B. Representatives of national institutions

Title	Affiliation	Date of interview
Budgeting and Contracting Unit	Estonian Health Insurance Fund	06.08.2013
Healthcare Chief Specialist	Estonian Health Insurance Fund	15.08.2013
Healthcare Department	Estonian Health Insurance Fund	23.08.2013
Audit Manager	National Audit Office of Estonia	12.08.2013
Parliament representative in the Supervisory Board of the Health Insurance Fund	Parliament of Estonia, Social Affairs Committee	23.08.2013
Member of Parliament	Parliament of Estonia	29.08.2013
Healthcare Department	Ministry of Social Affairs	27.08.2013
Deputy Secretary General	Ministry of Social Affairs	28.08.2013
Health Information and Analysis Department	Ministry of Social Affairs	30.08.2013

VI. Program of Interviews: Romania
1. Preliminary interviews

Title	Affiliation	Date of interview
Management board	Ministry of Health, World Bank Unit	06.08.2012
Consultant	Independent consultancy	07.08.2012
Associate Professor	Titu Maiorescu University	07.08.2012
Medical Doctor	Private healthcare industry	08.08.2012
Counselor	Ministry of Health	08.08.2012

(*continued*)

(continued)

Title	Affiliation	Date of interview
Management board	Center for Research and Evaluation of Health Services, National School of Public Health and Health Services Management	09.08.2012
State secretary	Ministry of Health	09.08.2012
Management board	World Bank Romania	10.08.2012

2. Main interviews
Hospital management representatives

Title	Hospital	Type of hospital	Date of interview
Management board	Medical Services Unit, Cluj-Napoca	n.a.	06.02.2013
Medical Doctor	Cluj-Napoca Municipal Emergency Hospital	Local (decentralized)	07.02.2013
Management board	County Clinical Emergency Hospital Cluj-Napoca	Regional (not decentralized)	08.02.2013
Medical Doctor	Bucharest Clinical Emergency Hospital	Regional (not decentralized)	13.09.2013
Medical Doctor	Sfântul Luca Chronic Disease Hospital, Bucharest	Regional (decentralized)	16.09.2013
Management board	Louis Țurcanu Children Emergency Clinical Hospital Timișoara	Regional (decentralized)	20.09.2013
Management board	County Clinical Emergency Hospital Timișoara	Regional (not decentralized)	19.09.2013
Management board	Infectious Disease and Pneumophysiology Hospital Timișoara	Regional (decentralized)	21.09.2013
Management board	County Children Hospital Pitești	County (decentralized)	24.09.2013
Management board	Dâmbovița County Hospital	County (decentralized)	25.09.2013
Management board	Hospital and Health Services Administration, Bucharest	n.a.	30.09.2013

VII. Program of interviews: Norway
A. Hospital management representatives

Title	Hospital	Type of hospital	Date of interview
Management board	Oslo University Hospital	University hospital, South East RHA	13.06.2014
Management board	Østfold Hospital Trust	South East RHA	26.06.2014
Management board	Sunnaas Hospital Trust	South East RHA	27.06.2014
Patient safety and quality	Oslo University Hospital	National and regional, South East RHA	02.07.2014
Management board	Haukeland University Hospital, Bergen	University hospital, West RHA	03.07.2014
Management board	Health Forde Hospital Trust	West RHA	08.07.2014

B. Representatives of central institutions and other organizations

Title	Affiliation	Date of interview
Member of Health and Care Services Committee	Norwegian Parliament, Conservative Party	04.06.2014
Professor of Public Administration	University of Oslo	19.06.2014
Department of Health Legislation	Ministry of Health and Care Services	24.06.2014
Department of Specialist Services	Ministry of Health and Care Services	25.06.2014
Young Doctors' Association	Norwegian Medical Association	25.06.2014
Management board	South East Regional Health Authority	04.07.2014
Management board	South East Regional Health Authority	05.07.2014
Emeritus Professor	Department of Healthcare Management and Health Economics, University of Oslo	04.07.2014
Deputy Director	Office of the Auditor General	09.07.2014
Deputy Director	Office of the Auditor General	09.07.2014
Management board	Norwegian Medical Association	11.07.2014

INDEX

A
Aaviksoo, A., 65
academics, 2, 6, 9, 17
access, 70–2, 154, 167, 179, 189
accountability, 2, 14, 39, 102, 144
administrative management model, 22
agencification, 14, 40
agency theory, 31, 33
Aker University Hospital, 212
Alexander, E.R., 24
Alonso, M.J., 22
Anglo-Saxon countries, 18
autonomy reform, 3, 10, 18, 19
  of hospital management, 147–52
  public management reform and
    coordination, 12–14

B
Benefits Agency, 41
Beuselinck, E., 38, 39
Birchall, J., 15, 16, 20
Blair, Tony, 185
Bloom, N., 21

Bossert, T., 20
Bouckaert, G., 10, 38, 40
Burns, L.R., 38
business methods, 11
business-type managerialism, 11

C
Calvert, R.L., 33
caste behavior, 173
Central and Eastern Europe (CEE), 3,
  12
central healthcare institutions
  English version, 243–5
  Romanian version, 246–8
central hospitals, 86, 87, 103, 111,
  125
centralized decentralization, 187
Central Sickness Fund, 77, 81
Chawla, M., 21
Cheema, G.S., 14
Chhotray, V., 26
Clark, J.C., 34
Clifton, J., 22

© The Author(s) 2017   255
S. Dan, *The Coordination of European Public Hospital Systems*,
DOI 10.1007/978-3-319-43428-5

Clinton, Bill, 185
Collins, D., 20
competitive decentralization, 15
conceptualizations, 24, 34–41
coordination, 23–5
   addressing specific theoretical and
      practical issues, 67–8
   conceptual and analytical
      approaches, 34–41
   culture and, 29–31
   definitions of, 35
   dimensions of, 37
   Estonia; conflicting interests and
      hospital system culture, 121–8;
      expensive medical equipment,
      purchase of, 110–12; hospital
      network, 106–7; information
      asymmetry and imperfect
      monitoring, 116–21;
      mechanisms and instruments
      of, 101–3; medical personnel,
      104–6; positive and negative
      incentives, 113–15
   governance and, 25–7
   Norway; conflicting interests and
      goals, 206–10; hospital
      network, 197–201; mechanisms
      and instruments, 188–91;
      process *versus* coordination of
      quality, 201–4
   organizations, institutions and, 27–9
   principal-agent theory and, 31–4
   in public hospitals, 219–30
   Romania; centralizing public
      procurement, 161–3;
      conflicting interests and goals
      and hospital system culture,
      170–6; financial resources,
      156–61; information
      asymmetry and imperfect
      monitoring, 167–70;
      mechanisms and instruments

   of, 152–5; positive and negative
      incentives, 164–7
   salient approach, 38
   theoretical framework of, 50
corporatization, 19–20, 22
Crowston, K., 34
cultural differences, 70–2
culture
   and coordination theory, 29–31
   hospital system, 49–54

D

decentralization reform, 2, 5, 55, 225,
   229
   public management reform and
      coordination, 14–16
   Romania, 140–7
decision-making autonomy, 148, 240,
   241
decision space map, 20
decomposition, 26
de-concentration, 15, 76
delegation, 15
devolution, 15, 76
Diaz-Fuentes, D., 22
DiMaggio, P.J., 38
Directorate of Health, 189, 203, 204,
   221
Downs, A., 32
DRG system, 159, 160, 168, 175,
   186, 195, 222, 231
Dunleavy, P., 10
Dunsire, A., 27

E

East Tallinn Central Hospital, 110–12,
   114, 116, 120, 128, 227, 231,
   232
economic theories, 10, 31
Eisenhardt, K.M., 33

elite medical profession, 52, 172, 210–16, 234
entrepreneurial behavior, 16, 17
Estonia, 63, 65, 71, 220–2, 225, 228, 230, 234, 239
  interview program, 250–3
  public hospitals in; conflicting interests and hospital system culture, 121–8; coordination, cases and problems of, 104–12; duplication, 108–10; hospital management autonomy and political decentralization, 79–82; Hospital Master Plan 2015, 83–101; and hospital trends, 75–9; information asymmetry and imperfect monitoring, 116–21; mechanisms and instruments, coordination, 101–3; positive and negative incentives, 113–15
Estonian Health Insurance Fund, 87, 102, 223
European Commission, 132, 176
European Observatory on Health Systems and Policies, 65
European public sectors, 13

F
Foundations Act, 85
Fountain, J.E., 38–9
Frederickson, H.G., 24

G
generic management theory, 11
Giordano, P.V., 34
good management practices, 21
Govindaraj, R., 21

H
Habicht, J., 65
Habicht, T., 65
Hall, R.A., 34
Harding, A., 22, 148
Health Action, 206
Health Board, 76, 102
Health Care Board, 84
healthcare institutions, 30
healthcare organization, 17, 38, 76
healthcare policies
  Estonia, 75–9
  Norway, 179–82
  Romania, 131–5
healthcare reform, 16–23, 93, 132, 133
healthcare sector, 3, 53, 232
Health Care Services Organization Act, 82
Health Insurance Act, 76
health policy makers, 5, 6, 104, 205
Health Services Organization Act, 84, 85, 101, 102
Health Systems in Transition (HiT) series, 65
Hood, C., 11
horizontal decentralization, 15
Hospital Act, 111, 182
Hospital Association, 122
hospital management autonomy, 220
  1991–2000, 80–2
  2000–2014, 82
  Norway, 191–6
  and political decentralization, 79–80
  Hospital Master Plan 2015 (HMP), 83–4
  compete/collaborate, 91–101
  and political decentralization, 84–91
hospital network, 106–7
  Estonia, 197–201
  Norway, 197–201

Hospital Network Development Plan (HNDP), 79, 83, 84, 86, 93, 102, 103
2002 Hospital Reform, 5, 180, 182–8
hospital system culture, 235
conflicting interests and goals and, 230–41
principal-agent theory, 54–6
Romania, 170–6
theoretical framework, 49–54
Huxham, C., 39

I
information and communication technologies (ICT), 201–3, 224, 232
information asymmetry, 54, 56, 116–21, 167, 205, 232
institutionalism, 7, 29, 50
institutionalization, 29
institutions, 27–9
internal decentralization, 15

J
James, O., 40

K
Kimberly, J.R., 38
Koppel, A., 65

L
Labour Party, 186
Lindblom, C.E., 34

M
Macdonald, D., 39
mainstream microeconomic theory, 31

Malone, T.W., 34
management boards, 102, 117
managerial autonomy, 22, 80, 147
March, J.G., 30
Maris, J., 65
market-type mechanisms (MTMs), 10, 11
Mills, A., 14
Ministry of Health, 5, 138–40, 142, 145, 147–50, 152, 153, 161, 162, 164, 168–70, 173, 222, 226, 237
Ministry of Health and Care Services, 180, 182, 184, 187, 200–1, 213, 221
Ministry of Public Health, 133
Ministry of Social Affairs, 81, 83, 84, 100, 102–7, 116–18, 123, 222, 223

N
National Audit Office of Estonia, 65, 109
National Commission for Hospital Accreditation, 152
National Health Insurance House, 133, 138, 152, 154, 156, 169
National Strategy for Hospital Rationalization, 133, 136, 137
Nemec, C., 16
neo-Weberian state (NWS), 12
networks, 24–6, 31, 108
new public governance (NPG), 12
New Public Management (NPM), 1–7, 9–11, 32, 39, 40, 186, 237
autonomy reform, 12–14
decentralization reform, 14–16
and healthcare reform, 16–23
Nordic welfare state, 186, 199, 209

North Estonia Medical Center, 103, 231
North Estonia Regional Hospital, 111
Norway, 5, 59, 66, 69, 71, 221, 224–6, 234, 239, 240
2002 hospital reform in, 230
interview program, 253
recentralization in, 227
Norwegian Medical Association, 206
Norwegian Ministry of Health and Care Services, 27
Norwegian Radium Hospital, 212
NPM-type reforms, 234, 238

O
Office of the Auditor General, 194
operational governance, 17
organizational reform, 3, 219–30
organizational theory, 25, 27–9
Oslo University Hospital, 211, 212, 224, 227, 232, 233
Oxford Handbook of Public Management, 15

P
Patient Rights' Act, 186
Peters, B.G., 26, 30, 34, 38, 40
Pierre, J., 26
political decentralization, 15, 79–80, 226
1991–2000, 80–2
2000–2014, 82
self-governed hospitals and, 84–91
political science, 12, 14, 23, 235, 236
politics, 39, 109, 124–7
Pollitt, C., 10, 11, 13, 15, 16, 20
Popa, A.E., 66
Powell, W.W., 38
Preker, A.S., 22, 148

principal-agent theory, 7, 10–11, 25, 113, 116, 127, 233, 235, 236
and coordination theory, 31–4
hospital system culture, 54–6
Norway, 204–5
research design, 59–60
Romania, 169, 171
privatization, 13, 15, 20
public administration, 1, 6, 7, 13, 23, 28, 220
public choice theory, 10, 31, 32
public hospitals
addressing specific theoretical and practical issues; access, cultural differences and language, 70–2; coordination, 67–8; defining coordination problems, 68; perception *vs.* evidence, 69–70; thinking in before and after terms, 69
case selection, 59–61
coordination in, 219–30
English version, 245–6
in Estonia; conflicting interests and hospital system culture, 121–8; coordination, cases and problems of, 104–12; duplication, 108–10; hospital management autonomy and political decentralization, 79–82; Hospital Master Plan 2015, 83–101; and hospital trends, 75–9; information asymmetry and imperfect monitoring, 116–21; mechanisms and instruments, coordination, 101–3; positive and negative incentives, 113–15
Norway; conflicting interests and goals, 206–10; elite medical profession, 210–16; healthcare policies, 179–82; hospital

public hospitals (*cont.*)
management autonomy, 191–6;
hospital network coordination,
197–201; 2002 Hospital
Reform, 180, 182–8;
mechanisms and instruments of
coordination, 188–91; process
versus coordination of quality,
coordination of, 201–4
preliminary interviews, 62–3
primary data collection methods,
61–2
Romania; centralizing public
procurement, 161–3;
conflicting interests and goals
and hospital system culture,
170–6; decentralization reform,
140–7; financial resources,
coordination of, 156–61;
healthcare policies, 131–5;
hospital management
autonomy, 147–52;
information asymmetry and
imperfect monitoring, 167–70;
mechanisms and instruments of
coordination, 152–5; positive
and negative incentives, 164–7;
rationalization, 135–40
Romanian version, 249–50
secondary data collection methods,
65–7
semi-structured interview program,
63–5
type of, 60
Putman, R., 15, 16, 20

R
rational choice theory, 25, 31, 32
rationalization, 135–40
recentralization, 3–5, 19, 59, 225, 227

regional health authorities (RHAs),
182–4, 187–9, 191, 192, 197,
200, 210, 213
requisite theory, 22
Rikshospitalet University Hospital,
212
Rockel, M.V., 34
Romania, 5, 66, 224, 225, 234,
239
interview program, 251–2
public hospitals; centralizing public
procurement, 161–3;
conflicting interests and goals
and hospital system culture,
170–6; decentralization reform,
140–7; financial resources,
coordination of, 156–61;
healthcare policies, 131–5;
hospital management
autonomy, 147–52;
information asymmetry and
imperfect monitoring, 167–70;
mechanisms and instruments of
coordination, 152–5; positive
and negative incentives, 164–7;
rationalization, 135–40
Rondinelli, D., 14

S
Schröder, Gerhard, 185
self-governed hospitals, 84–91
self-seeking behavior, 11, 21
Semashko-type Soviet system, 132
semi-autonomous organization, 13
Simon, H.A., 30
Smith, D.L., 14
Smith, K.B., 24
Social Insurance Law, 133
sociological institutionalism, 30, 51,
52, 216, 236

South-East region, 210–11
Soviet Union, 75, 132
steering, 26, 27
Stoker, G., 26
Stoltenberg, Jens, 185

T
Tabibzadeh, I., 14
Tallinn Children Hospital, 103
Tartu University Hospital, 103, 110,
  231
Telemark Hospital, 211
transparency, 14, 70, 144, 149
*Transylvanian Review of
  Administrative Sciences* (2011),
  14

U
Ullevål University Hospital, 212,
  214

V
Vaughan, J.P., 14
Verhoest, K., 38

W
Walston, S.L., 38
West, E., 17
Williamson, O.E., 31
World Bank, 66, 82, 83, 137
World Health Organization, 109